THE UNIVERSE IS ONE

Towards a Theory of Knowledge and Life

Paul A. Olivier

University Press of America,® Inc.
Lanham • New York • Oxford

Copyright © 1999 by
University Press of America,® Inc.
4720 Boston Way
Lanham, Maryland 20706

12 Hid's Copse Rd.
Cumnor Hill, Oxford OX2 9JJ

ISBN 0-7618-1437-X (cloth: alk. ppr.)

Contents

Jenny, I don't know if Mama was right or if it's Lieutenant Dan.
I don't know if we each have a destiny,
or if we are all just floating around accidental-like on a breeze.
But I think, maybe it's both.
Maybe both, it's happening at the same time.
— from the movie *Forrest Gump*

ειϛ εστιν ο κοσμοϛ
"the universe is one"
Philo of Alexandria
De Opificio   171

Foreword

Isabelle Stengers

Often the richest encounters are the most unexpected ones. When I received during the winter of 1992 a text called "The Universe is One," and saw that its author was juxtaposing names such as Bohm, Capra, Barrow, Wheeler, Prigogine and Stengers, with references to God, Word and Spirit, I certainly had every reason to fear the worst. Here was still another book presenting what is called "New Age Science" as some magical potion capable of reconciling what our history has separated, capable of creating a unitary perspective where scientific and religious truth are led to speak a common language by means of the far too simple miracle of analogy. As a philosopher, I try to discern and disentangle the many and varied bonds between science and power, bonds which are sometimes quite explicit, and sometimes implicit or hidden. As a rule the more a scientific author seems to achieve a synthesis between science, religion and wisdom, the more numerous are these bonds. However, in spite of this first negative reaction I decided to give the text a chance. And after I read it, my initial mistrust had been transformed into interest and surprise. Why was this author, in contrast with so many others before him, able to handle scientific writers not only with respect but also with a certain freedom that would enable him at the same time to challenge and demand? From where came the power to escape that deadly trap of the mind and imagination which scientists so often set, whatever their intellectual standing, and so easily and so unthinkingly fall into, when they cannot resist transforming the latest developments within their narrow specialty into some general model? It is only when I came to the fourth and final chapter of this book, to the study of the New Testament texts of John and Paul that I understood: this power sprang from an inspiration completely outside the domain of science. It sprang from the depths of what could only be described as genuine *religious* experience.

I take as a testimony to the value and truth of this religious experience the quality of its impact upon the author: Paul Olivier bears witness to this experience through his generous and lucid ability to really listen to what scientists are saying, even going so far as to share their passions and dreams, but at the same time refusing to go any further with them in their quest for truth the moment they begin to evoke images of power, the moment they try to take this unique Universe of ours and to force it to conform to some rigid model arising only with the framework of their particular domain of specialization.

I am not a Christian and to me the Christian notion of "grace" was always associated with the dark story of conflict, hate and terror, a story which began, if we follow Paul Olivier, when the "single greatest heresy in the history of Christian thought" (p. 108) led the emphasis to swing "from cosmology to soteriology." Whatever this historical thesis, it is the very experience of reading "The Universe is One" which forced me to understand and accept "grace" in the cosmological perspective which the reader will discover, namely, the power of images emerging from within Mind, or more precisely Mind itself in the act of its emergence, in the act of self-organization and selection which constitutes its truth. Yes, a powerful image guided Paul Olivier and gave him the power to select, from among the many scientific references at his disposal, those elements which should feed and nourish this image, all the while not allowing science to manipulate or unduly fascinate.

For a process philosopher as I try to be, the experience of reading "The Universe is One" is also an odd one. Indeed there is a very deep affinity between Olivier's position and Whitehead's cosmology, while in some respects the divergence is obvious. I discovered that Olivier has certainly heard about Whitehead but never read him and I wondered if this was something to regret. My proposed answer would be "no." One of the aims of this introduction is to explain why.

Whitehead's cosmological work was first and foremost a philosophical one, and we know that if he could have done without God, he would have happily done so. The starting point of Paul Olivier is quite different: it is the worship experience. When he speaks about God, and more precisely, when he denies being able to speak about God, he is not speaking about a philosophical God, as the Gods of Leibniz or Whitehead. He is not speaking from within the constraints of experimentation with concepts, which demands that the philosopher be free to construct or eventually destroy the concept of God. He is speaking from within the constraints of the worship experience, which allows him to affirm and experiment that the Universe is one.

The philosophical Gods of Leibniz and Whitehead express the essential distinction between philosophical and scientific endeavors. They are part of a demanding conceptual experimentation which provides not only intellectual tools, but also powerful images which help to resist what Whitehead has called the "bifurcation of nature," its separation into knowing subjects and knowable objects. I needed those philosophers' daring quest for coherence in order to be interested in science and scientists, while holding on to the possibility of not "believing" in science itself, knowing full well that it is precisely this belief which transforms science into an arrogant denial of whatever escapes its grasp. However as a daughter of my time, I never thought I could become interested in a religious approach to the Universe. The Gods of Leibniz and Whitehead were philosophical, the very mark of the difference between the speculative coherence of a system and what we may call the "scientific dialogue with nature." Indeed whatever its scope, the scientific dialogue always starts with the active invention of demanding questions through which definite answers may be obtained from our world. As a consequence, science's own invention of itself cannot be included in what it describes. We cannot formulate a demanding question leading to a definite answer about our own act of inventing such a demanding question. In contrast, the struggle for coherence which defines speculative philosophy aims at including within the same consistent framework the most simple aspects of what we call matter and the very act of man's creation of himself through his questions and speculations. Thus philosophical Gods were not in themselves something which could be a source of inspiration and emotion. You may need a speculative philosophical system in order to resist the fascination of separations and simplifications, i.e. the fascination of power, and this makes an important difference. But this difference is nothing more than the strength to resist and create. In no way can it be the ground for a

xi

shared emotional, vital, collective experience.

I am still not a religious person in the sense that I have no faith which binds me to a particular denominational tradition, but I am now convinced that I cannot work for a future where science and philosophy would claim to form a closed alliance expelling religious experience, the experience of worship, as a crucial part of our human adventure. I had learned from Whitehead's philosophical adventure, culminating in "Process and Reality," that resisting the modern Western "bifurcation of nature" is not an easy task. We have never finished learning how deeply entrenched within us are the judgments we have inherited from this split and how powerful are the images it inspires. I have now learned that my indifference about religious experience, or more precisely my belief that it was a purely personal matter, was a part of this same heritage I wanted to resist. This part of our Western heritage fosters the notion of the human subject as having to accept bravely his or her essential loneliness. It leads us to despise all the traditional, vital experiences of togetherness, of a participation in a collectively shared Now, and to label them as rather infantile experiences, good enough only for those who have not the strength to accept the hard truth of human fate.

I want to emphasize this last point. Perhaps one of the most urgent tasks before us involves learning how our reactions and reflexes, our habitual ways of situating ourselves with respect to our past and with respect to other cultures, are part of our Western heritage. This heritage possesses no doubt an inventive, creative side open to real novelty, but it also possesses a destructive side, closed in upon itself, fearfully proud and arrogant. We can no longer hide the ravage and devastation which our history has generated on all levels relating to ecology, that is, on all those levels where we may speak of a togetherness of differences: the ecology of the Earth and of its living populations; the ecology of human beings with the diversity of their cultures, customs, and ethical systems; the ecology of the individual with the multiplicity of questions, needs, and meanings which must be constructed in order to construct a human life. But in order to undertake this urgent task, we must first liberate ourselves from the arrogance, which has permitted us to destroy, to singularize, to judge and to condemn, all, of course, in the name of progress and rationality. This arrogance is that part of our Western heritage which is both the most crucial and the most difficult to fight, since it can even lurk behind, infect and influence the very creative initiative we deploy in order to escape its grasp.

To protect ourselves from this arrogance, the words which Paul Olivier quoted from the apostle Paul's Letter to the Romans are so precious: "For we know that the whole creation groans and suffers the pains of childbirth together up till now" (p.135). A new image arises, that of a multileveled Universe, at the same time both one and many, where all that manifests itself in the irreversible creation of a "now," in the very act of generating an experience, a thought or a choice, brings together the whole of a groaning and suffering creation. This image forbids us the very tempting solution of escaping our heritage by denouncing it, that is by simply taking the side of its many victims. When we fight for justice, it denies us the right to be blind to the fact that those whom we are struggling against are "groaning together" with us. It demands that we dare to live, to think and to struggle driven by the image that in each act of life and thought we share not only the suffering but also the hope, not only the sorrows but also the joys, of the whole of a single creation, inanimate, dead or alive. It is very easy for me, as a daughter of a Western middle class, to take a distance from my forebearers who ignored the suffering and hopes of the workers whose exploitation they accepted, or the sorrows and joys of the populations whose colonization they celebrated as a progress for humanity. But it is much more demanding to live knowing that each one of my thoughts and actions share in the suffering and groaning of the whole of the Universe, that each one bears the mark of all that which I cannot hear or feel.

Also at the same sad level as the arrogance of denunciation, we find the arrogance of a faith in a new kind of knowledge which supposedly has the power to smooth over all of our mistakes, to bring together everything which we have separated. This arrogance characterizes, I fear, many of those who speak of a "New Science" or a "New Age Science." At a certain moment in his life it was the sad mistake of Gregory Bateson when he dreamed of a new kind of science, cybernetics, which should deliver us from the illusions of mechanistic objectivity and give us access to a true science of living things, of human beings and their social interaction. This is equally the weakness of so lofty a thinker as David Bohm or even of so sober a thinker as the biologist Stephen J. Gould, when he accepts meaningless chance not only as a present-day scientific answer to scientific questions but as a truth to be accepted by everybody or a source of general wisdom. In this context let us not even begin to speak of the speculations of the two Johns,

Wheeler and Barrow. In each case it seems that science is able to soar beyond the limits which define it, as it tries to enter into dialogue with the philosophical or spiritual traditions of humanity, as it tries to serve as a source of wisdom and reconciliation. But in each case a fearful ingredient is at work - a hidden pride. In each case, linked to each positive inspiration, to each new image which inspires the life and thought of the scientist, we find the arrogance of power. Each new image serves indeed not only to unify but also to deny and to disqualify all which falls outside of its domain.

Thus, when David Bohm, for example, uses his implicit order to explain that a particle - and with it all that could enter into a relationship of observation including the observer - is nothing but an abstraction, he seems to rejoin certain forms of wisdom cultivated in the East. But at the same time and of equal importance, he speaks as a specialist of quantum mechanics, as the representative of a science which up to now has been unable to give to observable events (quantum jumps, atomic decays, and so forth) any other status than that of secondary and derived. The convergence between a tradition of wisdom which taught that what we experience is a tapestry of illusion, and a science which seems to authorize a similar lesson may appear fascinating. But this fascination is a trap, since it merely ratifies the power that theoretical physics claims on all Western sciences. The West and the East cannot be reconciled on the narrow and misleading basis of a similarity of discoveries arrived at through completely different methods and means - and what could be more different than the Oriental tradition of meditation and the Occidental tradition of theoretical physics, the latter so active and dominant, having conquered the very summit of the pyramid of sciences?

In fact, Paul Olivier is not interested in the history of our scientific struggles and conquests. He need not bother with all this. His notion of an "internal image" allows him to "feel" unerringly at what point inspiration turns into arrogance. This then is the power of his "epistemology of the sacred," the saving force of his image of the Universe as one. Through his worshipping sense of the oneness of the Universe, he not only escapes arrogance, our worse temptation, but he also "saves" the scientific thrust toward knowledge from its own arrogance. The self-preoccupation, the negation, the violence, woven into most scientific achievements just become insignificant aspects, easily dismissed because of the beauty of the whole of which each achievement is a part, saved through an understanding which makes them part of the "groaning and suffering whole."

For Paul Olivier no scientific achievement should be able to destroy or reduce in the name of scientific objectivity, because scientific achievements are themselves part of our single multileveled Universe. The very creation of scientific objectivity is, at the level it both expresses and produces, part of the process of becoming itself. He gracefully avoids the old struggle about scientific reality - in order to say it is not our own arbitrary representation devoid of truth, don't we have to claim it truly exists "out there"? - as he relates this reality to meaningful information, to differences which make a difference for the scientist. This implies that whatever we achieve in constructing "scientific reality," we will never be able to escape our own shoes, i.e. the very process of what we call reality is produced through an historical, technical, social and imaginative creation of meaning. But in so doing there is no "out there" which would escape us, since everything that exists produces its own existence through a similar process. Yes, we can never point to some more fundamental mindless reality existing beyond the context of meaningful creative relations. We may well try to decide if the warmth of the sun or the wavelength of the light it emits is part of an objective reality. Never will the sun "out there" confirm our decision. But we are not alone in deciding about this. Before we came to such an explicit question, answers were already being created. The growing plant and the cells of our skin meaningfully testify to the light that makes a difference. The cat seeking the sun's warmth affirms through its enjoyment the mutual creation of a warmth-giving sun and a sensually delighted cat. Never will we find a better proof of the sun's meaningful existence. Whatever the scientific and "objective" representations we produce in describing the sun, we should never forget that these representations are produced through a human history in which we systematically invent new ways for the sun to make a difference for us. Never should these human representations override or replace the cat's delight. They just add to it, each time creating a new kind of relation, a new way of selecting, abstracting and confirming. In this way, a new reality comes into existence.

Paul Olivier's image of a single living Universe is not meant to become a scientific statement replacing other scientific statements about the Universe, about life or human perception. In the same way, Leibniz's monadology or Whitehead's philosophical speculation was never meant to replace the active creation of meaning that we call science. Even before I met Paul Olivier and with him the problem of religious experience, I never thought that science and philosophy could ever come to some kind of simple unity, to some kind of all-encompassing position which would transcend their differences. I always saw them as complementary enterprises. Complementarity, if we generalize Niels Bohr's meaning of the term, does not put limitations on different ways of knowing, explaining or describing. It takes however each particular way as grounded in a particular relationship and as such, following definite constraints. A constraint is not a limitation we meet at some point or another; rather it is intrinsically bound to the very way we arrive at a certain point, and to the questions we ask. In so doing we "decide" both what we are looking for and what is the reality we address in order to provide an answer. Complementarity is a relational concept whose primary meaning is that we cannot think about getting an answer without first being responsible for the question. Questions always come before answers. Questions do not determine what the answer will be, but they do play a central role in shaping and constraining the kind of answer we will get.

It is in those terms that, as I already said, I had accepted philosophical Gods as both the manifestation and the stamp of the difference between scientific and philosophical questions. Never would science encounter any trace of the existence of such Gods or feel the need to relate to them, because never can a scientific description, whatever its scope, go beyond what I would call a "technically dualistic" position, meaning in Paul Olivier's terms, the active choice, selection and confirmation of a local truth. Never would it go beyond the inventive abstraction taking place within a particular local level. And never could this level "explain itself" in the sense of justifying unto itself that the questions it answers are the relevant ones. In contrast, philosophy, and primarily speculative philosophy, follows different constraints, since its very challenge is to create a language which would allow us to conceptualize the self-creation of both man and nature. It leads to very strange concepts indeed: Leibniz's monads and pre-established harmony, Whitehead's eternal ideas and the atomic temporality of the actual beings' self-creation. This is the normal outcome of their aim and constraints: speculative philosophical concepts should not resemble scientific concepts because they must not pass the same tests. As Whitehead said, both the domain and tools of philosophy are language, it is an experimentation with language, the mapping together of what we have learned to express about ourselves, and what we have learned to express about what we question. The crucial test of this mapping is not a verifiable local answer to a particular problem. It is the very fact that when reinvented following the constraints of the speculative language, our experience both of the world and of ourselves becomes more interesting. As Whitehead put it, "nothing is but anything," and the aim of speculative philosophy is that "anything" may lay claim to the full vividness of a self-creating reality.

Paul Olivier's worship, at the basis of his "epistemology of the sacred," is for me a new creative constraint grounded in that rather overwhelming *experience* of a single Universe. To proclaim that "the Universe is one" is a truly prophetic utterance that we must distinguish quite clearly from both the philosophical experimentation with concepts and from science's dialogue with nature.

We cannot appreciate a constraint in itself. We are only able to appreciate its effects, the level of risk and creativity it meaningfully generates. Paul Olivier's presentation of contemporary science compels us to explore the risks and creative opportunities of the constraint he proposes. His central point is not so much "what can we learn from science?" but "what can we learn from science when we listen to it with the assurance that the Universe is one?" I have already explained that it is the very nature of the result, its "saving grace" which selects, confirms and gathers up meaningful answers while letting fall with quiet surety the arrogance permeating these answers, which convinced me I could no longer ignore the "worship constraint." Through his worshipping sense of the oneness of the Universe, Paul Olivier indeed succeeds in transforming the meaning of his scientific references in such a way that each science becomes one creative local adventure among others.

To speak about distinct paths created through distinct constraints does not mean that they should be indifferent to each other. Far from that. I deeply appreciate Olivier's beautiful prophetic description of what would be a "worshipping scientist": "He may stand firmly and with great proficiency within a single discipline, or he may even stand at the philosophical crossroads of several disciplines, but at every instant he humbly and freely submits all to the lordship of the larger whole. He may delve as deeply as possible into the truth of a particular level, but never for a moment does he lose sight of that larger truth in which he participates. Not only does he meet regularly with others of the same discipline to share and exchange ideas, not only does he take part in interdisciplinary research and development, but even more importantly he assembles with his fellow scientists as well as other brothers and sisters in the deepest ecstatic and prophetic praise. His worship does not represent some peculiar personal eccentricity, but rather it forms the heart and core of his method as a scientist (p. 155)."

I believe that such "worshipping scientists" would be not only better citizens but also better scientists. Since its beginning, and today more than ever, science is not only an activity rich in invention, risks, surprises and even wonders, but it is also plagued both by contempt and ignorance for what is not scientific, and by power struggles within science itself. For many scientists, science is a conquest, with the world being defined in terms of sheer possibilities of expansion, as if it were consigned or delivered, so to speak, to their questions. As a consequence the success in one field is not celebrated as a new access which will add new ways of understanding, as a creation and discovery of a new level within a multileveled reality. It is seen at last, truly scientific approach, all other approaches being dismissed as belonging to opinion, which may be of cultural value but has nothing to do with science. For example, as their ultimate triumph some brain specialists even dream of the disappearance of all scientific practices that would address the human mind and spirit through language, emotion and meaning. The will to expand and dominate is at the root of many such irrational and stupid scientific claims. In contrast the image of "worshipping scientists" corresponds to a far more enlightened and rational science.

In order to create a true complementary relationship however, it is important to give a precise meaning to such terms as, "to submit all to the Lordship of the larger whole." To achieve a true complementarity, never should one adventure, be it scientific, philosophical or religious, limit some other adventure in its positive risks and hopes. Each should generate for the other more exciting and exacting demands. This means that the Lordship of the larger whole cannot be conceived in terms of some kind of positive, factual or theoretical knowledge which would be a matter of belief or authority, but rather as a perpetual recall that no scientific result, however wonderful it may be, can ever lead to claims which would reduce other levels to simple consequences. The "Lordship of the larger whole" is indeed a perpetual recall that the only truth which can ask for submission is that of a Whole for which we have no scientific or dogmatic words, but which nevertheless is able, through the worshipping sense of wonder it inspires, to generate new levels of interest, new possibilities of meaning, as well as a deep and broadened sense of responsibility for the quality of the togetherness of our experiences. This Whole is neither a philosophical concept nor a scientific reference. It is an image produced by the very "Now" of the worship experience. And the power of this image is the bringing together, the gathering up of these two elements that science, ever since Galileo, has disconnected: the successful production of an "objective knowledge," that is of a reliable bond with a reality which this bond designates as "preexisting," discovered and not fabricated, and the deep and passionate feeling that this production is a novelty, an event creating new beings, new meanings, new possibilities.

Also philosophy and worship may learn from each other on the condition that each explicitly refers to the domain of practice on which it depends and which it cannot transcend.

Whitehead once stated that the adventure of Western rationality is the adventure of hope. This is a philosophical statement that opens up philosophy to something it requires but cannot ground. Rationality furthermore can never claim to have fulfilled this hope, to have created a language that would give a terminal expression to the coherence of our many experiences. This is why the relation between philosophy and hope is not a stable one. Philosophy is always in danger of forgetting about hope. It then becomes a prisoner of language, fascinated by the many traps, the many paradoxes it can produce. It then may enter into a competitive and vindictive relation with scientists. Indeed forgetting its own specific risks and challenges, it can no longer understand that scientists are abiding by different constraints. I thus think that the philosophy of today needs as badly as science a perpetual recall to the hope without which the concepts it creates become meaningless, just empty and sterile words. This recall cannot be expressed in philosophical terms any more than it can be an object for scientific reference. Hope can be recalled only as felt and concretely experienced. This is precisely, following Paul Olivier, the experience actually produced and embodied in the "here and now" collective act of worship, the "here and now" fulfillment of hope.

The act of worship, generating an endlessly new and powerful set of images that draw together and emotionally relate the many words we use in our many quests for meaning, is not a good starting point for philosophical practice. It cannot bear the philosophical demand for analytical freedom, a condition for the experimental creation of concepts whose first aim is to make explicit the propositions and problems we are able to formulate during each historical period. But it does bear witness to the intrinsic constraint of this experimentation: through its own conceptual tools, philosophy cannot create and share the actual experience of the coherence its aim is to construct.

Paul Olivier gives us the powerful image of the interplay of Word and Spirit producing new and always unexpected levels of meaning, creating that living worshipping experience of the relation between the unfolding of these meanings and the multiple unity of the Universe. Neither Word nor Spirit corresponds to scientific references or philosophical concepts. The interplay of Word drawing upon Spirit is neither a psychological experience, which could be commented on in anthropological terms, nor is it some speculative philosophical reference. I think it would also be a misunderstanding to make Word and Spirit a matter of theological definition or discussion. The interplay of Word drawing upon Spirit exists in its own right insofar as it is actually experienced as such, thereby creating its own present, its own actuality. I would even say, using a Whiteheadian expression, that living Logos "tells no tales about itself"; the only tales to be told are the ones which are produced in the interplay between Word and Spirit, endlessly constructing and creating a Universe, including our own experience. Living Logos does not belong to science or philosophy, but as a powerful image, it creates a living ground - something that contemporary science sadly lacks and which philosophy by itself cannot provide. This living ground forms the basis for what can be called a creative, ethical, dynamical relationship among the many ways of our experience, for what Gregory Bateson called an "ecology of mind."

However, as a living ground for togetherness, the religious, worship experience also needs to be embedded in a tradition with its own constraints. Indeed we know this experience to be a dangerous and fragile one, so easily diverted towards all kinds of fanaticism, superstition, and ferocious rivalry. It needs its own words and syntax in order to construct its own truth, quite different from scientific and philosophical "truths," and in order to enhance and share the specificity of the relation it creates. I believe that this is the goal and crucial importance of "The Universe is One." As such it is then inheritor of what has long been called "theology," and leads us to understand the specific aim and constraints of this tradition we call theology. It is not as a logos "about"

God that theology can contribute to human (and cosmic) togetherness but as ecology of the sacred, as the research and learning about those words and practices which authenticate the quality of the worshipping experience. Just as science and philosophy may learn from each other and from theology, theology may then learn from science and philosophy many a valuable lesson derived from the very nature of the risks and openness of experimental traditions.

Both Paul Olivier and I as well as most of the readers of "The Universe is One" are part of our Western tradition. The very distinction between science, philosophy and theology is a Western creation. As long as we keep in mind that arrogance is our worse enemy, hopefully we will not allow ourselves to believe that we are free to step outside of our tradition and to speak in the name of some kind of general all-encompassing truth. This, however, is again a constraint and not a limitation. Moreover, our tradition is also the one responsible for the present historical situation: the statement "the adventure of humanity is one" is not only a prophetic truth but also today a problematic matter of fact. As inheritors of the Western world which is responsible for this situation, we have little choice: our task is to work within this tradition with a single ever-evolving purpose in mind, that we become worthy to bear the incredible responsibility that what concerns us now concerns the whole of humanity. Following Paul Olivier, this also means that we will allow ourselves to experience deeply the brilliance and brightness of the glorious image of a Universe in becoming - a Universe suffering and groaning together with us in our quest for meaning. I sincerely hope that, whatever their religious beliefs, whatever the difficulty of entering "where angels fear to tread" as Bateson put it, the readers of this book will owe to Paul Olivier the quiet assurance that the very experience of the power of this image is a perfectly legitimate and integral part of the human quest for meaning, and that they will also share with him and with me the conviction that both an epistemology and an experimental ecology of the sacred are crucial aspects of the demanding task which lies before us.

Acknowledgements

Grateful acknowledgment is made to the following for permission to reprint previously published material:

From *WONDERFUL LIFE:* The Burgess Shale and the Nature of History by Stephen Jay Gould. Copyright (1989 by Stephen Jay Gould. Reprinted by permission of W.W. Norton and Company, Inc.

From *WORD BIBLICAL COMMENTARY, ROMANS 1-8* by James D.G. Dunn, 1988, Word Publishing, Nashville, Tennessee. All rights reserved.

From *JESUS AND THE SPIRIT* by James D.G. Dunn, SCM Press, 1975, by permission of SCM Press.

From *CHRISTOLOGY IN THE MAKING* by James D.G. Dunn, SCM Press, 1980, by permission of SCM Press.

From *THE PARTING OF THE WAYS* by James D.G. Dunn, SCM Press, 1991, by permission of SCM Press.

From *THE EMPEROR'S NEW MIND* by Roger Penrose, Oxford University Press, 1989, by permission of Oxford University Press.

From *THE NEW BIOLOGY* by Robert Augros of Saint Anselm College and George Stanciu of Magdalen College,1987, by permission of Professors Augros and Stanciu.

Thanks to Eric Bishop and Jennifer Chamberlain of the *Waxahachie Daily Light* for editing this book. Special thanks to Isabelle Stengers, George Deschrijver, Pete A.Y. Gunter and Mieke Camerlynck for their endless encouragement and support. A final thanks to my parents, Robert and Mildred Olivier, who, by their presence from beyond death, are indeed the true authors of this book.

Introduction

In *Mind and Nature,* the well-known anthropologist Gregory Bateson begins his introduction by quoting Saint Augustine:

> Plotinus the Platonist proves by means of the blossoms and leaves that from the Supreme God, whose beauty is invisible and ineffable, Providence reaches down to the things of earth here below. He points out that these frail and mortal objects could not be endowed with a beauty so immaculate and so exquisitely wrought, did they not issue from the Divinity which endlessly pervades with its invisible and unchanging beauty all things.[1]

A few pages later Bateson eloquently set forth the main lines of his epistemology:

> This book is built on the opinion that we are parts of a living world. I have placed as epigraph at the head of this chapter a passage from Saint Augustine in which the saint's epistemology is clearly stated. Today such a statement evokes nostalgia. Most of us have lost a sense of unity of biosphere and humanity which would bind and reassure us all with an affirmation of beauty. Most of us do not believe that whatever the ups and downs of detail within our limited experience, the larger whole is primarily beautiful.
>
> We have lost the core of Christianity. We have lost Shiva, the dancer of Hinduism whose dance at the trivial level is both creation and destruction but in whole is beauty. We have lost Abraxas, the terrible and beautiful god of both day and night in Gnosticism. We have

lost totemism, the sense of parallelism between man's organization and that of the animals and plants. We have lost even the Dying God.

We are beginning to play with ideas of ecology, and although we immediately trivialize these ideas into commerce and politics, there is at least an impulse still in the human breast to unify and thereby sanctify the total natural world, of which we are.[2]

These paragraphs from Bateson also serve as a fitting introduction to this book. What follows here is not an exposition of his thought. Generally it proves to be far too elusive and unsystematic to be taken in full seriousness by science, philosophy or even theology. Yet Bateson was a courageous explorer travelling the uncharted waters of mind, and from time to time he made a few amazing discoveries which we feel are indispensable in building a sound epistemology of the sacred. We have followed him with great enthusiasm into many a strange place, and no doubt we have taken his thought into areas where certainly he himself would never have gone. Maybe we are one of the fools who have rushed in where angels fear to tread - an impulse Bateson so carefully avoided in his last book, *Angels Fear: Toward an Epistemology of the Sacred,* edited, re-written and published by his daughter Mary Catherine Bateson only after his death. Undoubtedly this is the case. But hopefully as a result of this very incomplete effort, doors are opened a bit wider to those much wiser and much better equipped to build a more comprehensive epistemology of the sacred.

Let us go back to this impulse to unify which Bateson mentioned in his introduction. Perhaps there is no impulse in the human heart more dangerous than the impulse to unify. The history of our entire Western culture may be summarized for future generations as the history of the decimation of diversity. We have been destroying on an unprecedented scale countless species of plants and animals, even rainforests and entire ecosystems, all in the name of the progress of man. Our missionaries have been decimating the rich cultural heritage of untold numbers of indigenous peoples, labeling them as crude and uncivilized, all in the name of a God in whom few people in the West truly believe. In substitution for the rich diversity of flora and fauna, we rush in with a few select breeds of coffee beans and cows. In the place of the vibrant animistic tribal religions of these indigenous peoples, we offer our stale tradition and lifeless rituals packaged under the righteous banner of either Protestant or Catholic. Both our science, geared to grabbing hold of reality and describing it objectively in a single clear language, and our religion, so glibly offering us a single divine supernatural viewpoint encapsulating all truth, like to brandish the sword of eternal verities and to reinforce within us a deadly and simplistic impulse to unify.

But just look at the title of this book: *The Universe is One*. The subtitle is perhaps even more pretentious: *Towards a Theory of Knowledge and Life*. In chapter one we propose a comprehensive theory of knowledge, while in our second chapter we elaborate and expand it into a theory of life. In chapter three we test our theory for its aesthetic appeal, for its power to convince, and in our fourth and final chapter we commit perhaps the greatest folly of all in correlating the insights which we have gathered from modern process science to our Judeo-Christian heritage. With wholesale abandon, we have given in to this almost irresistible impulse to unify.

Yet at the same time, we are forced to admit that not a single truly significant distinction made anywhere in this book is original to its author. Most of the ideas from science were gathered from the popular science section typical of any large English-speaking bookstore. Isabelle Stengers, Ilya Prigogine, Erich Jantsch and Stephen J. Gould were without doubt the most influential authors from the world of science. From the New Testament we have drawn from a single source, James D.G. Dunn, Lightfoot Professor of Divinity at the University of Durham. As a New Testament scholar not particularly concerned with scientific or dogmatic questions, Dunn offers us a clear view into the world of inter-testamental and New Testament times. So in this book, insights from modern process science mingle freely with those of Philo, John and Paul, and in this strange and hopefully happy confluence, many ideas which have been separated in the West as far back as the Second Century AD, have found their way back together again.

In the volatile, turbulent, organismic, animistic and apocalyptic setting of the Eastern Mediterranean 2,000 years ago, Stoicism, Platonism and Judaism underwent a series of transformations in the hands of the early Christian writers to produce that rather unique cosmological synthesis which we will attempt to describe in our fourth and final chapter. We follow Philo and John in their transformation of the Stoic concept of Logos as a principle of order within the Universe. Likewise, modern process science, as presented to us by Prigogine, Stengers and Jantsch, speaks of self-ordering and self-organizing on the level of the whole of the Universe. What are the similarities and differences between these ancient and modern notions of universal self-ordering? How are we to understand self-organization? Is it nothing but the blind and indifferent collocation of bumping bits of matter as mechanistic science since the 17th Century has proposed? Can the unpredictable all by itself bring about order?

By definition, the unpredictable remains thoroughly unpredictable and does not possess even the tiniest ability to select. This then brings us to the more Platonic aspect of this ancient synthesis. As we seek to unravel the dynamics of self-organization, we need a selective element which is truly selective, which is clearly distinct from chance, and which in its radical distinctiveness has genuine power to effect the continuous transformation of chance into meaningful pattern and purposeful project. Not only should this selective principle have the power to organize an entire Universe from within itself, but as an integral part of a valid principle of explanation within science, it should also have the power to rid the human mind of all that cheapens and degrades it in its effort to explain. If we really want to pinpoint that which has power to order and impart direction, and if at the same time we want to free the human mind from the magic of cheap and easy answers, we begin nowhere other than with the concept of mind. We need not hide it, disguise it or call it by any other name. We speak of mind with all its distinctive features of selection, anticipation, memory and imagination, yet mind in no way reduced to narrow notions of human rationality or exalted to more grandiose notions of divine rationality.

But as we set out in chapter one to explore the dynamics of mind, we quickly discover that mind represents but a single pole in a highly complex process dynamic. Turning away from itself, away from any idealistic preoccupation with itself, the perceiving mind orients itself towards something so very unusual, something we should never expect to find in a Western context. For what presents itself to mind in a rush of heuristic excitement is not matter, not even the most chaotic matter in motion, but something far more interesting: chaos itself. This takes us far beyond a simple static Platonism and sets up a state of tension where reality emerges not in the selective, not in the random, but only in the event of their dynamic interaction. Here the selective does not randomize, the random does not select, and neither one defines itself without the other. Hardly could we imagine two principles so opposite and yet so complementary, and as we bring them together in all their radical distinctiveness, we find ourselves describing nothing less than the dynamics of a living organism. For in a living organism we uncover the dynamic of mind selecting over and against some element of the new and unexpected.

This selection and incorporation of the inherently unpredictable assures that the evolution of a system is never simply the unfolding of that which was there all along. The process could never unfold in the same way twice since at all steps and stages we witness a constant influx of the unexpected bubbling up anywhere from within a multiplicity of interrelated levels. No one can deny that there is pattern to the process, but since this pattern is continually bombarded with newness, it quickly distinguishes itself as *unique* and *individual.* In a world of *irreversible* processes where the element of real chance comes into play, we can never rewind the tape of life and watch history repeat itself in the same way twice. In a world of living systems, nothing ever happens according to the inevitability of laws that never change. Lady Luck makes her presence felt not only in the evolution of life on Earth as Stephen J. Gould so correctly maintains, but at each and every step and stage in the evolution of our Universe right on back to its earliest beginning in time. Since every law within our Universe bears the ethereal imprint of random fluctuations, every law has an irreversible story to tell, and since nothing is ever fully stable in the presence of the unpredictable, even those laws that govern the evolution of our Universe are themselves subject to evolution.

Therefore, with the selection and incorporation of the inherently unpredictable, the notion of time acquires meaning. The Now stands out and distinguishes itself over and against both past and future. What meaning could we give to the present if it is nothing more than the unraveling of that which was there all along? Likewise what meaning could we give to the present if it is being pulled, drawn or attracted by some divine energy or force situated in a far-distant future? With nothing either in the past or in the future to guarantee its evolution, the present state of a natural system is filled with *risk.* The inherently unpredictable is just loaded with risk, and its selection and incorporation implies real *responsibility.* It continually calls into question the comfort and security of the confirmation of the past, and it propels us into a future that is in principle wide open. With a past distinct from a present, and with a present distinct from a future, time acquires directionality.

This irreversible movement of time brings us to one of the many Jewish aspects of this ancient synthesis. In the Hebraic view of history, almost unique in the ancient world, time was no illusion. Moving forward instead of endlessly repeating itself, time had a beginning and an end. Filled with promise and hope, time for the ancient Hebrews moved ever so tenuously toward an end or goal. Christianity held on to this ancient notion of time and transformed it even further by radically sharpening the arrow of time in its thrust toward the fullness of an immanent End. In an apocalyptic setting where time rapidly draws to a close but never closes off completely, we find ourselves standing precariously at the edge of time, relatively free from the confirmation of the past, ecstatically disposed to and constantly overwhelmed by that surprising element of the new and unexpected. Just about anything can happen in the flurry and excitement of a real Pentecost. Even the purpose or goal of the entire historical process can suddenly shift or change in new and unexpected ways.

So from within this fluid and open-ended perspective, we need not be afraid of the impulse to unify. Our Universe no longer resembles a vast mechanistic clockwork wound up with incalculable precision by an external God. We dispense with both mechanism and supernaturalism as we delight in a Universe which continually self-organizes and renews itself. This Universe partakes of all the bumpiness and unexpectedness, all the risk and open-endedness which characterize the dynamics of any natural system. It indeed creates itself in that marvelous interaction or *mixture* of what modern process science describes in a variety of ways as chance and necessity, novelty and confirmation, contingency and law, disorder and order. The oneness of our Universe stands out, not in the flatness and uniformity of undifferentiated Being, but in that highly differentiated oneness of a Universe in becoming.

For as we look across the rich multiplicity of interrelated levels within our Universe, we begin to catch glimpses of a pattern which connects, of a pattern of patterns, of that wondrous metapattern which Gregory Bateson kept alluding to and hinting at so often. Each level within our Universe distinguishes itself not only in terms of a stable lawfulness, but also in terms of a highly unstable lawlessness. Einstein's God may not play dice, but the Universe enjoys nothing more. This lawlessness pervades every aspect of the natural world. She provokes change. She allows nothing to sit still. She continually generates diversity between levels as well as uniqueness and individuality within levels. For at every level within our multileveled Universe we see a complex blend of

the lawful and the unlawful,
the predictable and the unpredictable,
the stable and the unstable,
the regular and the irregular,
the logical and the illogical,
the certain and the uncertain,
the expected and the unexpected,
the explainable and the unexplainable,
the normal and the paranormal,
the ordinary and the extraordinary,
and even the commonplace and the miraculous.

We could go on and on attaching names to this fundamental bipolarity within our Universe, but what we want to emphasize above all else is this unmistakable and ubiquitous pattern of "pattern in the midst of inherent unpredictability." This metapattern appears on all levels, and we hope to show in this book how it has the power to unify and thereby sanctify the whole of the natural world of which we are.

Certain aspects of the dynamics at a particular level may appear stable enough to fit loosely a mathematical description, but other aspects, especially if we look closely enough, bear the imprint of tiny fluctuations and demand an historical interpretation. Stephen J. Gould teaches us that ultimately we must make use of the tools of history in our study of the unique and unrepeatable. Yet this amazing insight applies not only to the evolution of life on Earth, but also to that much larger picture encompassing the whole of reality. For as we reach back in time to the very beginning of our Universe, to those first few minutes, seconds and even fractions of a second of the Big Bang, we do not know "where to draw the line between those aspects of the Universe which are attributable to law and those which issue from the revolving doors of chance."[3] The two intermingle and blend in dynamic interaction right on up to that awesome point where randomness and lawlessness simply proliferate in the quantum nebulosity of the earliest imaginable Universe.

A profound randomness therefore characterizes our Universe, and this imparts uniqueness and individuality to it in its bumpy and somewhat less than perfect evolution. Our Universe was born in a cloud of unpredictability, and this same chanciness it has carried all along as the source of its ongoing self-creating potentiality. Free from all supernaturalism, our Universe truly *comes alive* as a single self-organizing and self-sustaining whole. As strange as it may sound in a Western context, we firmly believe that the Universe created itself according to the exigency of nothing *external* to itself. This means that the Universe should have created itself out of the logic of its own *internal necessity* coupled paradoxically to the fluidity of its own *inherent unpredictability*. In other words, the Universe should have created itself out of its own internal freedom and choice. No supernatural act of creation. No external Lawgiver, Architect, Mechanic or Programmer, ordaining, designing, winding up, programming or in any other way messing with, our Universe *from the outside.*

At no step or stage in the birth and evolution of our Universe must we posit some God-given intervention. For how can we impart meaning to the history of our Universe against the backdrop of an almighty and all-knowing God in whose aura all else fades into insignificance? But at the same time we need not strain credulity to a breaking point in positing nothing but the whim of pure chance. For how can we explain order by appealing to disorder alone? The Burgess Shale, the Amazonian rain forest and even man in this mindless scenario would all be reduced to insignificant details on a cold and utterly indifferent landscape. Every page of this book is devoted to the task of restoring risk, relevance and meaning to the story of our Universe, and we could never dream of accomplishing this task without making some fairly serious modifications to both the science and religion as generally understood and practiced here in the West. The supernatural and the mechanical have fed and nourished one another so forcefully within Western thought over such an extended period of time that to break the hold of the combined force of their mesmerizing power over the human mind, we must propose a viable alternative.

So in the place of the supernatural and the mechanical, we propose the cosmological in all its wondrous complementarity. We underline its organic wholeness as well as its raw potentiality, its ability to conserve as well as its ability to generate radical change. In short, we propose a Universe. Once we put *all within the Universe,* then this amazing reality comes alive and admits of a far greater complexity than anything which the method of classical science has been prepared to handle up until now. Once we put *all within the Universe,* then this same reality springs to life within the imagination with an immediacy and power which far exceeds anything offered within classical Western religion. As we abandon the simplicity of the mechanical and the superfluity of the supernatural, we find ourselves standing at a crossroads where science and religion no longer fight and oppose one another. On the contrary each plays a unique and indispensable role in stabilizing the human mind in its effort to know.

Unfortunately, most of us in the West are immersed in the magic of the supernatural and the mechanical. We equate being with the purely mechanistic notion of static spatial structure, and in this sense we identify and categorize all spatially extended objects around us as beings. If we are of a particularly superstitious twist of mind, we make things even more complicated when we take this fundamental structural bias and extend it in the direction of God. We then make a direct and thoroughly nonsensical leap from beings to Being. Underlying static spatial structure is some more fundamental ground of Being, a *substance ultime* as Jean Guitton would say, which we then call God.[4] Even though we may qualify our notion of Being, carefully distinguishing it and setting it apart from any particular being, such logical posturing gets us nowhere. At the end of the day we are forced to introduce so many qualifications that our concept of Being suddenly transforms itself into Nothingness. For within the apophatic tradition in Western theology, no matter what we say about God, it is always more false than it is true.[5] How can science and even religion tolerate such abuse within human discourse? The Western notion of God is a convenient way of explaining everything and nothing at all. Certainly science does not need this hypothesis, and religion suffers no great loss in dispensing with the mysticism of sitting in silence before the emptiness and coldness of the nothingness of Being.

Regrettably many theists will be shocked, hurt and even insulted with this last paragraph. Since many theologians of great intellectual standing have been writing most eloquently for thousands of years about the existence and attributes of a supreme Being, could I not be somewhat less confrontational and declare an openness to forge ahead in their metaphysical quest for a set of theological statements which logically cohere and which hopefully do not deny far more than they affirm? Would it not be possible for me to refine and qualify human discourse so that it could convey positive knowledge about God? By means of rational thought alone, would it not be possible to build up a plausible case for God in a way that would not end up in self-contradiction and denial?

In other words, what I am really asking is: would it not be possible to take one of the most superficial aspects of human intelligence, the faculty of rational thought, and bestow upon it the power to give access to God? In assigning so much power to the rational, do we not run the risk of mutilating, distorting and even falsifying our concept of God? Do our theological constructs not contain so much of the divine that they easily become a platform for extremism, fanaticism and fundamentalism? As the best of these formulations become fixed and frozen into doctrine and dogma, does this not reinforce within us a sense of superiority and power? From such a sublime theological position, are we not tempted to dismiss the faith of less educated peoples as so much naivete and superstition?

Our search for the sacred should have nothing to do with power. If our rationality cannot situate us securely on the lofty terrain of the divine and the theological, should we not turn to other modes of intelligence which we share with the natural world and which situate us on the far more humble terrain of the organismic and the cosmological? So much hangs in the balance, and in spite of the all the pain and confusion this may create, we must move on.

This brings us once again to what we have said earlier about a living organism understood primarily in terms of the complementarity of the selective and the random. A machine by contrast has neither a selective nor random principle which could explain the How or Why of its existence and ongoing operation. When we make the statement that the "Universe is one," we wish to emphasize that our Universe operates not as a machine, but in every respect as a single living organism. If the Universe does indeed resemble a single living organism, then we should expect to find both a selective and a random principle operating at that unique and distinct level of the whole of reality. This selective principle we call Word, and we hope to show in the most general way how Word has the power to organize an entire Universe from within itself. This random principle we call Spirit, and we also hope to show how Spirit serves as the source of the inherent creativity which our Universe possesses in and of itself. Insofar as our Universe comes alive in the interaction of Word and Spirit, it possesses everything that it needs to account for its existence and ongoing evolution. Since it does not require anything outside of itself to explain itself, not only do we face up to and dispense with the hidden need within mechanistic theory for a supernatural principle of explanation, but we also move far away from the dangers of a rigid, unitary and dogmatic concept of truth that so easily instills within us a sense of superiority and power.

According to the theory of knowledge we will attempt to set forth in this book, God represents a point of singularity or a state of perfect symmetry completely unknowable and unreachable even to the clearest intellect. Therefore it makes no sense, either in the context of science or religion, to talk about God in a direct and unqualified manner. Jewish monotheism had always experienced much tension in its effort to speak about God. When it spoke, for example, of the Hand or Finger of God, it struggled courageously with the utterly impossible logical task of trying to analogize the knowable and the unknowable. Such language may have been rich in poetic feeling, but it never came close to capturing anything of God as such. Without denying or eliminating God in any way, Christianity resolved this dilemma about how to speak about God by bringing to centerstage the two cosmological realities of Word and Spirit. Representing two very distinct yet complementary experiences, they operate so directly and immediately, so personally and intimately, that they can no longer be contained within the featureless and unknowable transcendence of God. They drop right out of God and into the heart of a living Universe.

We suggest that insofar as we say anything about God outside of the direct and immediate experience of Word and Spirit, then we have adopted a supernaturalist position. Let us define supernaturalism as any program of thought which claims to provide knowledge about God outside of the ecstatic and prophetic experience of a living Universe. As Word has to do with all that is selective and orderly within our Universe, and as Spirit has to do with all that is random and disorderly within our Universe, how could we ever attempt to reduce the rich polarity of these two completely opposite cosmological realities to the flatness and singularity of a supernatural Being? Logically the selective and the random exclude one another so forcefully that any rational effort to bring them together in a unitary manner implies a logical contradiction of the highest order. No refinement of human discourse will do the job, and even in what was supposed to be the most profound mystical silence, all that I have ever experienced was the deepest emptiness and void.

If we want to get a fairly good idea of what the vibrant interaction of Word and Spirit is all about, then let us turn to those letters which the apostle Paul wrote to the Gentile churches he had founded. Together with Paul we emphasize the *shared experience* of Spirit, which represents an entire worshipping assembly fused into a single state of *collective* ecstasy. Then what happens next is truly amazing and obviously quite difficult to follow within a Western setting. For it is out of the deep communion and togetherness of Spirit that prophetic images emerge within the *collective imagination.* Yes, you have read it correctly: not *my* imagination or *your* imagination, but that vibrant and vivid animistic domain of a *collective* imagination. C. G. Jung may have written quite accurately about a collective *unconsciousness,* but very few psychiatrists, philosophers or even theologians in Western thought have been prepared to write about the validity and sheer excitement of being on the inside of a collective *imagination.* Here we are no longer talking about the thought process of a lone individual but the thought process of a tribe or corporate entity. Note well its fundamental bipolarity.

On the one hand, we find the nebulous, fluid, random and unexpected movement of Spirit, expressing itself through a state of collective ecstasy wherein the assembly of worshippers are fused into a single corporate entity. The early Christians used metaphors of wind and water to describe the dynamic and unpredictable movement of Spirit. On the other hand, we find the more selective movement of Word, expressing itself in terms of prophecy, concretely understood by First-Century Christianity as the speaking of the very words of living Word. *Here they experienced the spontaneous generation of images within the collective mind of that new self-organizing entity they had become.* Since Word and Spirit were primarily cosmological realities, worship represented that truly awesome experience which situated them right at the very heart and core of a living Universe. Here it was not even a question of understanding or defining the Universe as a living organism but of actually *experiencing* it as such, and right within their experience of being transformed, transfigured and renewed in worship through the fullness of a living Universe, they were given a window out onto God which no rational formulation, unitary description or mystical silence could ever provide.

Long before our scientific culture elevated the faculty of rational computation to a status far above all other processes of thought, indigenous peoples throughout the world have benefited in innumerable ways from a mode of tribal reflection very similar to what we find within New Testament experience. How firmly embedded we are within a cultural tradition which arrogantly dismisses any suggestion of the validity of this direct and spontaneous mode of tribal thought. Yet as a product of the natural world, surely we must still possess deep within some kind of bond that unites us to our evolutionary origins. Surely there must be some remnant or residue within the human psyche of the way intelligence operates, not only within indigenous peoples, but also within and throughout the whole of the natural world. Could it be that what happens in worship is the closest we could ever come to an experience of how nature itself has been selecting, thinking, anticipating, and thereby evolving long before we ever came on the scene? This is not simply a matter of exploring some logical landscape in search of an analogy which links human thought to the creative thought processes of nature. It goes much deeper. It's a matter of finding a fundamental homology or relationship in kind which posits that both man and nature share a common *intersubjective* bond.

Perhaps the most difficult problem which the reader must resolve before he or she would be in a position to accept the possibility of a deep link between human and non-human subjectivity lies in that much debated arena of the relationship between mind and matter. As we move into this troublesome area, the reader may note a shift in emphasis from Logos to Mind. Even though we tend to associate Logos more closely with the ecstatic and prophetic thought process of *worshipping* subjects, and even though we tend to associate Mind more closely with the evolutionary thought process of *perceiving* subjects, still the reader will find throughout this book a certain ambiguity in the usage of these two words. Logos may cross over at times into the *imaginal* landscape of Mind, but Mind generally does not cross over into the more *numinous* landscape of Logos. Either Logos or Mind may function adequately in a description of the dynamics of perception, but Mind does not always function well in a description of the dynamics of worship. Perhaps at the level of the deepest link between human and non-human subjectivity, this distinction between Logos and Mind has no meaning. For we feel that Mind in the act of selecting and creating new biological forms and patterns of behavior, and Logos in the act of leading, guiding and organizing a tribal unit in the event of worship, are indeed one and the same.

In any case, returning to the problem of the relationship between mind and matter, we note three distinctive positions within the history of Western thought: idealism, materialism and dualism. On the one hand, if we try to explain everything in terms of mind, we end up with a fanciful idealism. Most scientists and philosophers have little problem in understanding that pure idealism, grounded as it is in nothing other than mind, does not offer us a satisfactory theory of explanation. On the other hand, if we try to explain everything in terms of matter, we end up with a very sober materialism. However, we cannot help but feel that pure materialism, since it does not and cannot take into account the mind and the imagination of the scientist or philosopher reflecting on this problem of the relationship between mind and matter, also does not offer a satisfactory explanation. Dualism, as articulated by the 17th-Century philosopher, Rene Descartes, had little concern for purity as it tried to overcome the tension and absolute contradiction of these two warring epistemologies.

The position taken in this book would appear at first glance to be nothing more than a variant of the idealist position. For we maintain throughout this book that *reality emerges only within mind.* Insofar as we identify even the smallest corner of our Universe as possessing an existence outside of the constructive operation of mind, then we have adopted a dualist position. We define dualism as that theory which accords an independent existence to objects outside of their relationship to perceiving subjects. Dualism posits the reality of mind over and against a pre-given and ready-made world of external objects. But if everything we could possibly say about objects only emerges within mind, then surely this has to be a clear-cut case of an idealist position. How could we ever hope to build a unified theory of knowledge upon the vacillation and whim of every perceiving subject?

Hopefully it will become apparent that mind is a whole lot more comprehensive than human mind, and that intelligence is infinitely more subtle than rational computation. In chapters one and two, we make a case for that highly differentiated Mind of a living and evolving Universe. In chapter three the effort to unify becomes paramount as we set out to describe the emergence and evolution of images within the comprehensive subjectivity of a Universe. In chapter four we explore with the help of First-Century Christianity how this same cosmological dynamic unfolds within the human imagination, while the appendix on Sir Isaac Newton represents an attempt to bind the vocabulary of the first three chapters to that of the fourth. All the while we emphasize repeatedly that Mind does not self-differentiate in idealistic isolation: it only selects and anticipates, evolves and grows within the context of that totally opposite yet fully complementary process pole of the inherent unpredictability of Spirit.

In order to obtain a better understanding of what this new process pole of Spirit could be, we turn to the three great intellectual achievements of the 20th Century: relativity theory, quantum physics and nonequilibrium thermodynamics. We examine them briefly, not to construct some definitive statement about the structure of our Universe, but primarily as an aid in shattering the neat deterministic picture of 17th-Century science. For within the new conceptual framework of 20th-Century thought, randomness becomes an essential and irreducible feature of the Universe. From the smallest to the largest structures within an expanding Universe, from the earliest to the latest stages in its historical evolution, randomness has always and everywhere played a central and indispensable role. All three of these great intellectual achievements point to the possibility that, at the junction of space and time, there is something over and against mind far more interesting and far more complex than the dullness and simplicity of bumping bits of matter. And here we feel justified in going beyond discussions of scientific probability or the lack of precision which accompanies every legitimate effort to know. For we cannot help but view the chaotic movement of Spirit in a far more positive sense as that endlessly creative source of newness and change which is indissolubly linked to the dynamics of every living and evolving system.

If our theory of knowledge were not grounded in this new process pole, then we would have no other choice than to accept the idealistic accusation in silence. But if Mind exists as Mind only in complete and utter dependency upon that rich and creative source of the newness and unexpectedness of Spirit, then the idealistic accusation cannot stand. We hope to show in the pages that follow, not only how the inherent unpredictability of Spirit grounds the truly historical evolution of our Universe in time, assuring that the future is not contained in a present which has all been predetermined from the past, but we also hope to show how Spirit grounds the historical acquisition of knowledge, assuring that the evolution of knowledge within our Universe is not simply the unraveling of some supernatural plan or eternal law which has been there all along. Spirit puts time back into history, and risk and adventure back into the quest for knowledge. She dismisses the logical necessity of some supernatural "world behind this world," which in the final analysis always underlies and justifies every purely mechanistic or materialistic program of thought. But most importantly, she grounds the self-organizing activity of Mind and prevents it from soaring away on an idealistic flight of fancy.

We propose that Mind exists and operates as Mind only over and against the newness and unexpectedness of Spirit. Without the incessant transformation and integration of newness, Mind quickly atrophies and dies. But if the reality of Mind is grounded in Spirit, then the opposite is equally true: Spirit exists and operates as Spirit only over and against Mind. The inherent unpredictability of Spirit does not exist in itself, but only over and against a mental or subjective frame of reference for whom all this newness and unexpectedness has meaning. As opposite as these two cosmological principles may be, neither one could exist without the other. Only within their deepest bipolarity, do we uncover the unity of an evolving Universe.

Therefore within a process theory of knowledge, we propose that *a Universe emerges afresh* in each and every act of the dynamic interaction of Word and Spirit. This is not idealism, materialism, dualism or supernaturalism. It is a far more complex theory grounded in our experience of a living Universe.

As we set out to elaborate this theory, we draw much inspiration from the late Erich Jantsch who wrote, "We stand at the beginning of a new synthesis."[6] In the same spirit the Nobel laureate Ilya Prigogine and Isabelle Stengers also believe that "we are heading toward a new synthesis, a new naturalism."[7] The old alliance between science and nature, between science and society, between science and religion has been shattered. "Our role," say Prigogine and Stengers, "is not to lament the past. It is to try to discover in the midst of the extraordinary diversity of the sciences some unifying thread."[8] In this book we hope to catch a glimpse of that unifying thread. Our hope is grounded in the simple intuition which Prigogine and Stengers have stated so clearly: "We are living in a single universe."[9] In other words, that unifying thread could be nothing other than the Universe itself.

Chapter 1

Towards a Theory of Knowledge

But in trying to catch glimpses of this unifying thread, we are confronted with many non-intuitive features that run in sharp opposition to most of the principle presuppositions of our modern Western culture. How thoroughly obsessed we are in the West with static spatial structure or matter. Our culture lies deeply entrenched in the fallacy of a naive materialism: "What we see and touch is real, and everything else is less real." With little reflection we hold on to the old Western stereotypes of structure-oriented thinking, and we define coconuts and pigs, for example, simply in terms of those spatially extended objects which fall from trees or lie in the mud. In trying to fashion some notion relating to the whole of reality, we continue along the same distorted logical pathway and conceive of the Universe as nothing more than a gigantic object spatially extended over billions of light years. Filled with a myriad of self-existent parts, it knocks about blindly and mindlessly with absolutely no pattern, purpose or logic. Finally things get even more complicated, as we have noted in our introduction, when we take this structure-oriented bias and extend it in the direction of God. Underlying static beings is some more fundamental ground of Being which we then call God. In the end we understand nothing of pigs and coconuts, we understand nothing of the complexity of our Universe, and what we understand of God only serves to create endless generations of agnostics and atheists.

Within our modern mechanistic framework we take parts or equilibrium structures as our point of departure. These parts exist independently of each other, they are extended in space, they lie outside of one another, and they are connected only by simple external relationships. When we focus on parts it becomes so very difficult to explain even the most common features of our world. How, for example, do we explain concepts such as life or mind within a static framework? Surely an equilibrium structure has no life or mind, and the only way to overcome this dilemma is to introduce some sort of vital or mental principle operating on the inside as mysteriously as a ghost in a machine.

Here in the West we are happy with explanations that explain everything and nothing at all. Our psychiatrists will label a person neurotic or schizophrenic as if the neurosis or schizophrenia was a property of an isolated self. They focus on fictitious inner drives and tendencies that come nowhere close to explaining the complex interrelatedness of the self.[10] Some of our theologians are not far behind in their excitement about supernatural forces, radial energies or other such intangible elements lurking within or behind a world of material objects. They supposedly delve right into the "inner core of things," explaining the "numinous psychical inner-side of matter" or the "intrinsic interior value of the physical world." Most biologists rightfully deplore these mysterious drives or energies as propounded by psychiatrists and theologians, but when these same biologists begin to talk of selfish genes, organizers, regulators, or even genetic programs, they impart to these mechanisms the power to produce global order, and as Prigogine and Stengers would say, they mistake the formulation of the problem for its solution.[11]

The physicist of the classical Newtonian school might ridicule the psychiatrist, the theologian, and the biologist in their misguided effort to explain. But when this same physicist begins to speak of some mysterious force called gravity operative between the isolated and self-existent elements of his mechanistic world and somehow explaining their interaction and behavior, then he too jumps into a fantasy world of no explanation. The notion of a force in physics may be nothing more than a convenient anthropomorphism, says the astronomer John Barrow.[12] Einstein's general theory of relativity no longer allows us to speak of forces acting between self-existent, rigid bodies. The presence of what we call particles of matter and their motion determine the local topography of the space in which they situate. Each body moves along "the most economical path available to it on the undulating space created by *all the particles in the Universe.*" "The concept of a force has been subsumed," says Barrow, "within the more elegant and powerful conception of a dynamic space-time geometry."[13] Matter in motion determines spatial geometry as well as the rate of flow of time, and symbiotically this space-time geometry dictates how matter is to move.[14] Space bends, time warps, and what we should abstract as isolated bodies within the dynamic fabric of space-time, they in fact are capable of expanding and contracting according to the flow of the larger whole. So we end up with an unbroken indivisible space-time continuum encompassing the whole of the Universe. Just as space without time and time without space is an abstraction, so too an independent rigid body or a static spatial structure floating about within absolute time and absolute space represents an abstraction from within a much more complex and unified whole. This moves us far away from static spatial structure or matter, far away from any magical energies or forces operating within or between these static entities, and into that absolutely exciting arena of space-time process where whole new logical panoramas open up to us as never before in our effort to explain the world around us.

An Interrelated Universe

If we let this concept of dynamic space-time turn around long enough in our minds, we soon come to the shocking realization that isolated things do not exist. *No object explains itself.* Nothing sits off in some relationally disjoint corner of the Universe and possesses its existence independently from everything else. We define existence in terms of relationship, and something that does not relate does not exist. More specifically when we say that something exists, what we really mean to say is that it stands in relationship to the whole of Universe. Its identity does not lie within itself but precisely in the way it situates, functions and interacts within the context of everything else.

Relativity theory supports this point of view. With the introduction of universal constants such as the speed of light and Plank's constant, the claim of science to absolute and universal truth was destroyed. Since light travels at a finite speed, we cannot define the absolute simultaneity of two distant events.[15] Simultaneity occurs only with respect to a particular frame of reference, and since an observer can only be in one place at a time and not everywhere at once, since no two observers can occupy the same frame of reference, objectivity is not so objective after all. In a static world, objectivity defines itself in the *absence of a frame of reference,* whereas in a relational world, objectivity defines itself only in the *presence of a frame of reference.* In the former, we contemplate truth from the outside in a detached and indifferent manner, completely separate from what we are observing, while in the latter, we participate in truth from on the inside, somehow as an integral part of what we are observing.

But as soon as pull away from the security of absolute objectivity, many of us here in the West start getting terribly uneasy. We feel that we are diving right into a pit of pure subjectivity where the lone observer is the measure of all truth. Western thought so easily oscillates between two barren and utterly sterile positions: either we know everything or we know nothing at all. Focusing only on isolated objects, the human mind is carried to messianic or even demonic heights in an almost savage thrust toward knowledge and toward the control that this knowledge imparts. Focusing only on isolated subjects, the human mind can wallow and float in an oblivious ocean of no knowledge. In contrast to these two radical extremes, we seek a richly differentiated knowledge arrived at in that delicate balance and incredible difference between knowing everything and knowing nothing at all.

Since no one but the most arrogant fanatic would claim to possess all knowledge, we leave him alone in his ivory tower. But we cannot ignore the more sinister position of the skeptic who laughs in the face of every legitimate effort to know. In spite of the most noble and heroic efforts of countless generations to understand our world, he would argue that knowledge of any real significance or meaning is not possible at all. But to deny the validity of the entire evolutionary thrust within man toward knowledge puts the skeptic in a rather difficult logical position. *To argue no knowledge demands knowledge, can only be done from a position of knowledge, and is therefore a self-contradictory idea.* Somehow we operate out of a higher knowledge or belief that knowledge is possible. Somehow we know that our effort to know is not a "doomed and hopeless task."[16]

Quantum physics also supports a relational understanding of reality. A quantum particle is not an independently existing object, says Henry Stapp of the University of California: "It is, in essence a set of relations that reach outward to other things."[17] Yet quantum physics introduces a very peculiar twist to our understanding of this relationality. Whether an electron behaves as a particle or a wave depends upon the experimental situation in which it is forced to react. In a static view we aim at the complete description of the object in question, attaching no importance to how we go about observing it. But in quantum physics we have to decide ahead of time which questions we are going to ask and how we intend to observe, and this determines the kind of answers we will get.

If we ask a particle question, we will get a particle answer. If we ask a wave question, we will get a wave answer. No single theoretical language allows us to grab hold of reality and describe it completely.[18]

But quantum physics not only teaches us that we need an irreducible plurality of perspectives, all of which may be complementary, but it also teaches the far more disconcerting truth that certain properties of what we observe do not exist in the absence of observation. Prior to the event of observation, existence is nebulous and ambiguous. We cannot explain this nebulosity in terms of a disturbance due to the clumsiness of our measuring instruments or in terms of local hidden variables.[19] The act of making a measurement, the very act of observation, transforms this nebulous wavelike state into certainty by "projecting out or selecting a specific result from among a range of possibilities."[20] This *selection through observation* brings about an "abrupt alteration in the form of the wave function often referred to as its collapse," and this "drastically affects it subsequent evolution."[21] The act of measurement takes place when some sort of record or trace is *irreversibly* generated, and when this record or trace conveys *meaningful* information to the observer.[22]

Quantum physics therefore grounds existence in the event of observation, and it would assert that elementary particles are not so elementary after all: "They are of a secondary, derivative nature. Rather than providing the concrete stuff from which the world is made, these elementary particles are actually essentially *abstract* constructions based upon the solid ground of irreversible observation events or measurement records."[23] Since in quantum physics the mind of the observing scientist remains at all times an irreducible feature of the experimental situation, not only do we define reality in relational terms, but we also define it in the quirkiness of its relationship to mind.

The Dynamics of Perception

This takes us away from the mechanics of self-existent objects and into the dynamics of perceiving subjects. As we try to understand the dynamics of the perceiving mind, we quickly learn that perception is not the passive mirroring of a pre-given world. Perhaps the quickest entry into this complex world lies in a brief analysis of the concept of *difference*. Gregory Bateson once said: "A sensory end organ is a comparator, a device which responds to difference."[24] Perception operates upon difference or more precisely the *news of difference.* What we perceive is not this or that but the difference immanent in the mutual *relationship* between this or that. As perceiving subjects, if somehow we could focus our attention upon the singular, we would find that it, too, by necessity would be subject to even further differentiation. The moment differentiation stops, we have not reached some ultimate substance or ground of being. Rather we stand at the limits of perception and peer into an abyss of nothingness. An undifferentiated sameness, a state of flat singularity, or a state of perfect symmetry is, as far as the perceiving mind is concerned, indistinguishable from nothing.

In reading this black and white text, where do we find difference? In a very real sense difference is not to be found anywhere. It is not in the ink or in the paper, not even in some supposed space between the ink and the paper.[25] As long as we keep on thinking in terms of substance or materiality, we miss the enormous difference that difference makes. To deal with difference correctly, we must adopt the language of space-time process, a language that incorporates in an integral way the element of *time.* Gregory Bateson once gave the example of a light switch to illustrate this crucial ingredient:[26] in the "on" position the switch functions as part of an electric circuit and does not exist as a switch, and in the "off" position it represents a gap between two conductors which themselves only operate as conductors when there is no gap. Since a switch is not an electric circuit or a gap in an electric circuit, a switch only comes into existence *at a particular moment in the event of change relative to a previous state.* A switch strictly speaking has no substance or materiality.

We could go on to compare a sensory end organ to a switch, noting that our senses are turned on and off by some sort of triggering which comes into effect when a certain sensory threshold has been reached, but this would take us too far afield. We return to the notion of difference, and we take note of its intrinsic immateriality. Once time incorporates itself into a thing, it no longer defines itself as a thing but as an *event.* We might venture to suggest at this point that *immaterial mind deals only with immaterial differences,* but we do not want to leave the impression that difference is not real. *The difference between the presence of a difference and the absence of a difference is precisely that incredible difference between reality and illusion.*

Now difference is difference, it only arises as difference, it only presents itself as difference *relative to mind.* In relativity theory, reality defines itself only with respect to a frame of reference. A camera, of course, does not constitute a frame of reference. Even a camera feeding data into a computer does not constitute a frame of reference, even though these mechanical objects may be quite useful in assisting human beings in acquiring one. Therefore in addition to the two "somethings" in whose relationship difference is immanent, we underline mind as an indispensable third leg in a sort of *perceptual triangle*. Only mind selects out or judges difference to be difference.

Mind is that irreducible frame of reference without which difference has no meaning. A difference that may be highly *relevant* with respect to one mind may be quite irrelevant with respect to some other mind. "How are we to specify ... edges, boundaries, texture and orientation, if not in relation to some perceiver for whom these distinctions are *relevant*."[27] In other words mind does not deal with just any kind of difference. Mind deals with differences that make a difference, that is, with *meaningful* differences or what we call information.[28] In quantum physics the act of measurement takes place when some sort of record or trace is irreversibly generated, and only when this record or trace conveys meaningful information to the observer.

Are we saying then that there is no Universe outside of our perceptual triangle? That there is no pre-given world outside of mind in its formation and transformation of difference? Yes, and we would even suggest that only in the event of the interaction of immaterial mind with immaterial difference does a Universe emerge from nothingness. What a strange Universe we live in, where difference is only difference relative to mind, where mind is only mind in its active construction and transformation of difference, and where neither one of these two immaterial principles defines itself without the other. More specifically, what emerges in the interaction of these two opposite yet complementary poles situates at the level of what we call an *image*. We would then suggest that *immaterial mind deals with immaterial differences in constructing images of a material world*. We rejoin Bateson's profound epistemological insight that he expressed in a rather amusing way: we do not have pigs or coconuts in our brain - only *images* of pigs and coconuts.[29]

A beautiful example of the constructive role of mind can be found in the perception of color. Drawing upon some of the latest findings in neuroscience, psychology, artificial intelligence and linguistics, we make the surprising discovery that there is no one-to-one correspondence between perceived color and locally reflected light.[30] There are structures at all levels of our internal visual pathways that participate in some way in our perception of color.[31] Color is not perceived in isolation from other attributes, such as the shape, size, texture, motion and orientation of an object.[32] Visual perception itself is in active exchange with other sensory modalities such as the perception of sound and our horizontal/vertical perception.[33] To this we might add the influence of a variety of cognitive expectancies and memories.[34] There are aspects of color perception, which are specific to the human species, since we know that other species have evolved different perceived worlds of color,[35] and there are even aspects of color which are specific to a specific culture.[36] Thus we actively organize and structure all the various hue/saturation/brightness combinations into a limited set of color categories, and we end up associating names with these categories.[37] These color categories arise from out of a tangled hierarchy of perceptual and cognitive processes that stretch far beyond the isolated observer. Sight, sound, taste, smell, texture - all conspire in forming and constructing within the imagination that which we call an image.[38]

If the intensity and wavelength composition of light fail to explain our perception of color, then color does not exist in a pre-given world outside of mind. What we call red has no ready-made existence outside of our imaginative construction of red, and *the same would apply to each and every property of material objects.* It might seem immanently obvious that there is nothing we can say about something that lies outside of our perception and enactment of it, but still we operate under the grand illusion that cognition is simply the representation of a pre-given world by a pre-given mind. Our minds do such a remarkably consistent job in constructing a Universe of meaning that we naively believe that this Universe has an independent existence outside of mind. But in the last analysis, our knowing can never reach beyond the world of images and penetrate into some other world. *We deny categorically any dualistic tendency in support of a world behind this world.* The Universe is one. We are living in a single Universe, and these internal images and pictures emerging within the imagination are all we have got. They indeed have a cogency and reality. They are what we know, and as hard as we may try, we have no way of ever knowing anything else.[39] Since we can never get behind an image to something more basic, we arrive at the very limits of knowledge.

At this point someone might object and say that we have worked ourselves into a fanciful idealism. Not really. We do not deny difference. But what could we possibly say about difference prior to its selection, formation and enactment within the imagination? *How could we possibly imagine that which comes before images within the imagina-*

tion? Let it suffice for the moment that we distinguish difference from a state of perfect symmetry or nothingness, which by definition contains no differences, and that we situate it firmly within our Universe as that primordial source out of which and from which all perception proceeds.

Our Western culture lies deeply entangled in the fallacy of a naive materialism. In true Cartesian style we situate the material world "out there" over and against immaterial mind "in here." We assume that materiality is the ground of perception as if mind played no role whatsoever in the construction of a Universe of meaning. We make the sad and dangerous mistake of putting materiality, which is but the end result of a process of perceptual abstraction, at its beginning. However, over and against mind we do not find matter but a completely different bipolar point of reference. Instead we find that rather strange and unusual process pole of the new, the unexpected, and the different.

The Dynamics of Natural Systems

So the emphasis shifts away from material objects to that marvelous reality of living subjects. In process terms our Universe on all levels could be none other than a Universe of living organisms. We define a living organism in terms of a self-organizing, self-referential, self-renewing, hierarchically structured, autopoietic whole or mind - selecting and differentiating, evolving and growing in constant interaction with some element of the new and unexpected.

With regard to itself, an autopoietic system is in the first place self-referential, geared to the renewal of itself, whereas an allopoietic system or machine refers to a function from the outside, such as the production of a specific output.[40] In terms of the arrangement of process, a living system is hierarchic: we discover systems within systems within the total system in question. With regard to its structure, as we have noted previously, it is not a question of static spatial structure but of dynamic space-time process. With regard to its environment, an autopoietic system is open - open not only with respect to the exchange of energy and information but most importantly open with respect to the new and unexpected. It is not a structure-preserving entity de-evolving toward a state of equilibrium or death, but a space-time entity evolving toward a state of non-equilibrium or life. And finally in terms of total system dynamics, a living system organizes itself from the inside, in strong contrast to a machine that is organized by man from the outside.

We do not doubt for a moment our purposeful intentions in making machines. But if machines should possess purpose from the outside through the agency of man who makes them, why should we make such a fuss about attributing purpose to an autopoietic system which contains its purpose from within itself? Even the strong biological reductionist Jacques Monod was forced to admit that living organisms are endowed with a purpose or project, and this he recognized as essential to their very definition as living organisms.[41] The purpose of a living organism unfolds from within the dynamics of its own internal self-organization, and to deny purpose with respect to a living organism amounts to a denial of self-organization. All self-organization by definition is purposeful, but this purposeful, guided or self-directed unfolding of a living organism becomes difficult to pin down since it always takes place in constant interaction with that degree of the new and unexpected available to it at its particular level of self-organization. Living organisms evolve, grow and even behave at times in a most unpredictable manner, and their goal or purpose can suddenly shift or expand in new and unexpected ways.

Classical mechanistic dynamics had focused attention on isolated self-existent rigid bodies mindlessly bumping about in absolute space and time. These rigid bodies moved along so deterministically within the idealized world of 17th-Century science that their motion was understood to be completely reversible with respect to time. Knowledge of their position and momentum in the present should eventually give access to both their past and future states. In this scientific fantasy world, where each cause had a measurable, predictable and controllable effect, the dynamics of a pool table were projected onto the whole of reality.

This neat deterministic picture was challenged in the 19th Century with the advent of thermodynamics. "Thermodynamics appears as the first form of a science of complexity."[42] Thermodynamics focused not on single particles but on *whole populations of particles*. It inaugurated an important shift in thought from the local and individual to the global and statistical.[43] It introduced for the first time notions of process and of average effects within processes. Around 1852 it came up with its well-known *second law* which stated that the entropy of an isolated and closed system increases until it reaches a point of thermodynamic equilibrium.[44] Entropy represents that part of the total energy in a system which is not freely available and which cannot be put to work in a direct way.[45] In other words it represents irreversibly wasted energy, and the second law says that entropy in a closed system never decreases. If we isolate a system, then in time it irreversibly runs down and dies.

In contrast to classical dynamics, thermodynamics introduced the notion of irreversibility or directionality in our understanding of time. "Here we reach the most original contribution of thermodynamics, the concept of irreversibility."[46] At the global level of whole populations of particles, the symmetry between past and future in Newtonian physics is broken. Time in this new conceptual framework now points in a direction, it has an arrow as Arthur Stanley Eddington called it, it moves from past to future. In a closed system, entropy will increase with the flow of time, and order will eventually degenerate into disorder. A closed system evolves toward its most probable state of maximum disorder: in short, it self-disorganizes and dies. The original formulator of the second law, William Thomson, made a "dizzy leap from engine technology to cosmology."[47] He imagined the Universe to be a closed system and applied the second law of thermodynamics to the whole of reality. What a horrible vision of a Universe burning like a furnace![48] Pessimism and gloom, death and despair, characterized this 19th-Century cosmology of the giant universal steam engine inexorably grinding down to nothingness and death.[49] Such a view had no foundation in science: it merely reflected the "social and economic upheaval of the time."[50] Even to this day cosmologists still speculate about the "heat death" of our Universe.[51]

But what happens if a dynamic system is not isolated and closed but open to its environment, like all living systems? Instead of running down, it enters into a far-from-equilibrium state by continuously importing free energy from its environment and by exporting entropy. In apparent contradiction to the second law of thermodynamics, entropy does not have to accumulate and increase. Surprisingly in open systems it can stay at the same level or even decrease. A continuous energy exchange between the system and its environment takes place, and as a consequence, *order spontaneously arises out of disorder.* Even "inanimate" systems can self-organize and renew themselves,[52] and this represents a highly improbable state, as the Viennese physicist Ludwig Boltzmann called it.[53] Nonequilibrium structures may even lead to situations that would appear impossible from the classical point of view.[54] If we should try to explain them mechanistically as the result of purely blind collisions, surely we would have to label them as totally miraculous.

It was the genius of Nobel prizewinner Ilya Prigogine and his school of thought to focus on thermodynamic non-equilibrium as a source of order, self-organization, self-renewal, and spontaneous dynamic structuration. This new ordering principle Prigogine called *order through fluctuation.*[55] Over and beyond classical dynamics and equilibrium thermodynamics, Prigogine introduced a third dynamic regime, the level of dissipative structures. He introduced the notion of a *dissipative structure* to emphasize the close association between structure and order on the one hand, and dissipation or waste on the other.[56]

A dissipative structure is never completely stable, and when fluctuations exceed a certain critical size, it becomes highly unstable.[57] At this point entropy production increases significantly, and the system spares no expense in its creative buildup toward a new structure. The system reaches a thermodynamic branch where two new structures, mirror images of one another, become spontaneously available.[58] Nothing determines at this point how the system will behave. Prigogine and Stengers underline that at this critical bifurcation point, an irreducible random element comes into play.[59] Not simply an expression of our ignorance or lack of information, the random is truly random. Since we have no way of predicting the path the system will take, a deterministic description breaks down altogether. Indeterminacy, no longer the sole property of quantum physics, asserts itself on the macroscopic level as well.[60] Since tiny fluctuations may override average values in a decisive way, the law of large numbers does not apply.[61] Always dependent on the previous history of the system, but in no way determined by this previous history,[62] a qualitative change takes place as the structure goes beyond a certain critical threshold into a new level of dynamic self-organization.

Prigogine and Stengers maintain a close connection between randomness and the irreversibility of time:

> Boltzmann already understood that probability and irreversibility had to be closely related. Only when a system behaves in a sufficiently random way may the difference between past and future, and therefore irreversibility, enter into its description. Our analysis confirms this point of view. Indeed what is the meaning of an arrow of time in a deterministic description of nature? If the future is already in some way contained in the present, which also contains the past, what is the meaning of the arrow of time? The arrow of time is a manifestation of the fact that the future is not given, that, as the French poet Paul Valery emphasized, "time is construction."[63]

In the context of true randomness, process becomes *historical* process. It could never repeat itself in the same way twice since at each critical step and stage in its development, we witness the intrusion of some surprising aspect of the new and unexpected. With the continuous incorporation of newness, each historical process differentiates itself in a unique and individual manner, and it is this continuous differentiation which marks the flow of time. This prevents us from viewing history as a kind of unfolding where everything now and in the future is simply the unraveling of that which was there all along. David Bohm's notion of the unfolding of time can easily be understood in this sense. We distance ourselves from the Eastern notion of an eternally recurring cycle of the same, and we situate ourselves firmly within our Judeo-Christian tradition which views history as a linear unfolding having both a beginning and an end.

The *historical* path that a system follows is characterized by a succession of both stable and unstable regions. In the stable regions, lawfulness abounds, but at the critical bifurcation points, lawlessness comes into play. Both elements are "inextricably connected," and it is precisely this "mixture of chance and necessity" which constitutes the "history of a system."[64] Instead of viewing chance and necessity in sequence as Jacques Monod had done - "the utterly improbable chance of a self-producing molecular combination being 'hit' is followed by the absolute necessity of survival"[65] - we view them in their full complementarity. Where do these two complementary principles appear? We do not have to look very hard before we come to the rather startling conclusion that they appear throughout the whole of the natural world.

For in trying to describe the dynamics that govern the interactions at various levels within our multileveled Universe, we immediately encounter extraordinary differences between levels. Since they have all been riddled with newness, no two levels are the same. Not only does each level have its own unique logic or law irreducible to that of any other level, but each level also has its own unique and peculiar way of drawing upon the new or unexpected. Moreover, to make things even more complicated, no level sits still. Self-organization at any one level can suddenly shift or expand in new and unexpected ways. Nevertheless, in the midst of all this complex interrelatedness, we begin to catch glimpses of a richly differentiated sameness crosscutting all levels, and we even suggest that this differentiated sameness lies at the basis of our intuition of a single Universe. We believe that the Universe is one, that it evolved from a common origin and that it is linked by the same homologous principles. We should have no problem finding evidence from a variety of disciplines in support of this belief.[66] Not only do we have a formal similarity among levels, but a true homology or relationship in kind. This fundamental homology displays itself on every level as the dynamic and complementary interaction of two poles. Running through the vocabulary of modern process science, we find many ways to describe these two poles: chance and necessity,[67] novelty and confirmation,[68] contingency and law, sometimes even chaos and order. Long before these distinctions were made within science, the Mexican Yaqui Indians spoke of the nagual and the tonal.[69] We understand the arrow of time and the irreversibility of life processes in terms of the transformation of the former pole into the latter. It is precisely their dynamic interaction or *mixture* which constitutes the *history* of a system. On every level of self-organization within our multileveled Universe we see some sort of selecting, ordering, forming, confirming, organizing, logical, mental or lawful pole, which we call *Word*, drawing upon that random, new, indeterminate, nebulous, uncertain, unexpected or lawless pole, which we call *Spirit*. This fundamental homology or metapattern of Word drawing upon Spirit appears on all levels and connects wide domains of reality,[70] unifying and also sanctifying the whole of the natural world of which we are.

Intersubjective Agreement

As our perceptual triangle would suggest, the observing subject and the observed object form an unbroken whole, they constitute an indissoluble and necessary unity. This, of course, would make it very hard for someone to doubt the existence of the Universe. Fortunately for us, there are not too many people who argue the non-existence of the Universe. Two rather unusual positions come to mind in this regard. On the one hand, the solipsist who observes that he alone exists has to contend with the observations of other solipsists who share a similar conviction.[71] Obviously their observations taken as a whole contradict one another. On the other hand, the observer who observes that nothing at all exists has to contend at least with the observation of his own existence.[72]

Both of these illogical positions underscore the simple but very important fact that we may never isolate the observer in the act of observation. The observer observes in continuous interaction with other observers, and every observation he makes is colored, shaped, influenced and even biased by the observations of these other observers. All their observations in turn derive their meaning within the broad context of a universal history of observation. This places an important limit on any one observation setting it apart from sheer enthusiasm and wishful thinking. This intersubjective aspect of all observation rescues the lone observer from a narrow and intellectually debilitating subjectivism. The observer observes only within the context and limitation of his interrelatedness with respect to other observers, and therefore we speak of ever-widening circles of observation, which in turn differentiate into an almost endless multiplicity of levels of observation. This eventually widens out to encompass the whole of observing reality. Thus we venture to say that in the observation of any one observer we ultimately find the whole of the Universe in its interrelatedness observing itself.

We stress that this intersubjective aspect of all observation involves a multiplicity of levels. Only in constant interaction with other observers, *who by no means are limited only to human observers,* do we observers construct and enact a Universe of meaning. Now if we define the Universe as the totality of everything enacted by observers, then these observers can no more doubt the existence of the Universe than they can doubt the existence of themselves. Since the whole of the Universe in its interrelatedness stands behind them and supports them in their act of observation, since this act opens up an entire Universe of meaning within their imaginations, since there is no pre-given world lying outside of their intersubjective enactment of a Universe, the non-existence of the Universe is a thoroughly self-contradictory notion.

However, if we remain within the framework of classical physics which focuses on solid spatial structure as somehow existing out there in the absence of observation and relationship, if there is no perceptual triangle binding observers to their Universe, then the question of the existence of the Universe, as obvious as it may appear, does in fact become quite problematic. For how can a Universe be said to exist, if it is made up of isolated parts that exist independently of one another? How can we speak of a Universe when its parts lie outside of one another and are connected only by simple external relations? Where are we going to find a Universe in the midst of self-existent parts which merely bump into one another in a most superficial way? How are we to understand a totally mindless Universe whose parts knock about with absolutely no pattern, purpose, or logic? How are we to situate even a single observer in such a senseless and lifeless setting? A mechanistic universe in its drab and boring simplicity in no way approaches the complexity and excitement of a Universe filled with observers.

When we focus on parts, we forfeit all possibility of understanding our Universe. Any theory of knowledge grounded in the structure of a universe scattered and broken into an infinity of superficially related, self-existent elements will be equally fragmented and superficial, thoroughly unconvincing and lacking any real explanatory power. When we focus on parts, we may have lots of bits and pieces, but we have no *whole* and in the end we have no Universe. When we say that the Universe is one, we are taking a strong epistemological stance in favor of viewing it primarily and predominantly as a whole. The model of a machine gives no intuition or vision of the whole. It may establish the existence of parts, but it does nothing to establish the existence of the Universe. When we focus primarily upon parts and try to argue for the existence of the Universe, we are faced with very much the same logical problem that the supernaturalist faces when he looks out upon his clockwork universe and tries to argue for the existence of God. In both epistemologies, that of the mechanist and that of the supernaturalist, there is no Universe and there is no God.

When we take the *whole* of the Universe as our starting point in a theory of knowledge, then the only model that applies to a whole is that of a living organism. The reality of a living organism can only be understood from the unique and dominant perspective of the whole. No part within the whole can logically or functionally replace the whole, and this whole is always more than the sum of its parts. It is this whole, on the level of all that is, which we call the Universe and whose existence we do not doubt.

But the model of a living organism not only gives rich insight into the unity of the Universe, but it also hints at another equally important aspect of the Universe - its inherent unpredictability. In view of the very structure of the perceiving mind, which only operates upon the meaningful news of difference, it should be difficult to conceive of a Universe that should present itself to us in a flat and undifferentiated way and not contain this element of the new and unpredictable. A Universe whose unity lies in an undifferentiated sameness could never exist, whereas a Universe whose unity is grounded in a richly differentiated sameness incorporating this most essential element of the new and unpredictable is just writhing with contradiction and life. In a sense it is the only Universe which we as observers could ever know, and consequently it is the only Universe which could possibly exist. Open at all times to the unexpected, this Universe does not merely unfold that which was there all along. Its random, unpredictable aspect guarantees a richly differentiated *historical* unfolding in which the future is not explained by a present, which in turn is all explained from out of the past. In other words, our Universe truly *evolves,* and it should come as no surprise, as we hope to point out in the next chapter, that it should do so in fits and starts vaunting lavish and beautiful displays of the unexpected. We accentuate not static unitary being but a richly differentiated process of becoming.

Not only would we argue that a theory of knowledge grounded in superficially related bits and pieces should be as superficial as the interrelatedness of its parts, but we would even be hard-pressed to demonstrate how a theory of knowledge in a deterministic framework could be called a theory of knowledge. How can we speak of knowledge when it is merely the unfolding of some predetermined knowledge or plan which was there all along? In view of the indescribable effort of countless generations to know and understand our world, we would then have to say that the entire enterprise had been nothing but a cruel and senseless game. All this heroic effort expended in the acquisition of knowledge, and it only served to uncover certain eternal verities or truisms that had been there all along!

Instinctively we feel there is a whole lot more. Instinctively we feel that we are part of a living Universe, an integral part of a truth that continually evolves and grows. From within our *experience* of life, we ground our every effort to know. Thus we move on from a theory of knowledge to a theory of life. The two are inseparably intertwined.

Chapter 2

Towards a Theory of Life

Roger Penrose invites us to get a feeling for the uniqueness of our Universe with the following reflection:

> Try to imagine the phase space (cf. p. 177) of the entire universe! Each point in this phase space represents a different possible way the universe might have started off. We are to picture the Creator, armed with a "pin" - which is to be placed at some point in the phase space (Fig. 7.19). Each different positioning of the pin provides a different universe. Now the accuracy that is needed for the Creator's aim depends upon the entropy of the universe that is thereby created. It would be relatively "easy" to produce a high entropy universe, since there would be a large volume of the phase space available for the pin to hit. (Recall that entropy is proportional to the logarithm of the volume of the phase space concerned.) But in order to start off the universe in a state of low entropy - the Creator must aim for a much tinier volume of the phase space. How tiny would this region be, in order that a universe closely resembling the one in which we live would actually result?[73]

After several pages of explanation and mathematical formulas, Penrose produces a figure that reaches as high as 10 to the 10th power to the 123rd power. Penrose comments on how extraordinary such a number is:

> One could not possibly write the number down in full, in the ordinary denary notation: it would be "1" followed by 10,123 successive "0"s! Even if we were to write a zero on each separate proton and on

each separate neutron in the entire universe - and we could throw in all the other particles as well for good measure - we would fall far short of writing down the figure needed. The precision needed to set the universe on its course is seen to be in no way inferior to all that extraordinary precision that we have already become accustomed to in the superb dynamical equations (Newton's, Maxwell's, Einstein's) which govern the behavior of things from moment to moment.[74]

Penrose's image of a creator armed with a pin allows us to appreciate only in a very limited way the truly special character of our Universe. As we have said in our introduction, the Universe is not a vast mechanistic clockwork wound up with incalculable precision by an external God, and therefore it would make very little sense to speak about its probability. Insofar as probability arguments move us away from the indifference of blind chance, they have a certain appeal, but insofar as the push us toward the indifference of a supernaturalist agenda, they confuse and cloud our thinking. What do probability arguments prove? Nothing beyond the simple observation that our Universe could not have emerged wholly as a result of blind processes. But even though there is pattern to the process, this does not mean that we should explain the evolution of our Universe in terms of anything outside itself. We dispense with all supernaturalism, and we rejoice in the wholeness and raw potentiality of a Universe which continually creates, sustains and renews itself as a single living system.

The Theory of the Big Bang

The theory of the Big Bang states that the entire Universe is in a state of dynamic inflation and evolutionary change. The Universe can be viewed as a single whole and traced back to a beginning in time. The theory was predicted by Einstein's general theory of relativity,[75] and strong observational data accumulated over the years to confirm Einstein's theory. In 1929 Edwin Hubble through the redshift effect[76] saw the whole Universe to be in a state of overall expansion. In 1965 Penzias and Wilson discovered a previously predicted microwave background radiation at 3 K, widely interpreted as a residual effect of the initial fireball. The Big Bang theory accurately predicted the abundance within the Universe of the lightest elements of hydrogen, helium, deuterium, and lithium. For these and other reasons, it remains to this day a sound and reasonable theory.

According to the standard theory of the Big Bang, the Universe should have originated in a singularity of infinite compression. This is usually depicted as a space-time cone tapering downward to a single point. James Hartle and Stephen Hawking argue, however, that as we move down this cone to a point of singularity, the familiar three dimensions of space and the one dimension of time become blurred by quantum fluctuations. The one dimension of time turns into another spatial dimension, and "in the beginning" so to speak, we end up with four dimensions of space. The point at the bottom of the space-time cone gets rounded off and replaced by something a whole lot smoother, and within this rather bizarre state of affairs, time emerges gradually from space as the rounded bell-bottom slowly curves upward into the space-time cone of a Universe.

Therefore according to the Hawking/Hartle theory, time does not stretch back infinitely into the past, and yet it has no clear-cut boundary as such. The Universe has a finite age but it had no abrupt beginning at a singular point in time. From this Hawking concludes:

> The idea that space and time may form a closed surface without boundary also has profound implications for the role of God in the affairs of the universe. With the success of scientific theories in describing events, most people have come to believe that God allows the universe to evolve according to a set of laws and does not intervene in the universe to break these laws. However the laws do not tell us what the universe should have looked like when it started - it would still be up to God to wind up the clockwork and choose how to start it off. So long as the universe had a beginning, we could suppose that it had a creator. But if the universe is really self-contained, having no boundary or edge, it would have neither beginning nor end: it would simply be. What place, then, for a creator?[77]

This whole line of reasoning is somewhat similar to the previous notion of the creator armed with a pin. Hawking argues that if the Universe has no beginning, boundary or edge, we would have no need of an external creator winding up the clockwork of the universe and choosing how to start it off. In his argument Hawking clearly presupposes a mechanistic universe. Of course, we have no problem with the idea of an internally self-contained Universe whose origin lies within itself. We agree with Hawking and Hartle that we need not posit some supernatural act of creation. But we will never find the means to avoid a supernatural conclusion as long as we accept the premise of a mechanistic universe. A clockwork by definition always needs someone to wind it up, and Hawking's jump to a realm where time as we know it has been eliminated is hardly convincing. Creators, according to many classical theologies, just love to inhabit the realm of the timeless and the eternal. As long as we leave the mechanical in place, the supernatural will always come back to haunt us.

But if we are looking for a truly self-contained Universe that does not require an external creator, then this Universe *had better come alive* and contain its own potentiality for creating itself. As we descend the cone of space-time, randomness and lawlessness begin to proliferate until we reach a thoroughly unimaginable state of pure potentiality, a potentiality *not within God,* of course, but somehow within an uncreated Universe on the verge of being born. As the Universe evolves from its state of origin, we can never eliminate randomness and lawlessness from its description, for here lies the source of its ongoing self-creating potentiality. Free from supernaturalism, our Universe comes alive as a single self-creating and self-sustaining whole.

A general philosophical attitude dating back to Copernicus says that man does not occupy a privileged place in the Cosmos. But over the last few centuries modern science has tended to take this attitude to an extreme and to view man as nothing but an "insignificant accident lost in the immensity of the Cosmos,"[78] or perhaps as a "more-or-less farcical outcome of a chain of accidents."[79] In the history of Western thought, we witness a shift from the highly ludicrous position where man is everything to an equally absurd position where man is nothing at all. We accept wholeheartedly that man is not the center, purpose or goal of our Universe, yet this does not mean that man is nothing at all. In the context of the irreversible evolution of a Universe, where nothing happens infinitely often, where nothing happens in the same way twice, each step is unique and individual, and each step, no matter how exploratory, tentative or incomplete, shares in all the risk and relevance of the larger whole.

The history of the Big Bang allows us to understand why the Universe, in the present scheme of things, is as big as it is: nothing would exist in one that was significantly smaller. Yet the history of the Big Bang does not establish the ironclad necessity of the present scheme of things. Even though the microwave background provides us with the means of measuring our position in space and time, even though it restores a unified sense of history which lets us understand in a general way our place within an evolving Universe, it does not establish that this is the only way a meaningful Universe could have evolved.

Even though the time we live in is not just any time in an infinite sequence of times where everything happens infinitely often,[80] even though the place we live in is not just any place, but planet Earth, where after ten billion years of cosmic evolution, the conditions were appropriate for the emergence of complex forms of life, other scenarios could have unfolded, and they could all be considered just as meaningful as our own when viewed from after the fact.

At each step, at each break in symmetry in the evolution of our Universe, we find an irreducible random element that imparts an irreversibility, a uniqueness and an individuality to the entire cosmological process. No longer the drab and boring grinding out of "laws that never change," this dynamic far exceeds in complexity anything which mechanistic science could have ever imagined: a self-creating process dynamic involving billions upon billions of *selective events,* all drawing from an infinite pool of randomness, constantly feeding back upon itself and shaping itself across a multiplicity of co-evolving levels, adjusting and re-adjusting, formulating and re-formulating, continually searching, exploring, experimenting and testing, with the largest and smallest, the highest and lowest, the earliest and latest, all locked into one another in the dynamic unity of an evolving Universe. In such a context nothing is insignificant.

The magnificent overview provided by the theory of the Big Bang allows us to sense deeply the unity surrounding the birth, growth, and development of our Universe. Right from the beginning the process unfolded in a coherent and rigorous manner with both the smallest and the largest levels bidirectionally impacting and creating one another. The mathematics and observational data that go into this theory are staggering. Nothing within the process is haphazard or left only to blind forces: all unfolds step-by-step in tight and critical interdependency. Yet in spite of all this exquisite order, we have no right to conclude that everything had to happen the way it did. No law, blueprint or program emanating from some all-knowing Lawgiver, Architect or Programmer existed in some timeless domain to guarantee the evolution of our Universe. We underline that our Universe should have created itself according to the exigency of nothing external to itself, and at each break in symmetry, we find an irreducible random element assuring a fundamental freedom to the process. The Universe created itself as it went along, not under the compulsion of any external factors, but only out of the *logic of its own internal necessity coupled paradoxically to the fluidity of its own inherent unpredictability.* Let us not hide behind words.

What we really mean to say is that the Universe created itself out of its own internal freedom and choice.

Each choice in its ongoing evolution entailed constraint as well as further levels of freedom. No choice ever jumped over its previous history - its lawful aspect, yet no choice was ever strictly determined - its unlawful aspect. As we hold these two aspects together in all their rich complementarity, our Universe comes alive as a single self-contained entity, taking on all those characteristics we normally associate with any natural system. Soon we begin to get intuitions of a purposefulness, a guidedness or a directedness similar to that found in the growth and development of any living organism. These intuitions can never be formulated with exactitude or precision, yet they drive all wonder and curiosity. They evoke the inescapable yet utterly simple question: why?

The Anthropic Principle

How do we account for the near infinity of interdependent coincidences that appear to surround our existence as observers? From our limited Western point of view, not too many explanations are forthcoming. On the one hand, the supernaturalist will stop all thought and explanatory effort by pointing to a supernatural Being. God can be used to explain anything we cannot explain ourselves, and he conveniently fills in all the gaps in our knowledge. On the other hand, many a scientist would argue that if all these happy coincidences were not in place, we would not be around to take note of them.[81] There is no problem with his argument so far, but if he then goes on to say that, because we exist, our very existence guarantees that these coincidences must be so, that there is no point in asking why, and that there is no point in probing any deeper into the matter, then we can only conclude that he, just as the supernaturalist, has put an end any further thought or explanatory effort.[82] This is somewhat similar to the situation when a small child asks his parents "why this?" or "why that?" and gets the answer, "things are so just because." Whenever we follow the logic of pure chance, we can admit no purpose, and as a consequence our reasoning is always circular. We shall encounter a similar circular logic when we examine the thought of Charles Darwin.

Now if the weak formulation of the anthropic principle leaves us dissatisfied, perhaps we should turn to its strong formulation. Some scientists would then say that the Universe *must* have those properties which allow life to develop within it at some stage, or that the Universe *must* be such as to admit the existence of observers within it at some point in its evolution. Of course, many within the scientific community rightfully protest, saying that such a point of view implies that the Universe could not have been structured differently. Which position should we take? Did all have to happen the way it did or did nothing have to happen the way it did?

We cannot take a position in a debate where both sides presuppose a mechanistic universe. Both sides begin with an initially lifeless and mindless universe that for the most part has remained quite desolate except for that most improbable corner of the Universe called Earth, which very mysteriously contains static entities which appear to be alive and conscious. Those espousing some grand design assert that everything had to happen the way it did, saying forcefully: "there is a God," while those espousing pure chance assert that nothing had to happen the way it did, saying with equal conviction: "there is no God." One side ignores the chaotic aspect to the evolution of our Universe, while the other side ignores its orderly aspect. Of course, we care for neither one of these indifferent options, since a Universe is a complex blend of both internal necessity and inherent unpredictability.

Everything we know about our Universe right from its very beginning as well at every step and stage in its ongoing evolution leads us to recognize and identify the hand of Lady Luck. But if we include randomness right at the heart of our understanding of the evolution of our Universe, then we are implicitly admitting that its internal organization is far more complicated than that of a simple machine. We prize machines for their predictability, and when they are in breakdown mode and no longer functioning correctly as machines, we generally rush in to restore them to their original clockwork state. Randomness does not characterize the clockwork precision of machines, but it certainly matches the sudden and unexpected twists and turns in the evolution and behavior of living organisms. Living organisms evolve and grow in very unpredictable ways, and somehow we take their deep-seated unpredictability as a sure sign of life.

The proponents of the strong anthropic principle ignore the fact that our Universe is characterized by a profound randomness, and this imparts a uniqueness and individuality to it in its bumpy and somewhat less than perfect evolution. As Stephen J. Gould so correctly explained in his dialogue with former U.S. President Jimmy Carter, we may not use probability arguments within the context of the unique and individual. If we only possess a single sample, how can we compute its probability? Probability cannot be calculated for a singular occurrence known only after the fact. It only makes sense when attached to predictions made at the beginning of a sequence.[83] Since our Universe in every aspect appears to be unique, since we have no other universes with which to compare it, since we only experience living in a single Universe, it makes no sense at all to speak of its probability. Therefore Gould's position with respect to the anthropic principle is quite correct:

> Many physicists have pointed out - and I fully accept their analysis - that life on earth fits intricately with physical laws regulating the universe, in the sense that were various laws even slightly different, molecules of the proper composition and planets of the right properties could never have arisen - and we would not be here. From this analysis, a few thinkers have drawn the wildly invalid inference that human evolution is therefore prefigured in the ancient design of the cosmos - that the universe, in Freeman Dyson's words, must have known we were coming. But the current fit of human life to physical laws permits no conclusion about the reasons and mechanisms of our origin. Since we are here, we have to fit; we wouldn't be here if we didn't - though something else would, probably proclaiming, with all the hubris that a diproton might muster, that the cosmos must have been created with its later appearance in mind. (Diprotons are the prominent candidate for the highest bit of chemistry in another conceivable universe.)[84]

Did all unfold according to some God-given plan? Certainly not, if we accept Gould's thesis with respect to the role of chance in the evolution of our Universe. But it is one thing to accord a highly significant role to chance in the evolution of our Universe, and it's quite a different story to say that *all* unfolded according to nothing other than the whim of pure chance. If we accept that the unpredictable is truly unpredictable, then by definition it is not in a position to generate the least amount of order and certainly not the manifold and highly differentiated order that we see throughout our Universe. Of course, someone could always argue that the order that we see is simply an illusion and that the Universe only *appears* to be orderly. To this rather weak argument we would have to reply that his argument only *appears* to be reasonable.

The anthropic principle operates under the presupposition of a mechanistic universe, and, of course, implicit in this mechanistic understanding is the Cartesian split between mind and matter. In its weak version, the anthropic principle posits that matter, by virtue of the most fortuitous streak of luck, just happens to be structured so as to give rise to mind and to thinking beings. In its strong version, the anthropic principle posits that matter, by virtue of some God-given necessity, has been deliberately structured or tinkered with so as to give rise to mind and to thinking beings.[85] "I think; I am a thinking being; thinking beings exists; therefore the universe just happens to be structured or has been deliberately structured so as to bring about the existence of thinking beings." The anthropic principle extends Descartes' *cogito* in a cosmological direction and leaves its naive materialism firmly in place, and in so doing it contributes very little to our understanding of the evolution of our Universe. The scientific community had at its disposal all the elements of a living Universe - its orderly and disorderly aspects - and in formulating the anthropic principle, it missed the point completely.

How can mind evolve from matter when, as we have seen in chapter one, every property of the physical world involves a constructive input from mind? In the place of the evolution of mind from matter, we see an evolution from beginning to end never outside of or divorced from mind. Over the last 15 billion years, images of a material world, dynamically enacted and mutually reinforced within and throughout a multiplicity of co-evolving levels, have taken on such vividness, concreteness and sharpness of resolution, that we humans, who have come on the scene only within the last few moments of cosmic time, have fooled ourselves into believing, of course, not without a bit of help from Descartes, that somehow they have an independent existence outside of mind. No doubt Bateson would have to agree that we are indeed fools who have rushed in where angels fear to tread.

Living organisms do not require some *master plan* as they go about the business of *ordering* their existence. They often grope about, intuitively formulating and continually re-formulating their internal self-organization over and against a constant influx of the unexpected bubbling up anywhere from within a multiplicity of co-evolving levels. A comet hits and all hell breaks loose. Dinosaurs and vast arrays of plants and animals are decimated. But comets hitting planet Earth, even in combination with an almost infinite series of other such contingent events, do not give rise in all their prolific randomness to *Homo Sapiens*. A selective element is required, and in the case of a multi-leveled Universe, this selective element spreads out over or is internal to a broad range of co-evolving levels.

Living organisms select, and their selection is anything but blind. "blind selection" is a thoroughly meaningless juxtaposition of words:

something cannot be both blind and selective at the same time. If it is blind, by definition, it cannot see or select by means of the power and brightness of images, and if it is selective, it cannot possibly be blind. We could point to a "seeing blind man" or a "hearing deaf man" only by severely distorting the ordinary meaning of vision and hearing over and against blindness and deafness. In their selection, living organisms may not have a view of everything, but this does not mean that they have a view of nothing. They have a *limited* view within that unique portion of the highly differentiated space-time in which they situate, and there they select within the constraints of the *limited* freedom available to them, and there again, according to *limited* goals and purposes. These goals and purposes constantly shift, not necessarily for functional or adaptational reasons, as Gould explains so often,[86] but at times for no other reason than some minute intrusion of the unexpected.[87] A living organism creates itself as it goes along, in a process fraught with *danger and risk,* and in constant interaction with the whole of a living environment. As we try to understand more closely how this dynamic unfolds, we cannot ignore the tremendous intellectual legacy we have inherited from Charles Darwin.

Charles Darwin

Charles Darwin's theory of chance variation and natural selection remains to this day a topic of lively and heated debate.[88] Even though Darwin formulated his controversial theory as early as 1838, he waited more than twenty years before he finally got around to publishing it. Of course, the question naturally arises, why did he wait so long? Was he simply waiting for further evidence or additional documentation to back it up? No, says Stephen J. Gould in a delightful essay called *Darwin's Delay.* Gould examines two of Darwin's early notebooks, the "M" and "N" notebooks written in 1838 and 1839, and he finds good evidence to support the idea that Darwin was not so much afraid of his belief in evolution as such, since evolution was widely and openly discussed by most of the great naturalists of the first half of the 19th Century. Darwin feared something he considered to be far more heretical than evolution. According to Gould it was his belief in philosophical materialism that caused him to withhold publication so long, that is, his belief "that matter is the stuff of all existence and that all mental and spiritual phenomena are its byproducts."[89]

While other evolutionists of the 19th Century spoke of such things

as "vital forces, directed history, organic striving, and the essential irre-
ducibility of mind,"[90] Darwin went down a radically different path. The
primary feature that distinguished his theory from all other evolutionary
doctrines at the time was its "uncompromising philosophical materialism."[91] In spite of his desire at one time to become an English country
clergyman,[92] Darwin developed a deeply materialistic position that, of
course, was not very congenial to the 19th-Century understanding and
practice of religion. Little wonder then that he held back on publication,
says Gould: "He was not about to compromise a promising career by
promulgating a heresy that he could not prove."[93] Like his two famous
contemporaries, Marx and Engels,[94] Darwin had chosen the drab simplicity of the mechanical as a principle of explanation, and this, of
course, put him at serious odds with many of his fellow naturalists as
well as the whole of 19th-Century established religion. With the publication of *The Origin of Species* in 1859, the battle lines between mechanism and supernaturalism were clearly drawn, and fierce fighting has
waged on ever since.[95]

Darwin's insight into the dynamics of evolutionary change was simple and brilliant: chance variation supplies the raw material and natural
selection imparts direction. Here we have a random source constantly
generating newness, over and against what was supposed to be a selective principle providing order and direction. With the random and the
selective Darwin uncovered the two complementary poles basic to the
evolution of all natural systems, but unfortunately his "uncompromising
philosophical materialism" placed enormous restrictions upon him in
explaining their complementarity. How can we speak of a truly selective element within a materialist setting? Since bumping bits of matter
do not think, choose, plan, see or imagine in any way, we should have
a hard time attributing to them even the smallest ability to select. Let us
look more closely at Darwin's selective principle.

How does the environment select? By letting the fittest survive. But
how do the fittest within that environment come to be so superbly fit?
All that Darwin proposes is that they just happen by chance to be fit,
and they are subsequently selected as such by their environment. If we
follow carefully this line of reasoning, we find ourselves caught up in
the unavoidable circularity of a mechanistic explanation. Darwin's
selective element is so weak and so devoid of any real selective power,
that it does not *explain* how the fit become so fit. He simply proposes
that the fit are fit because they are fit, and the central question of how
they became so fit, he does not and cannot explain. As a true mechanist

and materialist, Darwin was obliged to side-step the problem of selection altogether, and like his supernaturalist counterparts with whom he supposedly had little in common, he left things safely tucked away in the realm of the mysterious.

If we define fitness in terms of survival, then survival of the fittest is in fact nothing other than "the survival of those who survive."[96] The only way to avoid the obvious tautological thrust of such a statement would be to disconnect the notion of fitness from the notion of survival, but this implies that somehow nature would have to identify and select the fittest beforehand and not simply as a consequence of their survival. Nature would have to superintend the creation of the superior design and not merely toss out misfits.[97] When an animal or plant breeder selects certain favorable traits, he knows *beforehand* those traits that he wishes to preserve. Here identification, selection and choice take place prior to and independent of the question of survival. Those who survive are not simply those who survive but those who were *selected* to survive. Surely a whole lot of chanciness may accompany selection, but real selection stands out on its own and logically distinguishes itself from survival, otherwise why speak of selection at all?

In his *Origin of Species* Darwin devoted most of the first 40 pages to the artificial selection of favored traits by animal breeders.[98] He made an analogy between the *artificial* selection of an animal breeder and the *natural* selection of an environment. But what a world of difference between a living subject who intelligently selects desirable traits and a materialistic environment which *blindly* and *insensibly* eliminates misfits! Here we go back to that unbridgeable gulf separating subject and object which Rene Descartes set in place: subjects who think, choose, select, plan and even anticipate, over and against blind and insensible objects which do none of these things. To impart the ability to select to material objects, we would have to invest them with some mysterious power or force that would lie completely outside of the framework of rational scientific discourse. If we accept the Cartesian gulf separating subject and object, with artificial selection and natural selection each on opposite sides, then we have no chance in the world of constructing a valid analogy between the two, and if the principle of natural selection really depends upon the validity of this analogy as Gould says, then Darwin's theory would appear to be in big trouble.[99]

Still however we believe that Darwin was on the right track. A valid analogy can be drawn between the selection of an animal breeder and the selection within an environment, provided, of course, that we view the environment not as insensible machine but as a multiplicity of living subjects capable of limited but true selection. What prevents us from delicately transposing Darwin's concept of natural selection from one side of the Cartesian divide to the other? According to the dynamics of natural systems that we examined in our first chapter, we have a rich vocabulary at our disposal to enable us to make his important shift. This then leaves us with living subjects all possessing genuine selective ability, and consequently with living subjects who can all be legitimately analogized. Gould realizes the importance of getting them on the same side of the Cartesian divide, but unfortunately it would appear that he chooses the wrong side. On the one hand, he says that "nature is not an animal breeder; no preordained purpose regulates the history of life."[100] Is he saying here that there is nothing in nature that can be compared to the purposeful self-organizing subjectivity of an animal breeder? On the other hand, he says: "in artificial selection, a breeder's desire represents a 'change of environment' for a population."[101] Is he then reducing the breeder's mindful choice to the mindless "choice" effected by some random change within an environment?

Stuart Kauffman, in his new book, *At Home in the Universe,* makes an analogy between technological evolution and biological evolution. Even though Kauffman admits at the beginning of his argument that technological evolution is "guided by intent and intelligence," to get his analogy right and to make sure that both technological and biological evolution operate on the same side of the Cartesian divide, he actually tries to persuade the reader that human technological evolution operates without real understanding and intelligence:

> I suspect that much technological evolution results from tinkering with little real understanding ahead of time of the consequences. We think; biological evolution does not. But when problems are very hard, thinking may not help that much. We may all be relatively blind watchmakers.[102]

Yes, we humans think rationally, and the rest of the natural world does not. But does this mean that the natural world does not think intelligently? What leads Kaufmann to suppose that rational thought is the only kind of intelligent thought? Moreover, does he honestly believe that we humans are ultimately blind watchmakers? What would such a formidable intellect have to say about the evolution of his own thought processes? Did he develop such a complex theory of "order for free" simply as a result of some blind force? If we humans do not understand fully the consequences of our theories and inventions, if we do not understand the implications of every aspect of a larger evolutionary process of which we are an integral part, if we are perplexed at times with those aspects of human intelligence which operate at a much deeper level than the rational, does this mean that our thought processes are so weak and blind that they end up on the mindless side of the Cartesian divide? Likewise, if evolution within the natural world does not proceed rationally, and if nature is not guided either directly or indirectly by means of some form of supernatural energy or force, does this mean that the natural world evolves so unintelligently that it too ends up on the mindless side of the Cartesian divide?

For example, what is mindless within nature about the female choice of a breeding partner? Does her choice not involve the selection of a mate according to criteria of beauty constructed and enacted deep within the recesses of her own imagination? Even though her choice is not rational, does she not have a mind and is her choice not a product of the selective powers of this mind? Limited as it may be, does her choice not proceed squarely from her own subjectivity, and does it not constitute one more event in a myriad of selective events which shape and impact the subsequent evolution of her species? Furthermore, could we not make a similar argument with respect to the male desire to procreate? Obviously non-human males are totally "blind" with respect to our modern theories relating to the transmission of a genetic heritage. But in their desire to procreate are their imaginations not filled with dazzling images of female beauty, which lead them to compete relentlessly with one another for the ultimate prize of sexual union? Is this competition among males not initiated and sustained through the power of images? Does it not constitute still yet another event that shapes and impacts the subsequent evolution of their species? How could we argue that the female choice of a mate or the male desire to procreate operates on the mindless side of the Cartesian divide?

If we limit our search for points of similarity to nothing other than that rather superficial ability to engage in rational thought, then obviously it would be very difficult to make an analogy between artificial selection and natural selection. But does this mean that we cannot make a perfectly valid analogy between a broad range of thought processes deeply shared by both man and nature? To construct an analogy between "tissues and terra-cotta,"[103] Kauffman tries to situate both analogs on the same side of the Cartesian divide, and true to the same dualistic heritage that he shares with Darwin and Gould, he sadly chooses the wrong side. If we should have any doubt that Kauffman's "order for free" is anything but blind, we should turn to page 207, where he uses the word "blind(ly)" four times in describing the dynamics of the evolutionary process. At the same time Kauffman says that "The *miracle* is so wondrous, the more so because there is no choreographer."[104] A bit further on the same page he describes an ecosystem as "a tangled bank of interwoven roles - metabolic, morphological, behavioral - that is magically self-sustaining."

We fully agree that the natural world does not need a Choreographer, but why assume that the natural world operates unintelligently? Are we humans not somewhat arrogant in making this biased assumption? Do we really believe that we are the only intelligent beings on Earth? The rapid and almost instantaneous formation of an image within the imagination involves the highly intelligent processing of a myriad of meaningful differences, and the subsequent presentation of this image to the selective powers of mind is anything but blind. Kauffman supposes that the natural world operates blindly, and the only explanation he gives to account for the emergence of order is to say that it happens as if by "magic and miracle." What is the validity of a principle of explanation that makes appeal to a proliferation of magic and miracle? Right at the moment that we are expecting real explanation, the ghost of supernaturalism suddenly appears. Although Kauffman gives powerful reasons why Darwin's chance variation and natural selection both fall far short of explaining the abundance of order within the Universe, is his universe not just as cold and insensible as that of Charles Darwin?

Darwin posited the origin of superior design primarily through its chance appearance in a changed environment. According to this logic, chance variation would appear to be the real source of superior design. But keep in mind, this same random source also generates a whole lot of inferior design. Only *after* the random generation of both superior and inferior design does natural selection get around to eliminating the inferior. But surely the mere elimination of the inferior could not have been that major creative force within evolution that Darwin had in mind. Maybe what Darwin really meant to say was that some *previous* decimation of *inferior* design by natural selection in an *earlier* stage constrained the level of probability for the chance appearance of *superior* design at a *later* stage.[105] By introducing time into the logic of evolution, we momentarily eliminate some confusion, but we are still left with the very annoying problem of the origin and purpose of complex design undeniably present in some earlier stage. Evolution is not the random meandering of chance but the selective transformation of chance according to the constraints of a *previous history,* and we may not forget that this previous history also demands explanation. We will return to this problem toward the end of this chapter.

So if we follow Charles Darwin in our search for meaningful explanation, we soon end up staring into an abyss of an infinite regression of incipient stages. This infinite regression overwhelms and dazzles as it grinds out mechanically towards the ultimate explanatory principle of God. As long as we accept the premise of a mechanistic universe, we cannot escape the supernatural conclusion that Charles Darwin fought so valiantly to dismiss. We reject not just the supernatural but also the mechanical as legitimate principles of explanation within science, and this forces us to look for the origin of superior design *within* the dynamics of the evolutionary process itself. Here we see movement from one stage to the next, but this movement is anything but mechanical. Sometimes it appears slow and gradual, effecting only trivial change. At other times, however, it appears momentous and sudden, effecting large-scale shifts to qualitatively new biological forms and patterns of behavior. We might state the obvious, that there is no movement without survival, but we haven't explained *why there is movement in the first place.* Why should one purposeful and more or less functional design ever shift and change into another?

On the one hand, we might offer the trite response of local environmental "pressure." But what may we ask is this mysterious force relentlessly driving evolution within a local environment? Do we really believe that we are explaining evolutionary movement when we appeal to the magic of some force that lies completely outside the realm of rational human discourse? What allows us to take properties that belong exclusively to living subjects and attribute them to insensible objects? On what grounds do we justify viewing the environment in mechanistic terms? On what grounds do we justify isolating it and viewing it as a static entity? If our environment consists of a variety of species in evolution, then surely this environment is on the move, as it evolves and grows within the context of the whole of a living planet. Is the local environment not an integral part of the larger evolutionary problem that demands explanation?

On the other hand, we might be tempted to turn *within* and try to explain everything on the level of genes. In this most unusual explanatory extravaganza, evolutionary movement is assured through selfish

Gaia as unit of evolution

genetic ambition. But do genes, operating on the level of the purely physiochemical, formulate strategy and display ambition? How could anyone seriously put forward such blatant anthropomorphism within the context of science? Is this not another strange analogy illogically straddling both sides of the Cartesian divide? Since genes themselves undergo evolution, since they mutate and are subject to *drift,* should we not view their evolution as an integral part of the larger evolutionary problem that cries out for explanation?

In another attempt at explanation from within, some biologists propose that evolutionary movement is assured through the logic of a genetic algorithm or program.[106] Nowhere can we find a better illustration of how a mechanistic explanation ultimately grinds to a halt at the gates of heaven. *Since no program has ever been known to write itself,* this idea logically demands an external Programmer, and in the place of explaining things from within, it ultimately ends up offering explanation entirely external to the evolutionary process. One could point to a program that has been programmed in a sense to write itself, constantly rearranging its own internal logic or even inserting itself into the logic of other programs. But as we marvel at the power of computer viruses and other such sophisticated high-level software, let us keep in mind that this software never appears within the memory of a computer outside the agency of some *external* human programmer who put it there.

To understand what we are saying, let us construct a thought experiment with the most powerful piece of hardware imaginable. First let us erase any remnant of an operating system as well as all application software. Then let us guard this hardware with great diligence, making sure that it remains completely cut off from hackers, robots, modems or any other contact with the outside world. Finally, after leaving it in total isolation for whatever period of time satisfies the requirements of this thought experiment, do we have any reason to expect that this sophisticated piece of hardware could ever create its own software and thereby execute even a single logical step?

Even if we were to conclude that such a software feat would be possible within the framework of what lies solely within the hardware itself, we would still have a hard time explaining why this piece of hardware would be compelled at a certain point in time to suddenly begin functioning as a computer. How does a mindless and totally indifferent machine arrive at the enormous will and intentionality needed to engage in the rigors of rational computation? If it did in a sense "turn itself on" to the idea of functioning as a computer, surely we would have to label this spontaneous emergence of order as entirely magical and miraculous. The appearance of the extraordinary and unexpected in an organismic setting does not sound so very unusual, but the appearance of the extraordinary and unexpected within a purely mechanistic setting reeks of supernaturalism.

Imagine how neat and tidy everything would be, if right at the moment of the spontaneous emergence of order, we could make appeal to some sort of supernatural input which would fire up our computer and set it in motion. In imparting so many strange mental properties to computers, are not Kauffman and the other believers in artificial intelligence in fact advocates of a new and curious form of supernaturalism? How do they manage to take software, which is a product of mind, and attribute to it properties that belong exclusively to mind? If we were to take the words which we speak or write, and attribute to them a logic and intentionality of their own, as if they originated and evolved independently of human intervention, would this not be a similar error? There may be nothing magical about imparting mental properties to mind, but whole armies of ghosts and goblins are just crawling out of the woodwork the moment we impart mental properties to the products of mind! Outside of the agency of man or some other external form of natural intelligence that created them, how do mindless allopoietic systems generate that initial sense of purpose and intentionality which would enable them to function as computers? Again, we must insist, that if we want a principle explaining evolutionary movement from one stage to the next, let us focus squarely on what is taking place *within* the evolutionary process itself.

We agree with Stephen J. Gould that it would be dead wrong to look for some preordained purpose in place from all eternity, and, of course, we can only clap and cheer when he says that it would be wrong, and even ludicrous, to put man as the goal and purpose of this incredible evolutionary movement.[107] But having failed to ground purpose in either God or man, are we then going to conclude that this universal thrust toward life unfolds without purpose and meaning? Does this not contradict and deny what evolution is all about? Evolution involves in its very essence *the continuous transformation of purpose and meaning,* and it always transcends the many human and divine categories we rigidly impose in our deplorable efforts to master and control it for our own limited goals and purposes. In saying that the story of evolution unfolds without purpose and meaning, have we not simply cleared the stage for the arrogant imposition of our own purpose and meaning?

This leads us to suspect that there is a serious logical error in the formulation of Darwin's theory of natural selection. Since we can never distinguish a truly selective principle in a mechanistic program of thought, and since most mechanists rightfully abhor a supernatural explanation within science, then there remains no other possibility open to them than to reduce everything ultimately to the logic of pure chance. But as rational human beings, somehow we know that chance alone cannot explain the emergence of superior design. If we could prove the emergence of superior design through chance alone, then we would find ourselves in the rather peculiar logical position of being able to prove just about any absurdity imaginable. We would have to give no reasons and produce no evidence in substantiating even the most ridiculous claims. We would have to point to nothing more than some mysterious origin in the clouds of pure chance. How can pure randomness select, thereby creating meaningful pattern or purposeful project? When we take the position that the amazing order inherent in superior design originates purely by chance, not only do we contradict the obvious meaning of words such as "order and disorder," "selective and random," but we also do something far more dangerous: we destroy the logical foundation upon which we construct meaningful statements.

If we were to claim, for example, that the argument we are making now concerning pure chance has little to do with its own internal logic and consistency, that it is true for no other reason than that it just happens by chance to be true, then the reader of this book should have every reason to throw it away and to look somewhere else for meaningful explanation. The logic of pure chance excludes logic and all forms of meaningful discourse. Note well that we do not deny that chance plays an extremely important role in the origin and evolution of natural systems, but all by itself chance does not explain. Pure chance or unselected chance by definition offers no explanation; whereas selected chance, or chance that has been integrated and *transformed* within orderly pattern and purposeful project, indeed has a logical and meaningful story to tell. Evolution is not the random meandering of the possible but it is, as Gould himself would say, "the transformation of the possible,"[108] and this transformation takes place by means of a selective principle truly distinct from chance.

But do we really understand the selective and the random? All too often we have heard these words in a mechanistic context where we easily lose sight of their basic meaning. What do we mean by selection? By what strange logic do we attribute selection to insensible objects? What is there to select when everything in a sense has already been pre-determined or pre-selected through the agency of some mysterious law or force? What is there to select in the absence of the new and unpredictable? What is there to select outside of a certain range of unpredictability? Can we speak of the selection of the necessary as true selection? How do we define selection in a totally indifferent framework where any one choice is as good as any other?

Likewise, what do we mean by randomness? How do we define randomness in a mechanistic context? By what strange logic do we attribute randomness to machines that literally fall apart in the presence of the random? Does randomness not squarely contradict the notion of a pre-determination or pre-selection through the agency of some mysterious law or force? How do we define randomness, newness and even time in the absence of a subjective frame of reference? Outside of living subjects, the act of selection proceeds without the least bit of anticipation and excitement, and in this boring and indifferent context where time has been forgotten, surely any one choice is as good as any other.

Since it was impossible for Darwin to explain the complementarity of the selective and the random within a mechanistic framework, his theory has never been terribly convincing. Therefore the classical objection to natural selection still stands: "natural selection may act as an executioner of the unfit, but cannot create the fit."[109] In more recent times Lynn Margulis expressed this objection using a gentler metaphor: Darwinian selection has the power to edit the story of life, but it does not have the power to author this story. Surely it is one thing to say that natural selection serves as the executioner, headsman or editor of the unfit, but it is an altogether different thing to say, as Darwin claimed, that natural selection is that creative force within nature which truly explains the origin and evolution of new life forms. To create and construct the fit, not just once but over and over again, not just in a few dull and monotonous forms, but in that seemingly endless multileveled diversity we find throughout our planet, and then to preserve certain aspects of the fit, sometimes over hundreds of millions of years,[110] in spite of all the multifarious chanciness within an environment that could so easily impact and destroy it - surely this involves an explanatory principle far more powerful than the disorderliness of chance alone.

Note how Darwin described selection:

> Natural selection is daily and hourly scrutinizing throughout the
> world, the slightest variations, rejecting those that are bad, preserving

and adding up all that are good, silently and insensibly working[111]

But when we look closely at the dynamics of the natural world, we do not find a simple, uniform picture of gradual transitions from one life form to the next. Fred Hoyle says it with much flair:

> Here we have an all-or-nothing situation, either a species continues with little change or it makes an abrupt leap, an expectation strongly supported by the fossil record, not "silently and insensibly." The thing happens with a flourish of trumpets.[112]

Where Hoyle speaks of a "flourish of trumpets," Gould speaks of a "bang," or a "Cambrian explosion:"

> Modern multicellular animals make their first uncontested appearance in the fossil record some 570 million years ago - and with a bang, not a protracted crescendo. This "Cambrian explosion" marks the advent (at least into direct evidence) of virtually all major groups of modern animals - and all within the minuscule span, geologically speaking, of a few million years.[113]

Drawing upon recent findings based upon rigorously determined radiometric age dates, Gould argues that the entire Cambrian explosion fits into an extremely short period of about 5 to 10 million years.[114]

But one of the greatest developments in evolutionary history according to Lynn Margulis and Dorian Sagan occurred long before the Cambrian explosion on the level of single-cell life. It had to do with the transition from non-nucleated bacterial cells to cells with a nucleus. Margulis and Sagan contend that this difference is "far greater than that between plants and animals,"[115] and furthermore, they find that it was so sudden that "it cannot effectively be explained by gradual changes over time."[116] Given such a sudden transition, we should expect to find no intermediate transitional development:

> All cells either have a nucleus or do not. No intermediates exist. The abruptness of their appearance in the fossil record, the total discontinuity between living forms with and without nuclei, and the puzzling complexity of internal self-reproducing organelles suggest that the new cells were begotten by a process fundamentally different from simple mutation or bacterial genetic transfer.[117]

symbio-genesis

Not only in the beginning, at the level of single-cell life, but over and over again, throughout the entire sweep of biological evolutionary history, we witness the same bizarre pattern of sudden and unexpected change with no intermediate forms.

At this point we make a very important distinction between Darwin's special theory which has to do with microevolution and his general theory which has to do with macroevolution.[118] Microevolution features rather trivial evolutionary changes such as those that Darwin observed in the finches on the Galapagos Islands or in the breeding of domestic animals. Darwin's special theory sets forth very convincingly that species are not immutable, that they can undergo a considerable degree of evolutionary change, and that new species can evolve from preexisting species as a result of fairly ordinary processes in which natural selection plays a key role. But it was not Darwin's special theory that had such a revolutionary impact in his day. The big revolution in human thought occurred when Darwin took his special theory and extended it into a general theory, that is, when he took his special theory and began to extrapolate and generalize it into a theory to explain all the diversity and adaptive design of life on earth. Here we move from trivial editing to full-blown authorship.

Darwin made the first real attempt to bring the study of life into the conceptual framework of the new scientific method espoused by Bacon and Descartes, and epitomized by the grand Newtonian synthesis. But just as Newtonian physics cannot be extrapolated and extended into relativity theory, quantum physics, and non-equilibrium thermodynamics, Darwin's special theory cannot be extended into a general theory of life. Because a certain degree of random variation has been shown to occur as in the case of microevolution, it does not mean that all evolution occurs through purely random processes. In his essay *Return of the Hopeful Monster,* Stephen J. Gould explains that it is wrong to postulate that macroevolution is simply the extrapolation of microevolution:

> Geneticists can study the gradual increase of favored genes within populations of fruit flies in laboratory bottles. Naturalists can record the steady replacement of light moths by dark moths as industrial soot blackens the trees of Britain. Orthodox neo-Darwinists extrapolate these even and continuous changes to the most profound structural transitions in the history of life: by a long series of insensibly graded intermediate steps, birds are linked to reptiles, fish with jaws to their jawless ancestors. Macroevolution (major structural transition) is nothing more than microevolution (flies in bottles) extended. If black moths can displace white moths in a century, then reptiles

can become birds in a few million years by the smooth and sequential summation of countless changes.[119]

We can solve very simple problems by trial and error, but the moment we encounter fairly complex problems, trial and error is exceedingly inefficient. Trial and error, as a mechanism for gradual microevolutionary change where only one element changes at any one time, is conceptually possible, but as a mechanism for macroevolutionary change where a multiplicity of interdependent elements must all evolve together, it is conceptually impossible within a finite period of time. If we change, for example, only one letter at a time in a three-letter word, we may arrive at another meaningful word fairly easily. But if we change only one letter at a time in a fairly long word or even in a very short sentence, we are faced with an entirely different dynamic where the odds of constructing anything meaningful are extremely improbable.[120] Now to transform one meaningful sentence into another meaningful sentence, the odds are even more unlikely - we would have to make two or more single word (not simply single letter) substitutions simultaneously, that is, we would have to make a radical macromutational change. To go even further and change one paragraph into another we would have to make a gigantic macromutational change that means in effect we would probably have to rewrite the entire paragraph. The odds then of constructing anything meaningful are beyond conceptualization.

Random shuffling is a highly unlikely mechanism for generating order. As the physicist Paul Davies explains, it merely produces stochastic drift with no coherent directionality. "Random shuffling tends to produce a jumble. It turns order into a jumble, and a jumble into a jumble, but practically never turns a jumble into order."[121] Referring to the possibility of coordinated motion arising within a closed state merely through random processes, Roger Penrose says: "It is an effective certainty that such coordinated motion will *not* be present! Such co-ordination could occur only by the most amazing fluke - of a kind that would be referred to as 'magic' if ever it did occur."[122]

Any computer programmer will shout and scream if we go into even the shortest and simplest program of his and make the smallest random change.[123] Analogously, sickle cell anemia results when a single change is made in only one amino acid in only one protein within the human red blood cell.[124] If we go into a watch and change the size of a single cogwheel, its chances of functioning correctly are very small. If we change any part in a complex system, we are obliged to change many other parts simultaneously, that is, we are obliged to change the whole if the system is to continue to function in an integrated and purposeful manner. Whenever we are dealing with complex systems where function arises from the combined activity of a number of co-adapted and interdependent parts, then gradual step-by-step random change as a mechanism of major functional change can be totally excluded.[125]

But for Darwin, evolutionary change had to be gradual, otherwise it would have been of supernatural origin. Darwin was a strict adherent to the ancient motto: *Natura non facit saltum,* nature does not make jumps.[126] God jumps but nature proceeds gradually. Moreover, according to the logic set forth by Darwin, a natural evolutionary process must be infinitely gradual requiring a myriad of transitional forms. A slow, gradual process of random evolutionary change over a long period of time would inevitably generate an "infinitude of connecting links." But Darwin faced the serious problem of how to uphold a theory of gradual macroevolutionary change given the almost total absence of any direct empirical evidence of transitional forms.

The only explanation Darwin could give for this lack of empirical evidence was to point to the extreme imperfection of the fossil record.[127] But what evidence did he have that the fossil record was imperfect? The only evidence that he had was the very absence of the transitional forms that his theory was supposed to explain. This hardly sounds like science. An appeal to the imperfection of the fossil record was excusable to a certain extent back in Darwin's day, but today no one can be taken seriously in claiming that the fossil record is incomplete:

> Darwin invoked his standard argument to resolve this uncomfortable problem: the fossil record is so imperfect that we do not have evidence for most events of life's history. But even Darwin acknowledged that his favorite ploy was wearing a bit thin in this case. His argument could easily account for a missing stage in a single lineage, but could the agencies of imperfection really obliterate absolutely all evidence for positively every creature during most of life's history? Darwin admitted: "The case at present must remain inexplicable; and may be truly urged as a valid argument against the views here entertained." (1859, p. 308).
>
> Darwin has been vindicated by a rich Precambrian record, all discovered in the past thirty years. Yet the peculiar character of this evidence has not matched Darwin's prediction of a continuous rise in complexity toward Cambrian life, and the problem of the Cambrian explosion has remained as stubborn as ever - if not more so, since our

confusion now rests on knowledge, rather than ignorance, about the Precambrian life.[128]

Wonderful Life

In his truly wonderful book called *Wonderful Life,* Stephen J. Gould disputes the classical view that the history of life is the tale of the gradual and steady progress toward excellence, complexity and diversity.[129] Instead of viewing the evolution of life in terms of a tree or cone of growing complexity, or in terms of a ladder of predictable progress, Gould argues for a thorough inversion of the classical Darwinian cone or tree. The sweep of anatomical design, he argues, reached a maximum right after the initial diversification of multicellular animals at the beginning of the Cambrian period. After this extremely rapid and truly explosive diversification of life, the fossil record reveals massive decimation and extinction followed by differentiation to be sure, but a differentiation only within a few surviving stocks.

like neural Darwinism ↓ progress by means of pruning

To make his point Gould draws attention to that oldest fauna of exquisitely preserved soft-bodied animals - the Burgess Shale in British Columbia, Canada - deposited in Middle Cambrian times about 530 million years ago.[130] This truly amazing fauna was discovered for the most part by Charles Doolittle Walcott beginning back in 1909. But right from the start Walcott grossly misinterpreted these fossils by shoehorning every last one of them into some modern group. Gould then recounts the story of Professor Harry Whittington and his colleagues at Cambridge University. Starting in 1971 they slowly discovered, by painstaking and careful analysis, that most of the Burgess organisms do not belong to familiar groups at all, that they cannot be understood as primitive or less advanced in anatomical design, and that these creatures, from a small quarry about the size a single city block, exceed in anatomical range the entire spectrum of invertebrate life in today's oceans:[131]

> The Burgess Shale includes a range of disparity in anatomical design never again equaled, and not matched today by all the creatures in all the world's oceans. The history of multicellular life has been dominated by decimation of a large initial stock, quickly generated in the Cambrian explosion. The story of the last 500 million years has featured restriction followed by proliferation within a few stereotyped designs, not general expansion of range and increase in complexity as our favored iconography, the cone of increasing diversity,

implies. Moreover, the new iconography of rapid establishment and later decimation dominates all scales, and seems to have the generality of a fractal pattern.[132]

For nearly two-thirds of the entire history of life on earth, all organisms were single-celled creatures of the simplest prokaryotic design.[133] But when eukaryotes appeared some 1.4 billion years ago, multicellular creatures did not follow triumphantly in their wake. Multicellular life appeared only in Cambrian times, that is, very late upon the stage of life, and when it did appear, it appeared in a geological instant, with no direct simpler precursors to be found anywhere in the fossil record of Precambrian times.[134] Gould recounts the tale of life with remarkable eloquence:

> Nearly 2.5 billion years of prokaryotic cells and nothing else - two-thirds of life's history in stasis at the lowest level of recorded complexity. Another 700 million years of the larger and much more intricate eukaryotic cells, but no aggregation to multicellular life. Then, in the 100-million-year wink of a geological eye, three outstanding different faunas - from Ediacara, to Tommotian, to Burgess. Since then, more than 500 million years of wonderful stories, triumphs and tragedies, but not a single new phylum, or basic anatomical design, added to the Burgess complement.[135]

Then Gould challenges us to lay aside our usual preconceptions and to think deeply:

> Step way back, blur the details, and you may want to read this sequence as a tale of predictable progress: prokaryotes first, then eukaryotes, then multicellular life. But scrutinize the particulars and the comforting story collapses. Why did life remain at stage 1 for two-thirds of its history if complexity offers such benefits? Why did the origin of multicellular life proceed as a short pulse through three radically different faunas, rather than as a slow and continuous rise of complexity? The history of life is endlessly fascinating, endlessly curious, but scarcely the stuff of our usual thoughts and hopes.[136]

Open at all times to the unexpected, the Universe does not merely unfold that which was there all along; its random, unpredictable pole guarantees a richly differentiated *historical* unfolding in which the future is not contained in a present that is in turn all contained in the past. In other words, our one Universe truly *evolves,* and it should come as no surprise that it should do so in fits and starts vaunting lavish and beautiful displays of the unexpected.

Gould displays a deep feeling for the historical and contingent unfolding of biological evolution by asking us to engage in an interesting thought experiment called "replaying life's tape."[137] If we press the rewind button back to the time of the Burgess Shale and replay the tape of life, should we expect to find the same odd assortment of creatures as before? Not at all says Gould. Instead we have every reason to believe that evolution would head down a pathway radically different from the road actually taken. When we understand the unfolding of biological evolution in terms of a tree, cone or ladder, then the repetition of our tape should look very much like the original, but this is not how evolution unfolds, he argues. Gould challenges any paleontologist to go back to the Burgess seas, and without the benefit of hindsight, to pick out those creatures that were destined to survive and those that were destined for extinction. Impossible he argues:

> But if we face the Burgess fauna honestly, we must admit that we have no evidence whatsoever - not a shred - that losers in the great decimation were systematically inferior in adaptive design to those that survived. Anyone can invent a plausible story after the fact.[138]

A little further on he makes the same point:

> We do not know for sure that the Burgess decimation was a lottery. But we have no evidence that the winners enjoyed adaptive superiority, or that a contemporary handicapper could have designated the survivors. All that we have learned from the finest and the most detailed anatomical monographs in the 20th-Century paleontology portrays the Burgess losers as adequately specialized and eminently capable.[139]

Gould distances himself from any deterministic understanding of evolution, yet at the same time he says that he does not jump from the old determinism of predictable progress to the despair of pure randomness. Instead he develops the idea of the historical and contingent unfolding of biological evolution where even small events at some early stage can throw evolution down a completely different channel:

> But the consequent differences in outcome "in the replay of life's tape" do not imply that evolution is senseless, and without meaning-

ful pattern; the divergent route of the replay would be just as interpretable, just as explainable after the fact, as the actual road. But the diversity of possible itineraries does demonstrate that eventual results cannot be predicted at the outset. Each step proceeds for cause, but no finale can be specified at the start, and none would ever occur a second time in the same way, because any pathway proceeds through thousands of improbable stages. Alter any early event, ever so slightly and without apparent importance at the time, and evolution cascades into a radically different channel.[140]

Please note that Gould says quite clearly that evolution is not senseless, *not without meaningful pattern. Each step proceeds with a cause,* but because the evolutionary process is characterized by a fundamental contingency, no *finale* can be predicted. He then goes on to set forth his main thesis:

> This third alternative represents no more nor less than the essence of history. Its name is contingency - and contingency is a thing unto itself, not the titration of determinism by randomness. Science has been slow to admit the different explanatory world of history into its domain - and our interpretations have been impoverished by this omission. Science has also tended to denigrate history, when forced to a confrontation, by regarding any innovation of contingency as less elegant or less meaningful than explanations based on timeless "laws of nature."[141]

Gould at this point leaves us somewhat baffled. We agree with him in regards to the role of contingency, but how in the world does contingency alone create meaningful pattern? How does it proceed for cause? This book also has as its basic theme the truly *historical* unfolding of biological evolution. Any denigration of time and history takes us out of this world and into a fantasy world of no explanation. But at the same time, we want to tackle the central issue of how *meaningful pattern* originates in the midst of a process riddled by contingency. How do things *proceed for cause* alongside, together with and sometimes even in spite of Lady Luck?

Gould deplores the fact that the stereotype of the scientific method has no place for irreducible history:

> We talk about the "scientific method," and instruct school children in this monolithic and maximally effective path to natural knowledge, as if a single formula could unlock all the multifarious secrets of

empirical reality.

Beyond a platitudinous appeal to open-mindedness, the "scientific method" involves a set of concepts and procedures tailored to the image of a man in a white coat twirling dials in a laboratory - experiment, quantification, repetition, prediction, and restriction of complexity to a few variables that can be controlled and manipulated. These procedures are powerful, but they do not encompass all of nature's variety. How should scientists operate when they must try to explain the results of history, those inordinately complex events that occur but once in detailed glory? Many large domains of nature - cosmology, geology, and evolution among them - must be studied with the tools of history. The appropriate methods focus on narrative, not experiment as usually conceived.[142]

These reflections of a first-rate paleontologist and biologist on the method of science are very instructive. Elsewhere in explaining how historical explanations are distinct from conventional experimental results, he touches on themes which we talked about in our first chapter - themes involving things like the unpredictable, the unique, the irreversible, and the complex:

Historical explanations are distinct from conventional experimental results in many ways. The issue of verification by repetition does not arise because we are trying to account for uniqueness of detail that cannot, both by the laws of probability and time's arrow of irreversibility, occur together again. We do not attempt to interpret the complex events of narrative by reducing them to simple consequences of natural law; historical events do not, of course, violate any general principles of matter and motion, but their occurrence lies in a realm of contingent detail. (The law of gravity tells us how an apple falls, but not why that apple fell at that moment, and why Newton happened to be sitting there, ripe for inspiration.) And the issue of prediction, a central ingredient in the stereotype, does not enter into a historical narrative. We can explain an event after it occurs, but contingency precludes its repetition, even from an identical starting point.[143]

Gould ranks the Burgess revision and the Alvarez theory linking the Cretaceous extinction to extra-terrestrial impact as the two most important palaeontological discoveries in the past twenty years. Both of these discoveries illustrate the extreme chanciness and contingency of life's history:

Decimate the Burgess differently and we never evolve; send those

comets into harmless orbits and dinosaurs still rule the earth, preclud-
ing the rise of large mammals including humans.[144]

Gould says that the answer to the question "Why can humans reason?" lies "as much (and as deeply) in the quirky pathways of contingent history as in the physiology of neurons."[145] He argues that the modern pattern of anatomical design as we know it was not guaranteed by
basic laws, by natural selection, by mechanical superiority in anatomical design, or even by lower-level generalities of ecology or evolutionary theory. He says quite clearly: "The modern order is largely a product of contingency."[146] Nowhere does he make this point more eloquently than in the following:

> Finally, if you will accept my argument that contingency is not
> only resolvable and important, but also fascinating in a special sort of
> way, then the Burgess not only reverses our general ideas about the
> source of pattern - it also fills us with a new kind of amazement (also
> a *frisson* for the improbability of the event) at the fact that we humans
> ever evolved at all. We came *this close* (put your thumb about a mil-
> limeter away from your index finger), thousands and thousands of
> times, to erasure by the veering of history down another sensible
> channel. Replay the tape a million times from a Burgess beginning,
> and I doubt that anything like *Homo Sapiens* would ever evolve again.
> It is, indeed, a wonderful life.[147]

Yet having said this, Gould does not deny predictability altogether:

> Invariant laws of nature impact the general forms and functions of
> organisms; they set the channel in which organic design must evolve.
> But the channels are so broad relative to the details that fascinate us..
> When we set our focus upon the level of detail that regulates most
> common questions about the history of life, contingency dominates
> and the predictability of general form recedes to an irrelevant back-
> ground.[148]

Please note what Gould says here: contingency *dominates* and predictability *recedes* to an *irrelevant* background. This entire book has as
it overriding theme that delicate balance between the predictable and
the unpredictable, the stable and unstable, the expected and unexpected,
and so forth. This balance characterizes the history of all living systems,
and to the extent that Gould disrupts this balance, the story of life is
robbed of its deepest meaning. Gould's position resembles very much

that of Charles Darwin: "laws in the background and contingency in the details."[149] Laws set the channel, and the details lie in the realm of the contingent. In other words, the Universe in general runs by law, but the details are left to chance. The *crucial question* for Gould boils down to where to place the boundary between predictability under invariant law and the multifarious possibilities of historical contingency:

> Traditionalists like Walcott would place the boundary so low that all major patterns of life's history fall above the line into the realm of predictability (and, for him direct manifestations of divine intentions). But I envision a boundary sitting so high that almost every interesting event of life's history falls into the realm of contingency. I regard the new interpretation of the Burgess Shale as nature's finest argument for placing the boundary this high.
> This means - and we must face the implication squarely - that the origin of *Homo Sapiens,* as a tiny twig on an improbable branch of a contingent limb on a fortunate tree, lies well below the boundary. In Darwin's scheme, we are a detail, not a purpose or embodiment of the whole - "with the details, whether good or bad, left to the working out of what we may call chance." Whether the evolutionary origin of self-conscious intelligence in any form lies above or below the boundary, I simply do not know.[150]

Is man an insignificant detail? "Perhaps we are only an afterthought, a kind of cosmic accident, just one bauble on the Christmas tree of evolution,"[151] says Gould. Are the creatures of the Burgess shale also insignificant details? Perhaps they too are nothing more than cosmic accidents which no one should have bothered to dig up or write books about with such excitement, enthusiasm and sheer delight. Of course, we appreciate very much Gould's emphasis on history and contingency, but why does he draw a boundary between law and chance? Why should laws be "invariant" as Walcott presumed?[152] *Laws are invariant only with respect to machines, but in living organisms, as the entire theory of evolution suggests, they vary constantly over and against this element of real chance.* Why should contingency dominate below the boundary and law above? John Barrow, reflecting as a cosmologist from a broad universal perspective, is reluctant to draw any lines between law and chance:

> The laws of Nature will not allow us to infer what we see in the Universe. And we do not even know where to draw the line between those aspects of the Universe which are attributable to law and those

which issue from the revolving doors of chance.[153]

Our examination of the history of the Big Bang would suggest that in the context of the whole sweep of universal history, there is nothing so unusual about the role which chance or contingency has played in the unfolding of biological evolution here on Earth. Everywhere we look within the history of our Universe, we see the hand of contingency. We see endless strings of lucky accidents without which complex life as we know it would not be possible at all. We contend that Lady Luck, as Gould calls her, makes her presence felt not only within the evolution of life on Earth but at all steps and stages throughout the entire history of our Universe. This holds true even as we reach back to the very beginning:

> The closer one approaches to the apparent beginning "of the Universe," so the effects of symmetry-breaking and quantum randomness begin to proliferate and generate the intrinsically random elements whose legacy creates the subtleties of interpretation we have highlighted.[154]

Perhaps things would become clearer if we should go back to our brief analysis of the dynamics of natural systems.[155] The *historical* path that a system follows is characterized by a succession of both stable and unstable regions. In the stable regions, deterministic laws dominate, and in the unstable regions near the bifurcation points, chance comes into play. Both elements of law and chance are inextricably connected in the historical evolution of any natural system. It is precisely their *mixture* that constitutes the *history* of a system. What meaning could we give to history without the notion of chance or randomness? As we have learned from Prigogine and Stengers, only when a system behaves in a sufficiently random way can the difference between past and future and hence irreversibility enter into its description.

Our thesis suggests that chance and necessity, novelty and confirmation, order and disorder are therefore *complementary* poles of all natural systems. Every level in our multileveled Universe in displaying self-organization, displays pattern and law. But law is never completely fixed, immutable, unchanging, stable, invariant or necessary. In its constant openness to that aspect of the new and unexpected available to it at its particular level of self-organization, it too can enter into an unstable state and is therefore subject to change. Many if not all of the laws that govern the evolution of our Universe are themselves subject to evolution. The story of the Big Bang, the story of the successive and at times quite unexpected breaks in symmetry involving at all stages the highly complex yet complementary interaction of both chance and necessity, we do not hesitate to characterize as a single *historical* process.

Therefore we should ask Gould to turn life's tape back even further than the Burgess Shale. Let us go back in time to the very first moments of the Big Bang and play once more the tape of life. Would we then get a Universe that resembles in any way our present Universe? We venture to guess that less than one second into our replay, things would already begin to look radically different from that familiar scenario of events described by cosmologists in the Big Bang. It is indeed a wonderful life, and its truly wondrous character lies precisely in that delicate balance between chance and necessity. Here nothing recedes into insignificance: not man and surely not a single specimen buried deep within that ancient mudslide of the Burgess Shale.

Nature Jumps

Hopefully we are now in a better position to approach this question of the discontinuous and sudden jumps in evolution. Everywhere we look in nature we see organisms that possess features that do not evolve one at a time: a multiplicity of highly interdependent features must evolve together for organisms to change their nature and function. Pure chance could never explain all the interdependent processes that converge in giving rise to new biological forms and patterns of behavior. The evolutionary movement from reptiles to birds is a particularly fascinating example.[156]

Did some sort of running, gliding, leaping, jumping, dancing, sailing, fly swatting or netting stage precede avian flight? Did flight originate from the trees down (the arboreal theory) or from the ground up (the cursorial theory)? It may be difficult to determine with any assurance exactly what took place, but in any case, we witness the work of an extraordinary intelligence. What strikes us first is the enormous enlargement of the scaly reptilian foreleg area into a very efficient airfoil by means of feathers. But how does one fray the scale of a reptile into the extremely complex structure of a feather riddled with the intricacy of such things as shafts, barbs, barbules and hooklets?

> Take away the exquisite coadaptation of the components, take
> away the coadaptation of the hooks and barbules, take away the pre-
> cisely parallel arrangement of the barbs on the shaft and all that is left
> is a soft pliable structure utterly unsuitable to form the basis of a stiff
> impervious airfoil.[157]

Feathers are strong, light, versatile, adjustable, maneuverable and
marvelously aerodynamic. We know that wings evolved several times,
but the complicated structure of feathers evolved only once. Did feathers originally evolve for other purposes such as temperature control or
sexual display? Since there are simpler ways to control temperature and
to show off, and since we do not find feathers anywhere other than in
birds or bird-like creatures capable of flight, some scientists argue that
feathers have evolved almost exclusively for the purpose of flying.

But in addition to having feathers and wings, birds also possess a
fairly unique lung and respiratory system. Generally in most non-avian
lungs, air moves in and out through the same passageways, whereas in
avian lungs, the air moves in only one direction assuring a continuous
delivery of air. "No lung in any other vertebrate species is known which
in any way approaches the avian system. Moreover, it is identical in all
essential details in birds as diverse as hummingbirds, ostriches and
hawks."[158] How does such an utterly different respiratory system
evolve? Keep in mind that with the slightest malfunction of a respiratory system, even for a few minutes, our poor reptile in transition would
have died.

We find many other unique features in the biology of birds: the
design of the heart and cardiovascular system, the gastrointestinal system, the unique sound-producing organ called the syrinx and so forth.[159]
How do we explain the emergence of so many intricate and unique features all operating in such an interdependent and integrated way?
Obviously machines do not possess the flexibility or the internal self-
organizing ability to select and effect all of these interrelated changes in
such a short period of time, and since we cannot exclude the role which
chance has played in this or in any other evolving system, we cannot
ground a single avian feature in some God-given necessity.

What can a creature do with only five percent of a wing? Surely a
part of a wing cannot fly, a part of an eye cannot see, a part of an ear
cannot hear, and therefore none of these bits and pieces would offer
selective advantage. In his essay *Return of the Hopeful Monster,*
Stephen J. Gould tries to solve this dilemma by asking us to consider the
possibility of a *small* random genetic change in early embryology

effecting a *large,* abrupt and discontinuous change in the adult form of an organism.[160] This change need not give rise to a perfected form all at once. It need only generate a "Hopeful Monster" which would then serve as a key adaptation around which a large set of collateral alterations could accumulate in the more traditional and gradual manner that Darwin set forth. In this way Gould explains how a fully perfected form like a wing or an eye could originate.

As we come to appreciate in a limited way the subtle and fluid dynamic of change within living organisms, we know that it would be wrong to look for some preordained purpose in place from all eternity. Yet this does not mean that we should reduce all to the meandering of pure chance and conclude that purpose does not operate. To invoke the principle of preadaptation[161] or exaptation,[162] or to set forth the more sophisticated argument of the Hopeful Monster as Gould does in his fascinating essay, does not eliminate the question of purpose: it merely shifts it to a previous stage. If we persist in transferring explanation to previous stages, we soon find ourselves in the same logical dilemma as Charles Darwin, inextricably trapped in the classical mechanistic regression toward the infinity of a supernatural explanation. Even though we cannot deny that small or even massive doses of chance may provoke, initiate, influence, impact or accompany change, we still cannot avoid the obvious truth that chance all by itself does not effect meaningful change. At some point we must explain meaningful change. At some point we must face up to the stark reality of a previous evolutionary history which distinguishes itself from chance and which continually transforms chance into meaningful pattern and purposeful project. Cut off from this previous history, chance amounts to nothing more than a series of insignificant blips in a meaningless ocean of noise.

We have no problem with the fact that the purpose which operates at one or more incipient stages is not the same purpose as that which operates at the later stage of the fully perfected final form.[163] This is exactly what one should expect when purpose is continually bombarded with the element of real chance. *But what is central in this discussion, what shouts out from the rooftops, is not the absence of purpose and meaning, but the extraordinary evolution of purpose and meaning.*

Two principles in evolutionary theory illustrate well this theme of the constant transformation of purpose.[164] Perhaps they are both grounded in the notion that any complex structure has a range of potential uses by virtue of the complexity of its previous history.[165] The first principle is called the one-for-two principle. Here a single organ performs more than one distinct function. We readily see that this principle does not offer a lot of evolutionary flexibility, for if one of the functions performed by this single organ were vital to the survival of the organism, there would be very little freedom to change. But there is a second principle, the two-for-one principle, where several organs perform simultaneously the same function within the same organism. This second principle is especially rich in creative potential. It allows one organ to perform a vital function, while the other organ is free to drift on in a useless and redundant mode, available for some other purpose or function.

Complex parts that are perfectly adapted to their environment, superbly discharging one and only one function, are not very interesting in terms of evolutionary change. But complex parts that become useless and redundant are a precious resource for change. Since they may require very little modification to fulfill an altogether different function within their environment, they enable nature to solve very complex problems without having to start all over from scratch. Once these evolutionary sub-units accumulate in sufficient diversity, nature is free to combine and recombine, to test and explore radically new evolutionary pathways. Once these evolutionary sub-units are in place, the tempo of evolutionary change may increase dramatically, with new life bursting on the scene in an abrupt and discontinuous fashion. Therefore it is quite logical that evolution should proceed by means of mixing, matching, modifying and rearranging complex modular sub-units which have the freedom and flexibility to fulfill more than one function.[166]

The idea that organs or organisms are ideally suited for one and only one function is a vestige not only of old-style creationism in the sense that God created each creature with a fixed and fully formed purpose in place from all eternity,[167] but it also reflects the rigidity of old-style mechanistic science where man makes machines with clear and well-defined goals in mind. In the real world of change where everything, to a certain extent, interconnects, overlaps and duplicates with respect to everything else around it, the notion of purpose defies the rigidity of supernatural and mechanistic categories of thought and defines itself in a fluid and open-ended manner. In the real world of change where clouds are not spheres, where mountains are not cones, and where lightning does not travel in straight lines,[168] in the real world of change where everything is so messy, redundant, imperfect and incomplete, the concept of purpose does not disappear but defines itself in most unconventional manner with lots of ambiguity, tentativeness and open-endedness. Purpose, like truth, has none of the sharp edges or straight lines which characterize a supernatural or mechanistic description of reality.

As we try to come to grips with the idea of purpose within an organismic context, we soon run across the paradoxical but precious notion of the *usefulness of useless parts*. Someone could argue the ultimate uselessness of useful parts, but after all, what purpose would his argument serve? Western thought oscillates once again so easily between two empty positions: either some all-embracing, God-given purpose or plan which existed from all eternity - or absolutely no purpose at all. To argue from the perspective of some all-purposeful God-given plan is indeed ridiculous, but to take the completely opposite position and to argue no purpose at all puts us in another logical predicament. *To argue no purpose demands purpose, can only be done with a sense of purpose, and is therefore a self-contradictory idea.* What purpose would it serve to argue that life has no purpose? Or what purpose would it serve to convince someone else that his or her life is totally meaningless? In such questions we confront the futility and emptiness of evil itself.

At this point we propose a symbiotic version of the two-for-one principle. This new principle in its simplest version would involve two organs shared simultaneously by two *different* organisms. One organ is shared in a vital way by both organisms, while the other organ drifts on as a useless appendage free to explore other possibilities. But organisms, of course, do not evolve in isolation. The two organisms evolve in interaction with a multiplicity of other organisms, and eventually they all come to share symbiotically a broad range of vital functions. In this complex symbiotic web, not just organs but entire organisms can be made redundant, and in their apparent uselessness, they become available to explore radically new evolutionary pathways. As long as we do not exaggerate the importance of any particular evolutionary sub-unit within the process, perhaps we are justified in attributing the notion of progress to the process as a whole.

But how to pinpoint or identify progress in such a fluid and open-ended context where everything eventually cedes its purpose to the continually shifting purpose of everything else? We face the very real danger of looking back upon this previous evolutionary history and interpreting all in terms of the progress of man, as if the entire process had been nothing but a preparation for the rise and ascent of *Homo Sapiens*. Let us not be so arrogant. We forget all too easily that we are participators in a process far larger and far more meaningful than anything we could begin to imagine within the context of our limited categories of interpretation. Furthermore, to pinpoint progress, it is not enough to study the confirmation of the past, but somehow we must actively participate in the emergence of those images within our Universe which select and *anticipate* a future from out of the contingency and chanciness of the present moment. All selection within the unity of space-time has a certain temporal aspect, and therefore all selection implies anticipation, an idea we will explore in greater detail in our third and fourth chapters.

Therefore, in the symbiotic and fluid nesting of purpose within purpose which encompasses all levels and reaches back to the earliest moments in time, we move far beyond the rigidity of the mechanical with its hidden supernaturalist agenda, and we begin to get a far more realistic insight into the meaning of the word evolution.

Everywhere in nature we find a tight and critical interdependency and interlocking across space and time. On every level throughout the whole of our multileveled Universe, everything depends on everything else. The whole of the Universe is presupposed and even anticipated by all of its parts. Look at how complex things can be only on the level of a single cell:

> Proteins are needed to make catalysts, yet catalysts are needed to make proteins; nucleic acids are needed to make proteins, yet proteins are needed to make nucleic acids; proteins and lipids are needed to make membranes, yet membranes are needed to provide protection for all the chemical processes going on in a cell.[169]

How do we begin to isolate the purpose of any one element within the cell in the midst of such complex interrelatedness? Note again the tight and critical interdependency in central biochemistry:

> Pull out a molecule - any molecule. What is it? Aspartic acid? That is as good an example as any. Aspartic acid is one of the twenty protein amino acids. It is, then, a component of virtually every enzyme. Every chemical reaction in the cell to this extent depends on aspartic acid being there, which means that every molecule made by the cell depends on this molecule. But, as it is often the case, this molecule is also used as a building block of all sorts of other molecules - for some of the nucleotide letters, for example. And, of course, nucleotide letters are of central importance. Pull out another molecule, any one of the central set, and ask "What use is this?" and you will find the same thing: you will find several immediate answers, and then, when considering more indirect effects, *you will find that every molecule is required in some way or other by every other molecule.*[170]

In biochemistry we see that every molecule depends on every other molecule in a fundamental way. How do we define the purpose of a particular molecule in such complicated interrelatedness? This interrelatedness and interdependency of all life applies to all levels, and this brings us back to the theme which we announced in the first paragraphs of chapter one, namely that everything within our Universe depends on everything else in a fundamental way. From our rather limited perspective some levels appear to be more intensely interdependent, and we say that they are alive. Areas apparently less interdependent, we simplistically label as dead. Molecules go back to atoms, and to understand the genesis of most atoms we need to reach for the stars, that is, to stellar nucleosynthesis. For the elements needed in stellar nucleosynthesis we need to reach back in time to the birth of the Universe. It all interdepends tightly and critically across the whole of space and time.

But this idea of an interdependent Universe, with all its parts purposefully evolving together, meets with violent resistance in certain scientific circles, since it forcefully contradicts the notion of the Universe as an insensible machine evolving according to the logic of blind chance. Unfortunately, for many here in the West the only alternative to the logic of pure chance is the equally superficial notion of an external God stepping in from time to time to direct traffic according to some predetermined plan. Likewise in discussions relating to the origin of life on earth, the only alternative to the magical and totally inexplicable origin of life in some prebiotic soup is some supernatural energy or force breathed into lifeless matter by an external God. Is the time not ripe for the scientific community to abandon the rigidity of a mechanistic explanation as well as the emptiness of its supernatural counterpart and to search for fresh alternatives in line with 20th-Century thought?

Up until now Darwinism has offered the only explanation of life invoking well-understood physical and natural processes as the causal agencies of evolutionary change. Darwinism has dominated so much of modern evolutionary thinking mainly because there has been no other scientific alternative to Darwinism. The persistence and power of Darwin's thought goes back, not to its logic or rigorous empiricism as we have seen, but to the fact that there has not been any other truly scientific alternative put forward to replace it:

> Mark Ridley, for example, again and again makes the case for natural selection simply on the grounds that we have no other plausible

explanation (Ridley 1985). This perspective is understandable, perhaps persuasive.[171]

A scientific theory cannot be declared invalid, as Thomas Kuhn would argue, until an alternative theory is put forward to take its place. Just as Ptolemaic cosmology persisted until Copernicus put forward his new heliocentric theory of the heavens, just as the theory of phlogiston persisted until Lavoisier put forward the true theory of combustion, someone might argue that Darwinism will persist until a radically new scientific theory is put forward to explain the origin and evolution of life. But is it simply a question of a new scientific theory within an old epistemological framework? "New facts, collected in old ways under the guidance of old theories, rarely lead to any substantial revision of thought,"[172] says Gould. How do we begin to explain what goes on in embryology, morphology, regulation, regeneration, reproduction, instinct and adaptation? We feel strongly that none of this will ever be explained within the narrow conceptual framework of mechanistic science. We must move on to the concept of mind operating on the level of the whole of reality - mind possessing both memory and imagination - mind remembering and anticipating across the entire sweep of space-time, and here we step into an entirely different epistemology of science.

Beyond Darwin?

Rupert Sheldrake, formerly a biologist at the University of Cambridge, has proposed a daring alternative to Darwinism which he has put forward within what he would consider to be a scientific framework. It is certainly not a complete theory, but it points in the direction of a fresh alternative to neo-Darwinism so badly needed today.

Sheldrake puts forth the idea of morphogenetic fields that serve as blueprints or channels for the shape and movement of all things.[173] Not only do we have the four fields of physics, but we have many other fields which explain, for example, the shape of a molecule, the growth of a crystal, the regulation of a cell, the development of an embryo, the behavior of a crowd, the formation of a galaxy and so forth. According to Sheldrake an individual human being is made up of a multiplicity of living fields all directed in hierarchical interlocking order right on up to the general field of the self. The self interlocks with the other fields until we reach the one universal field of the Cosmos itself.

> All forms and patterns of things that develop in the world have
> their own organizing fields, and all are ultimately derived from the
> primal unified field, which remains the all-encompassing field of the
> world.[174]

All entities organized by a particular field feed information to that
field, and the field in turn transmits its total accumulated information to
each entity. As more information is fed to a field, the field becomes
stronger, and the likelihood in the future of a particular expression of the
field is increased. Sheldrake does not speak of laws of nature but of
habits reinforced by repetition. Those entities under the organizational
influence of a field tune into the field in a process called "morphic resonance."

Sheldrake's fields are not physical fields, since they exist in another
non-physical dimension not affected by time and distance. Once a field
comes into existence it does not die. His use of the word "resonance" is
metaphorical, since there is nothing of actual matter or energy in resonance. Thus according to Sheldrake, non-physical fields organize the
physical. He gives a very illuminating example of the organizational
power of these non-physical fields in his discussion of the physical
brain. This he understands from an altogether non-classical perspective.

Sheldrake says that memory does not reside in the brain, instead the
brain merely tunes into the field of a particular person where memory
resides. Fields work in conjunction with matter in very much the same
way that a radio works with respect to an electromagnetic signal. A
radio simply tunes into the information contained in the radio transmission. If we open up a radio we do not find tiny people engaged in con-
versation, instead we only find transistors, tubes and other mechanical
parts. Without the electromagnetic signal, the radio remains a useless
pile of bits and pieces. In this way Sheldrake can answer the objection
of the mechanist who might say that his theory of hidden fields is totally unnecessary to explain form and behavior. Sheldrake sees fields as
operating from dimensions far beyond the apparent correlation of
mechanical parts.

Sheldrake's hypothesis of formative causation takes us well beyond
current mechanistic and reductionist thought. It has an explicit holistic
thrust that at first glance would appear to accord well with the ideas we
are developing here. His idea of a habit replacing the idea of a law fits
neatly into an organismic framework. But at the heart of Sheldrake's

thought we detect a troublesome duality that unfortunately explains very little and in the end may only serve to alienate or confuse the large majority of his fellow biologists. Sheldrake's fields are distinct from matter and from the more conventional fields which modern physics understands. They represent an addition to physics that no classical physicist could ever accept. Although Sheldrake understands these non-physical fields as acting directly upon the physical, he does not explain very well just how this interaction occurs:

> Are they energy-carrying fields like the other fields of physics? If so, they require the definition of new forces and new forms of inter-action. But if this is so, then how is it that their strength does not fall off with distance and time as with other fields? And if they have nothing to do with the conventional fields of matter and somehow transcend the limitations of space, how exactly do they operate and by what means do they interact with material forms and become reinforced by them?[175]

No doubt Sheldrake has a lot of explaining to do if he is to be taken seriously by science. Sheldrake's fields are as mysterious in their operation as any of the old vitalist forces that he as a good biologist was taught to reject. Operating within the physical, we find a hidden world of invisible fields. Sheldrake's analogy of the material radio tuning into invisible electromagnetic signals is clearly dualistic: the objective physical body or brain tunes into the subjective immaterial self or mind. Such an explanation, we feel, falls far short of a sufficient holism. By constructing his epistemology around matter and mysterious fields operative within matter, he remains within a tradition of thought reminiscent of the supernaturalism of Teilhard de Chardin.

Does not his notion of a morphic field represent nothing more and nothing less than what we have been describing all along as mind? He says that his fields "contain an inherent memory."[176] Elsewhere he says that the world field has an imagination.[177] Would it not be a whole lot simpler, especially within an organismic context, to associate memory and imagination with *mind*? Why talk about fields, since nowhere in classical physics do we find fields having memory and imagination? In disguising the reality of mind behind the curtain of a physics which knows nothing of mind, Sheldrake leaves far too many of the presuppositions of mechanistic science firmly in place. But in contrast, when we move into that exciting domain of the dynamics of natural systems, a whole new vocabulary presents itself. Words such as metabolism,[178] communication,[179] information, choice,[180] knowledge, experience,[181] consciousness,[182] even mind,[183] memory and imagination, all become readily available in our description of even the simplest self-organizing systems.

Sheldrake apparently does not view the selective ability of mind in a complementary bipolar relationship with the random.[184] He therefore has a hard time explaining how a new form first comes into being before any field exists. In *The Rebirth of Nature* he speaks of the "evolutionary creativity inherent in nature herself,"[185] but he makes no real attempt to explain the creative *within* nature. In his book *Trialogues at the Edge of the West,* Sheldrake, along with Ralph Abraham and Terence McKenna, sets about explaining the creative by making direct appeal to the concept of God. All three of them speak often of the Divine Imagination.[186] God or novelty is situated at the end of time as the Cosmic Attractor of the entire cosmic process.[187] But if God or novelty is situated in the future, how then do we understand the arrow of time? In the place of trying to explain everything deterministically out of the past, by giving such power to the future, do we not run the risk of a trying to explain everything out of the future? We prefer to place novelty firmly in the present, and in the process by which novelty becomes ordered and transformed by mind, time acquires directionality.

If we want insight into the evolution of biological form, let us draw from both Gould and Sheldrake and hold their apparently contradictory positions in full complementarity. On the one hand, Gould has rightly emphasized the role of chance. Without doubt Lady Luck plays a very important role in the evolution of biological form, but unfortunately all by herself she cannot explain very much. No one can make a convincing case for the manifold order within our Universe by appealing to disorder alone. On the other hand, in spite of the all the confusion he has introduced with his talk of fields, Sheldrake has made an invaluable contribution to biological thought by drawing attention to a whole range of phenomena which can be explained in no other way than through the highly selective organizational power of mind.[188] But remember, mind alone quickly atrophies, it offers nothing new. Mind operates as mind only over and against that rather strange and unusual process pole of the new and the inherently unpredictable, which we have no trouble identifying as the source of the creativity inherent within nature. Of course, we place the New firmly in the present, and we dissociate it, as well as Mind, from any direct reference to God. In so doing we arrive at a Universe highly differentiated along a multiplicity of interrelated pathways, each level displaying in its own unique way the complementary dynamics of both the selective and the random.

Here we find a realistic alternative to Darwinism which, of course, has nothing in common with the simplicity of the mechanical. But at the same time, it has little in common with the epistemology of those scientists such as Sheldrake and Bohm who, correctly appreciating the limitations of mechanistic science, sadly remain within its fundamental framework and at the end of the day are forced to turn to the supernatural in their effort to explain. As we have said before, we deny both the mechanical and supernatural as legitimate principles of explanation within science, and, of course, we distance ourselves from any esoteric New Age mixture of the two.

But this no doubt implies a whole new understanding of science and the method of science. Freed from its god-like pretension of being able to convert local truth into global truth, forced to grapple with the concept of self-organization on the level of the whole of reality, confronted on every level with the bewildering complexity of the inherently unpredictable, and coming to realize, as Gould teaches us, that experimentation, quantification, repetition, and prediction do not encompass the whole of scientific methodology, science today is called upon to submit to a profound transformation in its own self-understanding. No less scientific in its demand for clarity and precision, this new epistemology of science operates in humble awareness of its limited and tenuous hold on truth. It remains at all times a "quintessentially human activity,"[189] subject to all the foibles and false starts,[190] to all the pride and passion, that characterize any human activity. It speaks neither with the arrogance of divine knowledge nor with insensitivity of a mindless objectivity. It represents a fragile group of human beings trying to understand an extremely complex reality of which they are an integral part. Since this living reality never ceases to evolve and self-differentiate right within their understanding of it, new areas of scientific investigation constantly emerge. No longer intimidated by what some other level says is true and no longer constrained by what some other level says is possible, each science defines itself in a semi-autonomous manner according to the truth and possibility uniquely available at its particular level of investigation. In the end each local scientific reconstruction plays its part within a continually expanding body of knowledge, each exploring with wonder and delight the highly differentiated beauty of a Universe in evolution.

Chapter 3

Towards a Theory of Explanation

Gods and Goddesses

When man first traveled out into space, he gazed upon our azure-green planet from a distance, and the impact of seeing it in all its global beauty gave rise to a whole new set of questions and answers.[191] It took several trips out into space involving hundreds of billions of dollars for Western man just to begin to understand what far less educated indigenous peoples have sensed intuitively all along, that our planet functions as a single living whole. Could it be that "the entire range of living matter on Earth, from whales to viruses, and from oaks to algae, could be regarded as constituting a single living entity, capable of manipulating the Earth's atmosphere to suit its overall needs and endowed with faculties and powers far beyond those of its constituent parts"?[192] Very much evidence exists today in support of the amazing insight that our planet functions as a single self-regulating whole, so much so that the American biologist Lynn Margulis and the British chemist James Lovelock took the fairly logical step of calling this whole Gaia in honor of the earth mother in Greek mythology.

Lovelock and Margulis discovered the strange paradox that the conditions necessary for life on Earth are created and maintained by life itself in a self-sustaining process of dynamical feedback. Life maintains the chemicals and gases here on Earth in a radical state of disequilibrium, and this highly improbable situation cannot be explained as the outcome of purely random processes:

> The climate and chemical properties of the Earth now and throughout its history seem always to have been optimal for life. For this to have happened by chance is as unlikely as to survive unscathed a drive blindfolded through rush-hour traffic.[193]

If Earth's atmosphere were the product of simple chemical equilibrium, instead of having 0.03 percent carbon dioxide, 78 percent nitrogen, and 21 percent oxygen, it would quickly settle down to a deadly gaseous mixture resembling what is found on Mars and Venus, comprised of 99 percent carbon dioxide. Raise or lower the percentage of oxygen on earth ever so slightly, and life as we know it would not be possible.

> Our experiments confirmed the theory and at the same time convinced us that the composition of the Earth's atmosphere was so curious and incompatible a mixture that it could not have arisen and persisted by chance. Almost everything about it seemed to violate the rules of equilibrium chemistry, yet amidst apparent disorder relatively constant and favorable conditions for life were somehow maintained.[194]

Another example can be found in the level of salt in the sea.[195] The concentration of salt in the sea has remained delicately balanced for the last 3.5 billion years at its present level of 3.5 percent in spite of the fact that salts have been added and are still being added to the sea continually. A salt level slightly higher than 3.5 percent would make life as we know it impossible. The regulation of salinity is an extremely complex dynamic involving a multiplicity of interdependent factors. Microorganisms form rocky reefs which in turn trap seawater in lagoons where salt evaporates and accumulates in large quantities and is later buried. The movement of continental plates plays a significant role in this process, and yet the movement of continental plates is partially directed by a living process through the sheer weight of the limestone deposited on the sea floor. We have come nowhere near to discovering all the interdependent processes involved in controlling salinity.

Another example of the self-regulating touch of Gaia lies in the control of temperature on Earth. Since our planet was formed, the luminosity of the Sun has increased by 30 percent,[196] yet the temperature on Earth has remained remarkably stable throughout its entire history in spite of this tremendous increase. At a time when the Sun gave much less warmth, the atmosphere on Earth contained much carbon dioxide which produced a greenhouse effect which prevented the early primeval oceans from freezing over. But as the Sun grew hotter and threatened to boil away these oceans, life gave rise to photosynthesis which synthesized a large portion of carbon into living material. This released oxygen and destroyed the carbon dioxide blanket surrounding our planet. The release of oxygen had another beneficial effect. It produced the vital ozone layer in the upper atmosphere which shielded the Earth from dangerous ultraviolet rays. The best computer modeling of the Earth's temperature produces scenarios of either global glaciation or runaway heating. It would appear then that the Earth's atmosphere is only marginally stable,[197] and yet throughout 4.5 billion years, the temperature on our planet has remained virtually constant. Many other examples could be cited to illustrate this powerful self-regulating planetary dynamic.[198]

Lovelock has brought together much evidence in support of the theory that our planet is alive, that it functions as a single self-organizing whole. He has pointed to many interdependent processes where we actually observe our planet in the continuous act of it own *internal* self-organization. But if Lovelock has succeeded in convincing us that our planet does not operate with the rigidity and simplicity of a machine, this does not mean that we should jump to the supernatural in our effort to explain. How easy it is for a Westerner to conceive of Gaia in the flatness and singularity of some sort of energy, field, power or force mysteriously animating that gigantic spatially extended object we call Earth. If Gaia represents nothing more than a ghost in a machine, however, then she serves us poorly in our effort to explain.

As we try to grapple with the concept of self-organization on the level of an entire planet, we should dispense with the mechanical and the supernatural, and we should draw inspiration from the whole of evolutionary biology which speaks forcefully of the dialectical interplay of the selective and the random. Our definition of a living organism fits quite logically into the framework of a dematerialized Darwinian dialectic, and we do not hesitate to apply this definition to the whole of planet Earth. This then leads us to understand the origin and evolution of life on Earth in terms of a highly differentiated planetary mind - a mind which has been selecting and anticipating over the last four and a half billion years with a real sense of purpose and project. Here we find a selective element which is truly selective and which really gets down to the job of explaining something with respect to the manifold order we see throughout our planet. Once the concept of mind has been divested of facile connotations of human or divine rationality, it may be used within a scientific context enabling us to come to grips with what Gould would call the *awesome*[199] and *overwhelming*[200] improbability of human evolution. Human evolution, together with the whole of biological evolution here on Earth, when viewed in a mechanistic setting, is so awesome and overwhelming that it borders on the totally miraculous, but when viewed from within an organismic setting, it bears testimony to an internal selective process which continually transforms the improbable into that which is regular and stable enough to be subjected to scientific investigation. As we try to formulate a scientific approach to the highly improbable history of biological evolution here on Earth, we should not forget that in our passionate search for beauty and truth, our own minds are an integral part of that internal selective power capable of organizing an entire planet from within itself.

All throughout its turbulent history, our planet has managed to regulate itself in a most remarkable and robust manner over and against many unexpected and sometimes even violent internal and external perturbations. As our planet selects and evolves in the presence of the unpredictable, it acquires a uniqueness and individuality characteristic of the growth and development of any living system.[201] But living systems, even if we are speaking of entire planets, do not evolve in isolation, and as we join with Lovelock in gazing upon the whole of our planet from out in space, we soon come to another equally amazing insight: that this entire self-regulating planetary process constitutes only a relatively small part of the much larger evolutionary problem before us. For astrophysicists and cosmologists pull us away from the comfort and security of a narrow point of view, and they teach us that questions relating to the origin and evolution of life on Earth must be framed against the background of questions relating to the origin and evolution of the Universe itself.

This awesome level of the whole of the Universe, no longer the exclusive domain of philosophers and theologians, has been subjected to serious rational inquiry from within science itself, and it holds its ground as a valid area of scientific investigation. Some cosmologists today even go so far as to ask questions such as, "How did the Universe actually begin?"[202] Or "Can the Universe be created out of nothing?"[203] Even though these scientists are far from outlining or defining every step and stage in this universal process, they are asking legitimate questions which rise up from out of the firm conviction that we are not simply dealing with a jumble of causally disjointed bits and pieces. As we join in their excitement in formulating a scientific approach to that thoroughly amazing history of an evolving Universe, again we should not forget that our own minds are an integral part of that comprehensive subjectivity capable of organizing an entire Universe from within itself.

At this unique and distinct level of the whole of the Universe, we must be especially careful not to give in to the magic of cheap and easy answers. If these cosmologists have succeeded in convincing us that our Universe does not evolve with the rigidity and simplicity of a machine, this once again does not mean that we should jump to the supernatural in our effort to explain. Insofar as we conceive of our Universe as alive, as containing both a selective and a random principle, we need never appeal to some supernatural or implicit order mysteriously lying behind and explaining the ever-changing world in which we live. We agree with David Bohm that all is flux,[204] but to the perceiving mind this flux always bears the marks of differentiation and broken symmetry. To the perceiving mind undifferentiated sameness lies beyond all possibility of observation and could never be used to describe a Universe filled with observers. As observers we can only exist in that kind of a Universe which should reflect a high degree of differentiated sameness. This differentiated sameness requires a principle of order as well as a principle which assures the continuous differentiation of that order. In a world of perceiving subjects, we look for pattern over and against a source of randomness which assures the continuous differentiation of that pattern. For without randomness, we have no differentiation, and without differentiation, we have no observation, and without observation, we have no Universe. A Universe filled with observers must continually change and self-differentiate in order to observe itself and thereby maintain itself in existence.

Yet as incessant as this change may be, each act of observation imparts in its own limited way a fundamental unity to the process. Note carefully that this is not a unity which exists "out there," but it is a unity enacted within and by the observing mind. But since there is more to our Universe than the observation of any one observer, since each observer only observes in constant interaction with other observers, the unity which imposes itself upon the entire cosmological process is the unity of a highly differentiated Mind. This Mind selects over and against a bountiful supply of randomness which assures its continuous self-differentiation. It operates out of an internal necessity deeply embedded in all that is contingent and on the move, and even though its necessity has nothing to do with the absolute necessity of an external God, it still has primacy in all things as the fundamental unit of evolution.

This mental pole within our Universe we call Word, and that random pole which assures the continuous differentiation of Word, we call Spirit. We can no more doubt the existence of Word and Spirit than we can doubt the existence of the Universe, and to doubt the existence of the Universe becomes extremely problematic, since in our perception of it, we are actively involved in its very construction and enactment. We speak therefore of two internal polar process gods of a self-organizing Universe, and we would then suggest that each level within our Universe reflects, mirrors and more precisely participates in the fundamental bipolarity of Word drawing upon Spirit. Bipolarity on each level reflects a fundamental bipolarity at the level of the whole, and therefore the oneness of our Universe is a peculiar bipolar oneness. But once again we must proceed with caution.

For only in and through its unbroken interrelatedness with every other level, does each level reflect and mirror the fundamental bipolarity of the whole. Such reasoning rules out categorically any understanding of Word and Spirit along the lines of classical Western categories of thought. Word and Spirit are *internal* gods, *internal* to human observers and *internal* to all other observers or minds on all other levels within our multileveled living Universe. Word and Spirit do not exist "out there," outside of observers in some more fundamental supernatural domain. Rather they come alive only within the event of observation itself. Each observer in the event of observation differentiates, orders and structures, thereby creating in his own limited way, not the whole Universe, of course, but that unique part which only he could create given his unique historical place and his unique observational perspective within this larger self-differentiating whole. Each observer participates in the organizational power of Word as he differentiates and creates, in a direct and unmediated way, from the primordial source of the newness and unexpectedness of Spirit. It is precisely as participator that he finds his identity within this one universal space-time process of becoming. As such he can never be relegated to insignificance. On the contrary he is that indispensable partner in and through whom the Universe creates itself.

The pattern which connects, the pattern which unifies and even sanctifies our world is the metapattern of Word drawing upon Spirit. Only in view of the fact that all levels participate in and reflect this fundamental bipolarity may we conclude that the Universe is one.

Symbiosis

In our last chapter we rejected both the supernatural and the mechanical as legitimate principles of explanation within science, and this forced us to look for the origin of superior design right within the dynamics of the evolutionary process itself. We noted that evolutionary movement can be slow and gradual, effecting only trivial change, or that at times evolutionary movement can be momentous and sudden, effecting large-scale shifts to qualitatively new biological forms and patterns of behavior. Concepts such as environmental pressure, genetic ambition and genetic programs did not advance us very far in explaining this evolutionary movement. We stated the obvious, that there is no movement without survival, but up until now we have not really addressed the question of *why there is movement in the first place.* Why should one purposeful and more or less functional design ever shift and change into another? Certainly Word drawing upon Spirit represents perhaps the beginning of an explanation, but we haven't really explained why Word should be drawn to Spirit or why Word should select from Spirit. After all, someone could argue that Word and Spirit are just neat words that could be used to describe just about any kind of natural transition from an old to a new state. As fancy words for Old and New, insofar as they do not touch the Why of change, they explain nothing at all.

Still another objection closer to home: we may situate Word and Spirit within the natural world, but let us look carefully at the dynamics within nature. Is nature not at war with itself, locked in that universal struggle for life where only the fittest survive? Is nature not as Tennyson described it "red in tooth and claw"? How could we possibly make appeal to these two internal gods in the midst of such ruthlessness and slaughter? We begin with this latter objection.

We should not try to answer this last question by ignoring or trivializing the enormous struggle, pain and risk which accompany all evolutionary development, yet at the same time we should be careful to situate this aspect of the natural world within the much larger context of harmony, cooperation, co-evolution, mutual interdependence and symbiosis. Biologists such as W.C. Alle, A. Emerson, O. Park, T. Park and K. Schmidt find it almost impossible to document instances of direct mutual harm between species.[205] Nature tends to isolate geographically many species that have the potential to inflict enormous damage on one another.[206] Even when they are in close proximity to one another, similar species avoid competition by dividing the habitat into ecological niches. Two species seldom occupy the same niche,[207] and these niches divide up both spatially[208] and temporally.[209] Periodic migration, food specialization[210] and many other types of cooperative behavior enable species to avoid competition. In fact, this elimination of competition is so widespread and universal within nature that it is even used by biologists as a principle of prediction and discovery:

> Whenever we find rather similar animals living together in the wild, we do not think of competition by tooth and claw, we ask ourselves, instead, how competition is avoided. When we find many animals apparently sharing a food supply, we do not talk of struggles for survival; we watch to see by what trick the animals manage to be peaceful in their co-existence.[211]

Nature engages all her ingenuity in developing an incredible variety of techniques to forestall competition and strife among species. Colinveaux writes that "a fit animal is not one that fights well, but one that avoids fighting altogether."[212] Even predation must be seen as a kind of balanced co-existence:

> There are many predator-prey stories, for example, bird and insect species which grow increasingly smarter. Such a "battle" is not won by any side - for the predator this would be the worst of all possible outcomes. But both sides are spurred to ever-new developments - they co-evolve.[213]

Of course, predation does not benefit the individual that is eaten, but it can benefit the rest of the prey population in a variety of ways. Predation often allows for a greater diversity in the prey species. "The addition of a single predator can increase the number of prey species that can live side by side in a given habitat."[214] Stephen J. Gould explains further:

> In considering the causes of organic diversity, we might expect that the introduction of a "cropper" (either a herbivore or a carnivore) would reduce the number of species present in a given area: after all, if an animal is cropping food from a previously virgin area, it ought to reduce diversity and remove completely some of the rarer species.[215]

Contrary to what we would normally expect, the introduction of a herbivore or a carnivore greatly increases the diversity of life:

Now, a cropper in such a system tends to prey on the abundant species, thus limiting their ability to dominate and freeing space for other species. A well-evolved cropper decimates - but does not destroy - its favorite prey species (lest it eat itself to eventual starvation). A well-cropped ecosystem is maximally diverse, with many species and few individuals of any species. Stated another way, the introduction of a new level in the ecological pyramid tends to broaden the level below it.[216]

Following the lead of Steven M. Stanley of John Hopkins University, Gould even explains the Cambrian explosion through the introduction of the cropping principle:

Consider the Precambrian algal community that persisted for two and a half billion years. It consisted exclusively of simple, primary producers. It was uncropped and, for that reason, biologically monotonous. It evolved with exceeding slowness and never attained great diversity because its physical space was so strongly monopolized by a few abundant forms. The key to the Cambrian explosion, Stanley argues, is the evolution of cropping herbivores - single cell protists that ate other cells. Croppers made space for a greater diversity of producers, and this increased diversity permitted the evolution of more specialized croppers. The ecological pyramid burst out in both directions, adding many species at lower levels of production and adding new levels of carnivory at the top.[217]

We must view predation then in an altogether different light. The lion, for example, is not angry when he attacks,[218] unavoidable struggle is always minimized, no wanton killing takes place, and even pain seems to be reduced to a minimum. Nature wisely holds predator and prey in dynamic balance for their mutual benefit.[219] If all of nature were at war with itself, then we should expect that only one species should survive. But what we find is just the opposite: the tensions within nature are held in dynamic balance to create the greatest possible diversity of life at a given time and within a given space. Man projects his feelings of willful aggression upon nature, and having lost a sense of oneness with the natural world, he sets out to dominate and control. Unlike his ancient forebears, man now has very few natural predators, and with very little to limit his ability to dominate, he himself has become a biologically monotonous predator, destroying the rich diversity of life on Earth on an unprecedented scale.

Even when members of the same species occupy the same niche, nature is not at all at a loss in finding methods to avoid competition. Nature uses a variety of techniques to separate individuals from one another. Dispersion mechanisms in plants and animals reduce competition to a minimum.[220] The territory principle allows animals to create the space they need to live without conflict.[221] Among gregarious animals, the dominance hierarchy minimizes aggression within the social unit.[222] A species can divide a habitat peacefully among itself by learned behavioral differences.[223] A complex set of habits governs the social interaction within a family, herd, colony, flock or a school. An endless number of examples could be cited to document the techniques by which nature minimizes competition. Almost any natural history television program richly illustrates the harmony in nature. One example is particularly striking: the male giraffe can easily dismiss a lion with a single kick, but when it must "fight" with a rival giraffe it only uses its stubby, harmless horns.[224]

When overcrowding becomes a problem, it is not simply predation, starvation, severities of climate, or disease which regulate population growth, as Darwin said.[225] We find innumerable internal mechanisms that either reduce the onset of sexual maturity, that lower the birth rate among the sexually mature, that inhibit altogether the breeding of large portions of the adult population, that vary the size of a litter or clutch, and so forth. We can even find examples of certain plants which, as they tend to become overeaten, produce phytoestrogens which inhibit ovulation in the birds and animals which feed upon them.[226]

> That populations are self-regulating fits well with the notion of life as directed self-movement. Nature is not at war, one organism with another. Nature is an alliance founded on cooperation.[227]

But we should not view the dynamics of natural systems simply in terms of the avoidance of conflict. What we find goes much deeper: nature in cooperation, harmony and symbiosis. In fact all living systems are characterized by a symbiotic relationship with at least one other living system.[228] Jantsch understands symbiosis as "the intensification of environmental relations by process links between two or more organisms" wherein "the individual organisms do not lose their identity and yet the symbiotic relationship establishes an autopoietic unit of higher order."[229] The thoroughly interdependent character of biological processes manifests itself in a variety of ways:

One organism can be helpful to another in several ways: by providing food, protection from predators, a place to live, or transporta-
tion, or by ridding the other organism of pests, or by preparing some
necessary condition for its life or welfare. The innumerable co-oper-
ative associations between different species constitute one of the most
intriguing subject areas in all natural science. The variety and subtlety of interdependence is astounding.[230]

Without doubt the variety and subtlety of interdependence is truly
astounding. Life cannot be described in any other way than as a cooperative symbiotic venture:

No single species could persist if it were alone on the planet. It
would eventually exhaust all the available nutrients, and, having no
way to convert its own waste products into food, it would die. Life is
necessarily a cooperative venture.[231]

Lynn Margulis underlines the deep interdependent and symbiotic
character of all life:

All organisms are dependent on others for the completion of their
life cycles. Never, even in spaces as small as a cubic centimeter, is a
living community of organisms restricted to members of only a single
species. Diversity, both morphological and metabolic, is the rule.
Most organisms depend directly on others for nutrients and gases.
Only photo- and chemoautotrophic bacteria produce all their organic
requirements from inorganic constituents; even they require food,
gases such as oxygen, carbon dioxide, and ammonia, which although
inorganic, are end products of the metabolism of other organisms.
Heterotrophic organisms require organic compounds as food; except
in rare cases of cannibalism, this food comprises organisms of other
species or their remains.[232]

Margulis points to symbiotic relationships in the most unusual
places. She put forward the very exciting theory of the endosymbiotic
origin of the eukaryotic cell. Here we have the fusion of various
prokaryotes, such as the mitochondrion, the spyrochaeta and the chloro-
plast (found only in plants), into a single eukaryotic cell.[233] After fusion
they maintain their identity as organelles, each with their own genetic
material, each with their own DNA, RNA and ribosomes. Jantsch says
that we may not simply add up the capabilities of these various

organelles. "The eukaryotic cell represents a newly emerged level of co-ordination, a new autopoietic system level."[234] Still higher levels emerge when eukaryotic cells come together into multicellular organisms,[235] and again when multicellular organisms enter into various symbiotic relationships within an ecosystem. "Just as the symbiosis of organelles secures the metabolism of the cell and the symbiosis of cells the metabolism of the organism, symbiotic systems of organisms secure the metabolism at the sociobiological or ecological level."[236] The dynamic of life on all levels from beginning to end is unmistakably symbiotic in character:

> One major question needing to be examined is the general attitude of nature. A century ago there was a consensus about this; nature was "red in tooth and claw," evolution was a record of open warfare among competing species, the fittest were the strongest aggressors, and so forth. Now it begins to look different . . . . The urge to form partnerships, to link up in collaborative arrangements, is perhaps the oldest, strongest, and most fundamental force in nature. There are no solitary, free-living creatures, every life form is dependent on other forms.[237]

There are no solitary life forms. All of life defines itself in a tight and critical interdependency and togetherness. Margulis and Sagan underline this important shift within evolutionary thought from a state of warfare to a strong sense of mutual interdependency and networking:

> Next, the view of evolution as chronic bloody competition among individuals and species, a popular distortion of Darwin's notion of "survival of the fittest," dissolves before a new view of continual co-operation, strong interaction, and mutual dependence among life forms. Life did not take over the globe by combat, but by networking. Life forms multiplied and complexified by co-opting others, not just by killing them.[238]

Therefore when we look closely at the dynamics of natural systems, we do not see nature blindly at war with itself locked in the universal struggle for life where only the fittest survive. We follow Lynn Margulis in her explanation of the endosymbiotic origin of the eukaryotic cell, and there we discover that a symbiosis of organelles assures the metabolism of the nucleated cell. Nucleated cells enter into symbiotic relationship with one another assuring the metabolism of an entire organism. Finally a symbiosis of organisms plays its part in assuring the metabolism of our entire planetary system. On all levels, large and small, we witness not just evolutionary movement but evolutionary movement of a very specific *symbiotic* character. We agree fully with Lewis Thomas that this urge to form partnerships, this urge to live together, is perhaps the oldest, the strongest and most fundamental dynamic within nature.

But how do we explain this symbiotic nesting of life within life? Of course, there is no symbiosis without survival, but why should there be symbiosis in the first place? How do we explain this urge to live together? How do we explain the attraction of one life form to another? To answer these questions in a convincing manner, we must bind the dynamics of perception a bit more closely to the dynamics of natural systems by stressing the very close connection between image-creation and self-organization.

Beauty

Up to now we have explained self-organization in terms of mental process, and mental process as we have suggested involves above all else, images turning around in memory and imagination. In strong contrast with living organisms, machines do not have a selective or a random element, and hence they cannot construct images which they somehow present to themselves within the imagination. Since machines cannot imagine, they lack the capacity to self-organize. This internal image-creating ability very clearly distinguishes a living organism from even the most advanced computer. In no way does a computer approach the complexity of an internal image-creating mind, and hence a computer remains at all times nothing but a machine. Only living subjects or minds construct or enact internal images, can imagine *from within* and thereby build up or accrue that highly selective ability by which and from which all self-organization unfolds. In strong contrast to Kauffman's mechanistic theory of self-organization, we would suggest that self-organization is image-driven from beginning to end. An imagination burning with the brightness of images is anything but blind.

In place of the Cartesian "I think," we prefer to say "I imagine" or perhaps more accurately "we imagine." In so doing we make a firm epistemological shift from ideas to images. Ideas take time to work out rationally, and for many philosophers they are the exclusive property of rational man. In contrast images rise up spontaneously within the imagination, and man operates them in solidarity with a much larger image-creating whole. In saying "I think," modern man so easily places the accent on the "I" who does the thinking, whereas in saying "I imagine," the subject takes a much more humble and realistic place within the larger imaginal whole. In the process of internal image-creation, the subject may have the distinct impression of letting happen, but in no way does he control. Images may flash forth so directly and immediately, so vividly and spontaneously, that at times he feels overwhelmed and even possessed by their brightness and beauty.

We could imagine immaterial mind as a kind of *home* where immaterial images come to dwell. Perhaps the picture of a laminar *stream* would better illustrate the fluidity by which images concatenate freely in memory and imagination mutually influencing, interpenetrating and illuminating one another. This seemingly endless array of internal images constitutes that selective *storehouse* of memory and imagination which underlies and drives all self-organization. In creative thought, mind *freely* selects, and yet this selection always takes place within the context of a *historically* accrued storehouse of internal images. The previous evolutionary history of a system does not determine, but it does limit and constrain. If a deterministic description should characterize mind, then mind would be no longer in a position to encounter the truly new and unexpected, and in such a dreadful state, it would surely atrophy and die. In creative thought mind *freely* selects according to those criteria which emerge from out of the totality of its imaginal storehouse.

But how should we define that which draws, attracts and entices mind down a certain selective pathway? In the context of symbiosis, we can rephrase this question as, what draws and attracts one particular life form to another? In a valid theory of knowledge and life, these two questions are one and the same. Remember that as we look for answers, we should never lose sight of that fundamental freedom which characterizes all truly creative thought.

Sigmund Freud would have answered these two questions with the purely mechanistic notion of cathexis, "an attachment of the libido to some object, whether internal or external."[239] The cathecting self is obsessed by an object and drawn to it in much the same way that "an electric charge or a magnetic force is directed towards an opposite polarity."[240] Note once again that if we really want explanation within a mechanistic setting, we must appeal to the magic of some sort of mysterious power or force, and if we possess tendencies toward the superstitious, we would have to add to this magical force some nuance of the supernatural or the divine. In the end there is no big difference between a mechanist and a supernaturalist, for neither one could begin to describe mind in the *free* act of creative thought. Look for a moment at how some immanent scientists describe their own creative thought processes.

David Bohm once said that "almost anything found in nature exhibits some kind of beauty both in immediate perception and in intellectual analysis."[241] Werner Heisenberg said that beauty "in exact science, no less than in the arts" is the "most important source of illumination and clarity."[242] The physicist Richard Feynman remarked that "you can recognize truth by its beauty and simplicity."[243] With regard to a sense of beauty in scientific discovery, the physicist Roger Penrose refers to Chandrasekar, Hadamard, Poincare and Dirac:

> My impression is that the strong conviction of the validity of a flash of inspiration (not 100 percent reliable, I should add, but at least far more reliable than just chance) is very closely bound up with its aesthetic qualities. A beautiful idea has a much greater chance of being a correct idea than an ugly one. At least that has been my own experience, and similar sentiments have been expressed by others (cf. Chandrasekar 1987). For example, Hadamard (1945, p. 31) writes:
>
> "It is clear that no significant discovery or invention can take place without the will of finding. But with Poincare, we see something else, the intervention of the sense of beauty playing its part as an indispensable means of finding. We have reached the double conclusion: that invention is choice, that this choice is imperatively governed by the sense of scientific beauty."
>
> Moreover Dirac (1982), for example, is unabashed in his claim that it was his keen sense of beauty that enabled him to divine his equation for the electron (the "Dirac equation" alluded to on p. 289), while others had searched in vain.[244]

James Lovelock says that we know we have found our place within Gaia through a sense of the beautiful:

> It may be that we are also programmed to recognize instinctively our optimal role in relation to other forms of life around us. When we act according to this instinct in our dealings with our partners in Gaia, we are rewarded by finding that what seems right also looks good and arouses those pleasurable feelings which comprise our sense of beauty. When this relation with our environment is spoilt or mishandled, we suffer from a sense of emptiness and deprivation.[245]

Stephen J. Gould describes science as "resolutely personal" and "profoundly beautiful:"

> Science is as resolutely personal an enterprise as art, even if the chief prize be truth rather than beauty (though artists also seek truth, and good science is profoundly beautiful).[246]

Beauty plays an important role in governing the kinds of questions we ask as well as the enthusiasm and excitement which accompanies us down a particular path of inquiry. *But what really shines forth in beauty is not so much ideas but images, and the power behind an image to excite, motivate, attract and even move mountains, is the power of the beautiful.* Mind selects according to no other criteria than that which fits and matches the beautiful. In its hunger and thirst for beauty not only does it sense that it is on the right track, but it also knows deep down on the inside that it is fundamentally free.

Darwin denied beauty and said that it was a purely subjective feeling. "The sense of beauty obviously depends on the nature of the mind, irrespective of any real quality in the admired object."[247] According to Darwin, the fittest should survive, but why should the beautiful survive? The thrill and excitement we experience in the presence of the beautiful takes us far beyond the concept of survival. Somehow we know that "if nature were not beautiful, it would not be worth knowing and life would not be worth living."[248]

But how to explain the overwhelming abundance of beauty in nature? To speak in terms of its survival value or its utility amounts to a total misunderstanding of what beauty is all about. Surely we can read much more into an autumn leaf or the feather of an eagle in flight, than the purely functional aspect of photosynthesis or avian flight. Somehow we construct them as they relate to us in all their raw, exuberant, self-representation and self-expression. Beauty defines itself as the incredible marvel of things in right relationship, and just as there is no life or mind in any one object in isolation from everything else, so too something is beautiful only within the context of its interrelationship to everything else. Precisely in its interrelatedness, it is perceived as beautiful, thereby reflecting and mirroring the beauty of everything else. The Universe is one, and so is the richly differentiated and multifaceted beauty coming to expression therein.

Beauty cannot be explained through subjective factors alone, and yet beauty excites us because it is not purely objective. It does not stand there over and against us in an independent, pre-given and isolated manner.[249] We stress the theme of the unbroken wholeness of reality: the observer of beauty and the beautiful object observed are an integral part of one another. Since it is mind which actively constructs and in the end perceives beauty, beauty does not exist "out there," but arises only in the interaction and interdependence of observer and observed. This also implies that beauty reflects the uniqueness and individuality of both observer and observed. The beauty of a rose is as multifaceted as the number of observers in interaction with it. Each time the observer gazes upon a thing of beauty, its beauty transforms the observer so much so that as he observes it again, it manifests a beauty of an even greater differentiation and splendor. Beauty mirrors and amplifies beauty in a creative cycle of mutual self-construction and self-transformation.

How anthropocentric to limit the perception of beauty to man alone! If a sense of beauty leads and guides scientists in their act of inventing and constructing science, would it be so difficult for these same scientists to imagine that everything else creates itself in a fundamentally similar way? If we find nothing within our Universe which falls outside of the aesthetic marvel of things in right relationship, then the key to unraveling the enigma of symbiotic evolutionary movement lies in the power and attraction of the beautiful. *Beauty is the driving force behind all symbiosis and togetherness.* What takes place within the mind and imagination of man in his search for beauty simply mirrors and reflects that passionate search for beauty throughout the whole of the Universe. The Universe thirsts and strives for beauty in all things, continually rejoicing in lavish and beautiful displays of the unexpected. The Universe unfolds according to the logic of its own internal necessity, which we define more precisely now as the logic and marvel of beauty itself. *The only purpose we can attach to this continuous self-expression and self-representation lies completely within the evolutionary process itself as the differentiation and manifestation of its own internal beauty and splendor.* The Universe represents that incomparable symbiotic event unfolding according to the selective power of the beautiful.

Creative Thought

Danah Zohar maintains that the human mind in creative thought resembles a quantum system in many ways.[250] But we should be careful not to conceive of a quantum system or any other system as having an independent ready-made existence outside of our knowledge and construction of it. Remember that quantum formalism is itself a construct of the human mind, and perhaps this explains more than anything else the uncanny similarity which Zohar has invented.

Nonetheless before a measurement is made, quantum reality is inherently nebulous. Only probabilities can be predicted, and these probabilities are infinite with the limitations of the wave function. A selection through observation brings about the collapse of the wave function, probability is transformed into certainty, and a specific result is obtained. Likewise if we were to continue along the lines of Zohar's reflection, we might be justified in seeing a link between creative thought and quantum dynamics. For when we are in a state of *alpha,* in a state of deep relaxation in which the mind is awake but not focusing on any particular idea, we have reached the level where Spirit operates. The mind at this point is flooded with a vast array of mental possibility, all mixed in the imagination as a fuzzy indeterminate whirlwind awaiting some act of selection and choice. Here we arrive at the precondition of all thought and at the basis of all creativity and freedom. The more or less conscious act of concentration brings about a selection or choice, collapsing the wave function of infinite mental possibility and bringing to actualization that which situates at the level of *images* and *pictures.* We might even link the collapse of the wave function in quantum physics to this formation of images within the imagination.

Roger Penrose in his analysis of creative thought refers to Albert Einstein: "The words or the language, as they are written or spoken, do not seem to play any role in my mechanism of thought. The psychical entities which seem to serve as elements of thought are certain *signs* and more or less clear *images.*"[251] Jantsch refers to Ortega y Gasset's exciting idea of a guiding image.[252] In trying to explain the creative workings of his on mind, Roger Penrose also speaks of images:

> A common experience, when some colleague would try to explain some piece of mathematics to me, would be that I should listen attentively, but almost totally uncomprehending of the logical connection between one set of words and the next. However, some *guessed image* would form in my mind as the ideas he was trying to convey - formed entirely on my own terms and seemingly with very little connection with the *mental images* that had been the basis of my colleague's own understanding - and I would reply.[253]

Penrose adopts a Platonic epistemology in describing the dynamic of creative thought:

When mathematicians communicate, this is made possible by each one having a direct route to truth, the consciousness of each being in a position to perceive mathematical truths directly, through this process of "seeing." (Indeed, often this act of perception is accompanied by words like "Oh, I see!") Since each can make contact with Plato's world directly, then they can more readily communicate with one another than one might have expected. The mental images that each one has, when making this Platonic contact, might be different in each case, but communication is possible because each is directly in contact with the same externally existing Platonic world![254]

How we love this notion of a direct route to truth through mental images. Yet even though "the physical world seems more nebulous than it had seemed before the advent of the SUPERB theories of relativity and quantum mechanics,"[255] Penrose unfortunately has a tendency to attribute an independent existence to this physical world.[256] In Western thought we have often tried to explain static matter in terms of an even more static Platonic idea. But nothing appears static within the framework of an organismic epistemology where internal images continually evolve and grow within Mind in its constant interaction with the new and unexpected.

In creative thought we actually participate in this marvelous interaction. Truly creative thought represents a *balanced* interaction between these two opposite yet complementary poles. Roger Penrose would situate creative thinking primarily in the conscious mind. He differs from the majority of thinkers who situate creative thought in the unconscious.[257] In contrast to both of these positions we suggest that the selective and more conscious aspect of thought must be held in balance with the random and more unconscious aspect of thought. True creativity arises only in the balanced interaction of the two. Note well what Penrose says in this regard:

My guess is that even with the sudden flash of insight, apparently produced ready-made by the unconscious mind, it is consciousness that is the *arbiter,* and the idea would be quickly rejected and forgotten if it did not "ring true".. This is an area where the unconscious seems indeed to be playing a vital role, and I must concur with the view that unconscious processes are important. I must agree, also, that it cannot be that the unconscious mind is simply throwing up ideas at *random.* There must be a *powerful selection process* that allows the conscious mind to be disturbed only by ideas that "have a chance"...

In relation to this, the question of what constitutes genuine origi-
nality should be raised. It seems that there are two factors involved,
namely a *"putting-up"* and a *"shooting-down"* process. I imagine
that the putting up could be largely unconscious and the shooting
down largely conscious. Without an effective putting-up process, one
would have no new ideas at all. But, just by itself, this procedure
would have little value. One needs an effective procedure for forming
judgements, so that only those ideas with a reasonable chance of success will survive.[258]

On the one hand, Penrose speaks of an "arbiter," of a "powerful
selection process," of a "shooting-down process." These elements we
associate generally with the selective power of Word. On the other
hand, implied in the idea of arbitration or selection is a certain multiplicity out of which arbitration or selection takes place. This "putting
up" process of Penrose we associate with the random probabilistic pole
of Spirit. To explain creative thought we need the complementary interaction of both the selective and the random. Under no conditions should
we ever let one dominate the other.

In the above Penrose speaks of a "sudden flash of insight" but then
goes on to use the word "idea" repeatedly. Let us not get involved in
defining words too closely, but we feel that the notion of an image fits
much better this notion of a "sudden flash of insight." As we noted previously, ideas take time to work out rationally, and for many philosophers they are the exclusive property of rational man. In contrast images
rise up spontaneously within the imagination, and we operate them in
solidarity with a much larger multileveled image-creating whole.
Images may flash forth so directly and immediately, so vividly and
spontaneously, that at times we feel overwhelmed and even possessed
by their beauty and brightness. In no way do we control and manipulate
this process, and yet at the same time it does not control and manipulate
us.

We may reflect deeply on the origin of these images within our
imaginations, and we may even place ourselves in that frame of mind
where they will more likely appear, yet these images are not our exclusive property. All of nature moves by their power. Self-organization at
every level is image-driven from beginning to end. Here images evolve
and grow within Mind where nothing is fixed or static. Spirit guarantees
the fresh injection of the New within and throughout a multiplicity of
co-evolving levels. New minds, new levels of self-organization, are

continually being generated, yet always within the framework of every-thing that has gone before. Out of that endlessly creative source of Spirit, Word selects, and the final result of this bipolar interaction can never be calculated in advance. Spirit (wind) blows where she wills in a multiplicity of possible directions, and the goal or purpose of this interactive process, as continually formed, reformed, and transformed by Word is truly open-ended and free. However something of this goal never changes. Erich Jantsch described it so beautifully as the "extraor-dinary intensification of life."[259]

A Universe in Evolution

Jantsch makes use of the marvelous story of bacteria to illustrate this fluid and open sense of purpose and direction within nature.[260] Bacteria are single-celled organisms without a nucleus, and they do not repro-duce by transferring genetic material to the next generation the way cells such as our own do. Instead they simply divide by making a DNA copy. Primitive bacteria dominated the earth at a time when there was no free oxygen, and they were very well adapted to their oxygenless environment. We still find anaerobic bacteria today in oxygenless places such as mud or in the intestinal tracts of animals. A strain of pho-tosynthetic bacteria then came on the scene, giving access to an inex-haustible energy flow and to a greater enhanced flexibility.

> Photosynthesis also marks the inclusion of a cosmic environment for the non-equilibrium system of the biosphere. Without such an inclusion, the energy rich organic materials would soon have been exhausted, the entropy of the biosphere would have increased and life would have come to an end.[261]

For some two billion years photosynthetic bacteria performed the incredible task of totally transforming the atmosphere: they began to pour free oxygen into the environment. The presence of free oxygen later enabled them to metabolize glucose 15 times more efficiently. Yet how did they know that, if they all worked together to produce free oxy-gen, its presence would eventually give them this greater efficiency? But the story doesn't end here.

Bacteria metabolize glucose most efficiently when the concentration of oxygen reaches the 10 percent level. Why then, if adaptation to the environment is the only criterion, do these bacteria go on to pour almost twice that amount of oxygen into the atmosphere thereby decreasing their own efficiency to metabolize glucose. But this rather stupid maneuver of the photosynthetic bacteria created just the right conditions for the development of oxygen-breathing organisms with cell nuclei and sexual reproduction. As far as we know only oxygen-breathing cells with a nucleus can form tissues and link with each other to form multi-cellular organisms. Still the story does not end.

The concentration of oxygen in the atmosphere has remained remarkably stable over a very long period of time. At a few percent higher or lower than its current level of 21 percent, life on earth as we know it would not be possible. The Gaia hypothesis maintains that this critical level of oxygen is maintained by life itself, by living organisms continually engaged in breaking down gases and recreating them. No one understands completely all the internal mechanisms within planet Earth by which this delicate balance of oxygen is maintained.

Up to now we have said that evolution, or more specifically co-evolution, involves the bidirectional unfolding from the top down as well as from the bottom up right across a multiplicity of hierarchically inter-related levels. This definition seemed adequate until we ran across Jantsch's story of the bacteria. Now this talk of large and small must also incorporate notions of beginning and end, if we wish to do justice to the unity of space and time. Jantsch's story introduces a definite temporal element whereby early moments in the evolution of life on earth seem to presuppose later moments. How do bacteria with a very limited individual life span, select, anticipate and foresee on a time-scale spanning a few billion years? If we focus on subjects in isolation, of course, we understand nothing at all. However, if we focus on the comprehensive subjectivity of a Universe, then evolution over large periods of time does not appear so magical and mysterious. As we have noted earlier, the unity that imposes itself on the entire cosmological process is the unity of a continually self-differentiating Mind, and this Mind does not simply anticipate and foresee within the context of some pre-given large and small, within the context of some pre-given beginning and end, but it actually creates and re-creates these space-time categories in the continuous act of its own self-realization.

This means that the problem of how isolated bacteria anticipate and foresee within a process lasting several billion years is no different in kind from the problem of how a single cell within a developing embryo anticipates and foresees its function and place within the whole, how it gravitates to a particular *place* at precisely the right *time* within the bubbling cacophony of billions of other dividing cells. These two problems are ultimately no different in kind from the one problem of the evolution and development of that single living organism we call the Universe. Whether we are speaking of several billion years or six weeks, we are still operating within the comprehensive subjectivity of a Universe. This subjectivity may be far more differentiated than the subjectivity of pigs, coconuts and scientists, but it is still one of a kind with them, containing all the basic elements which would permit the construction of a valid analogy. No scientist could ever deny his own subjectivity, for if he were to do so, he would deny the living ground out of which he invents and constructs science. Would it be that difficult then for him to imagine that everything else creates itself in a fundamentally similar way? Each subject defines itself only in terms of his interaction and interrelatedness with respect to other subjects, and therefore each subject reflects and mirrors in a limited way that unique and distinct subjectivity of a Universe. Each subject draws from the same source, from that pool of images abiding within the highly differentiated memory and imagination of a Universe.

Perhaps now we can begin to understand in a very general way how the spontaneous emergence of images in creative thought reflects our participation in a vast mental process which is image-driven from beginning to end: images in the human imagination as well as images throughout the whole of nature, images in evolution across the whole of space-time, all creatively interacting and concatenating in that one evolving, multileveled memory and imagination of a Universe. In the context of creative thought, images have the power to lead and guide, and in the context of evolutionary biology, images have the power to organize. If we want to explain the discontinuous and abrupt generation of new biological forms and patterns of behavior, we must turn to that selective pool of internal images abiding within the comprehensive subjectivity of a Universe. The unity that imposes itself upon the entire evolutionary process is the unity of a highly differentiated Mind - a Mind which remembers and anticipates, which continually tests and explores with a real sense of purpose and project. What amazes and astounds us at every level is not the absence of purpose and meaning but the incessant transformation of purpose and meaning. With no God-given plan either in the past or in the future to guarantee its outcome, and with the element of chance always at work, the Universe creates itself as it goes along in a process filled with danger and risk. The only guide or guarantee which it possesses lies in the power and attraction of the beautiful. It knows that it is on the right track, that real progress is being made, by an overwhelming sense of beauty which inevitably accompanies each free act of creative thought. How far we are therefore from the magic of those mysterious mechanical and supernatural forces which totally destroy all freedom and creativity!

Furthermore, this highly differentiated Mind within our Universe, we suggest, actually creates both space and time in the continuous act of its own internal self-organization. If small random fluctuations can tip the balance in favor of large-scale change, how do we understand concepts of large and small? If earlier moments in the evolution of our Universe seem to presuppose later moments, how do we understand concepts of beginning and end? If each local evolutionary step impacts and illuminates global evolution, how do we understand concepts of local and global? If the useless and redundant are suddenly transformed into the useful and highly functional, how do we understand notions of usefulness and uselessness? In no way do we deny any of these distinctions, but we must emphasize that they are not pre-given and absolute: they only come alive within the comprehensive subjectivity of a Universe. We even suggest that space and time acquire dimensional and temporal aspects peculiar to the dynamics of each level wherein Mind self-differentiates.

We humans pride ourselves in our ability to think rationally, and this distinguishes us and separates us from the whole of the natural world. But in our next chapter we want to emphasize that our true dignity as human beings lies in an altogether different yet complementary mode of thought. Here not only do we tap into that endlessly creative source of newness within our Universe, but we actually participate in the prophetic transformation and reconstruction of this newness. In our togetherness and oneness with the whole of the natural world, it is our duty and responsibility not only to study the confirmation of the past but also to participate in the formation and enactment of those images within our Universe which select *and anticipate* a future from out of the contingency and chanciness of the present moment. Out of our unity with the whole of the natural world, we are called upon to assist in the birth of a Universe.

Chapter 4

The New Testament

Christology

Up to now we have used two words, Word and Spirit, to carry forward our thesis with respect to the fundamental bipolarity at the level of the whole of a living Universe. Each time we were tempted to use these two words in an exact sense, we side-stepped the problem by attaching to them a long string of words to broaden and extend their meaning. Since each level within our multileveled Universe should offer us a unique pair of names to describe the bipolarity manifest at that particular level, we would have to attach to Word and Spirit the nuances and peculiarities of all levels, if we really were intent on describing things in an exact way. Moreover, since this living reality never ceases to self-differentiate within our experience and understanding of it, any effort to describe or define Word and Spirit in a rigorous manner would be impossible.

Someone might object that our use of Word and Spirit could never be the same as what we should find within the New Testament. Surely they are not the same in some flat and undifferentiated sense. Here, as everywhere else within our multileveled Universe, we do not seek to uncover the objectivity of an undifferentiated sameness. We emphasize a wealth of experience, then and now, which overflows any single language or logical framework. Precisely in their richly variegated difference and diversity should the thought categories of modern process science resemble and illuminate the thought categories of the Christian New Testament.

As we proceed into the New Testament, we quickly discover that all the leading figures within First-Century Christianity were Jews, and at no point did they understand themselves to be anything but Jews. They held on to all those elements which they understood to be fundamental to their practice of their Jewish faith, and they did not see themselves to be starting or promoting a new religion. Like all Jews before them, they were strict monotheists, and even in their effort to understand Jesus of Nazareth, they engaged in a kind of cosmological reflection which was typically Jewish. At first this ancient vocabulary will sound strange to modern ears, but hopefully we should be able to relax as the familiar theme of a universal bipolarity surfaces once again.

The Centrality of the Resurrection

Christianity began with the extraordinary event of the resurrection. The first Christian preachers claimed that Jesus had been raised from the dead, and this belief formed "the basis or hinge of their proclamation."[262] Paul says in 1 Cor 15.17: "If Christ has not been raised, your faith is futile and you are still in your sins." It would be hard to imagine a form of Christianity which did not have this belief "at its heart and basis."[263] The early Christians believed that something actually happened to Jesus of Nazareth in the event of his resurrection, and the earliest attempts to explain who he was, all grew out of the firm conviction that he had been raised from the dead. "The single most striking feature of the earliest christology," says Dunn, "is the impact of the resurrection."[264]

But there was nothing uniquely Christian about the category of resurrection. Many Jews at that time, especially the Pharisees, believed in the general resurrection from the dead. In Daniel 2.12 we find, for example, the belief that "many of those who sleep in the dust of the earth will wake." Note carefully, however, that these early followers of Christ were not simply claiming that this individual had been raised from the dead. They believed something far more significant had taken place. They saw his resurrection as the first fruits, as the first sheaf of a much larger harvest soon to come. His resurrection heralded the beginning of the long-awaited general resurrection of the dead at the end of time; it heralded the end of the Old and the beginning of the New Age. The early followers of Christ stood in a most precarious position poised between the transition of the ages, and in their eschatological excitement and anticipation, their minds were cleared of old categories of interpretation that would have dismissed this Jesus as simply a man or at best some great prophet. In the context of the whole of history rapidly drawing to a close, they believed that he had *become* something far more significant. In an event so momentous that it inaugurated the beginning of the end of time, what had this man become?

Jesus is Lord

Perhaps the most significant title associated with or attached to this risen Christ was that of Lord or Kyrios. This title of Lord was the principal confession of faith for Paul and his churches.[265] Although this title "was not uncommon in prominent cults of the time, particularly the cults of Isis and Sarapis,"[266] the early Christians applied it to Jesus in a very exclusive way. For them Jesus was not merely a lord among many lords, nor was he simply the lord of a particular mystery cult. In his resurrection and exaltation he was established exclusively as the *one and only Lord*. Perhaps no passage in the New Testament underlines this theme better than 1 Cor 8.5-6:

> For although there may be so-called gods whether in heaven or on earth - as indeed there are many gods and many lords; but for us there is one God, the Father, from whom are all things and we to him, and the one Lord, Jesus Christ, through whom are all things and we through him.

Just as God in Jewish thought was exclusively the one God, Jesus in Christian thought was exclusively the one Lord. As a Jew, Paul did not deny in any way the distinctiveness and oneness of God as God, and yet as a Christian, he did not hesitate to assert the distinctiveness and oneness of Jesus as Lord. Within the context of modern mechanistic thought, this distinction between God and Lord is thoroughly meaningless and anachronistic, but within the context of the pre-mechanistic and animistic world of the ancient Near East, this distinction is highly significant. In the latter we confront a Universe alive with gods and goddesses, angels and demons, greater and lesser principalities, rulers, powers, elemental spirits and lords (see also Gal 4.3). In 1 Cor 8.5-6 Paul did not deny the reality of any of the many gods and lords within the Universe, for they were inextricably bound up with the very structure of the Universe as generally understood in his day. Instead of denying them, he situated Christ among them as their sovereign Lord. The lordship of Jesus only acquires meaning relative to the very real power that these entities were understood to be exercising within the Universe. A bit further in Paul's first letter to the Corinthians (15.24-28), the same theme surfaces once more:

> Then comes the end, when he (Christ) delivers up the kingdom to God the Father, after destroying every rule, every authority and power. For he must reign until God has put all enemies under his feet; and the last enemy to be abolished is death. Scripture says, 'He has put all things in subjection under his feet.' But in saying 'all things,' it clearly means to *exclude God* who subordinates them; and when all things are thus subject to him, then the Son himself will also be made subordinate to God who made all things subject to him, and thus God will be all in all.

The Lordship of Christ extends to the whole of the Universe, clearly encompassing "all things," yet at the same time firmly excluding God himself. Jesus is hailed as Lord of the Universe, yet always subordinate to God who established him as Lord. This theme of the lordship of Christ also stands out clearly in Phil 2.8-11:

> Who being in the *form* of God did not count equality with God something to be grasped, but emptied himself, taking the *form* of a slave, becoming in the *likeness* of men. And being found in *form* as man, he humbled himself becoming obedient to death - even death on a cross. Wherefore God has exalted him to the heights and bestowed on him the name which is over every name, that at the name of Jesus every knee should bow - in heaven, on earth, and in the depths - and every tongue confess that *Jesus Christ is Lord,* to the glory of God the Father.

This passage in Philippians echoes Isa 45.23:

> Turn to me and be saved, all the ends of the earth! For I am God there is no other. By myself I have sworn ... 'To me every knee shall bow, every tongue shall swear.'

Dunn sees this Isaiah passage as "one of the strongest assertions of Jewish monotheism in the whole of the scriptures."[267] Should we conclude from this that Paul was equating or identifying Jesus with God? We have no indication that Paul ever thought of himself as anything else than a Jew, and for a Jew to equate Jesus with God would have been tantamount to a denial of the exclusive oneness of God so characteristic of

Jewish faith. Note well that at the end of the Philippian hymn, every-thing is done *to the glory of God the Father.* The early Christians did not hesitate to distinguish the one God from his Lord, and this point of view is confirmed by the ubiquitous New Testament phrase "the God and Father of our Lord Jesus Christ" (see Rm 15.6; 2 Cor 1.3; 11.31; Eph 1.3, 17; Col 1.3; 1 Peter 1.3). We cannot doubt that a clear distinction was made within the earliest christological thought between God and Lord. But how are we to understand this distinction?

In proclaiming Jesus as Lord, in no way did Paul or any of the other Christians abandon their strict Jewish monotheistic faith. In the same breath that Paul could proclaim Jesus as Lord, he could also make the fundamental confession of Jewish faith - "God is one" (see also Eph 4.5-6). With this one title of Lord, Paul very effectively accomplished two things: he was able to confess Jesus' significance *with respect to the Universe,* and at the same time he was able to distinguish Jesus careful-ly from the one God.[268] This risen and exalted Lord supplanted all other lords and very effectively absorbed their significance and rule both with regard to the Universe and with regard to redemption.[269] In his resurrec-tion and exaltation, Jesus supplanted the role of angels or any other intermediaries with respect to God, and furthermore, he even bound and routed Satan as was to be expected in the New Age.[270] But in no way did Jesus supplant God or take away anything with respect to the one God. Jesus was established as Lord in his resurrection and exaltation, and the primary reference of this title is with respect to the Universe. It is pre-cisely as *Lord of the Universe* that Jesus reveals God. When we lose sight of this simple truth, then it becomes difficult, if not impossible, to construct a meaningful christology.

Paul could say both "Jesus is Lord" and "God is one" without the slightest contradiction, because in between God and man was the full reality of a living Universe. Only if we bring to the foreground the con-cept of a living Universe can we understand and follow Paul when he situates Jesus as Lord within this Universe, and only then can we under-stand how his Lordship in no way infringes upon God as God. When we try to understand how this man revealed God, we must be careful not to jump directly from this man to God. *The point of contact between God and man is neither God nor man but the fullness of a living Universe.* Therefore it is not surprising that the main christological thrust in Paul centers around that change which took place in *Jesus' relationship to the Universe* - that is, in his resurrection and exaltation, he became its Lord. Only in this way can we affirm the oneness of God without detracting in any way from the lordship of Jesus, and only in this way can we affirm the lordship of Jesus without detracting in any way from the oneness of God. When we bring a living Universe squarely into the foreground, then we can say without contradiction both "God is one" and "Jesus is Lord," all the while remaining both Jewish and Christian. Any real tension between the lordship of Jesus and the oneness of God surfaces only when we lose sight of the fundamental reality of a living Universe. For Paul, God was very much *God,* (Paul the Jew) and Jesus was very much *Lord* of the Universe (Paul the Christian), but this a Universe very much *alive* with whole multitudes of living voices (Paul the animist). The full power of the Kyrios title becomes apparent only against this rich animistic and organismic background.

By virtue of his resurrection and exaltation, Jesus became sovereign Lord of the Universe. But for many of the early followers of Christ this also meant that he had become none other that man which God had intended Adam to be all along.

The New Man

Generally the early Christians understood the risen and exalted Christ to be more than just an individual. The many incorporative phrases such as "in Christ," "into Christ," "with Christ" as well as "body of Christ," all support the notion of the risen Christ as a corporate and collective individual. The principal idea here was for the believer to be transferred and incorporated into this larger living entity. We may point to a certain Hellenistic influence perhaps, for in Greek thought it was quite common to compare a *polis* (city) to a living organism. But to understand this corporate aspect of the risen Christ, we need not go any further than to the thoroughly Jewish thought surrounding the collective figure of Adam. The Hebrew word adam means man: "what can be said of Adam in general is true of men in general, what is true of men in general is true of Adam."[271] The early Christians, especially Paul, tried to express the importance of Christ by comparing him to Adam.

By virtue of the fact that he was created in the *image* of God and given a share in the *glory* of God (Rm 3.23), Adam before the fall had enjoyed direct and immediate knowledge of God. As the crown of God's creation, he was granted lordship over all things, and all things within the Universe were subject to him. But unfortunately Adam did not honor God as God. He rebelled against his status as creature before God by eating from the tree of the knowledge of good and evil (Gen 3).

In trying to escape his creatureliness, in trying to snatch at divinity itself (Phil 2.7), in trying to become more like God, he exchanged the truth of God for a lie (Rm 1.25) and became less than the man he was. He became empty and confused (Rm 1.21), exchanging the splendor of the immortal God for "an *image* shaped like mortal man" (Rm 1.23). Sadly the whole of creation in its dependence upon him shares in his futility, confusion, emptiness and ineffectiveness (Rm 8.20). Adam forfeited the glory he once had and failed to arrive at the fuller glory God had intended for him when he created him in the beginning. In line with a broad current within Jewish thought at the time, Paul believed that the glory which Adam had forfeited would be restored in the last days. In this respect his thought was thoroughly Jewish in character and content,[272] but here Paul went on to introduce an important difference.

Just as Adam represents the old age where sin rules humanity to death (Rm 5), Christ represents the new age, "the age of life through death and beyond death."[273] What is true of all men "in Adam" is true of all men "in Christ": "For as by a man came death, by a man has come also the resurrection of the dead. For as in Adam all die, so also in Christ shall all be made alive." (1 Cor 15.21-22). In moving *from* the corporate reality of the old man Adam *into* the corporate reality of the new man Christ, the believer is transferred from death into life. Note well that the key to this transferal is grounded in the transformation from the *image* of the man of dust (Adam) into the *image* of the man of heaven (Christ): "Just as we have born the *image* of the man of dust, we shall also bear the *image* of the man of heaven." (1 Cor 15.49). The same theme appears in 2 Cor 3.18: "And because for us there is no veil over the face, we all reflect as in a mirror the splendor of the Lord; thus we are transfigured into his *likeness,* from splendor to splendor; such is the influence of the Lord who is Spirit." A bit further in 4.4, Paul speaks of the "gospel of *the glory of Christ,* who is the *very image of God,*" and in 4.6, he says: "For the same God who said, 'Out of darkness let light shine,' has caused his light to shine within us, to give us the light of revelation - the revelation of *the glory of God* in the *face of Jesus Christ.*" In Phil 3.21, Paul says: "He (Christ) will *transfigure* the body belonging to our humble state, and give it a *form* like that of his own *resplendent* body, by the very power which enables him to make all things subject to himself."

God created man in his own image as the crown of his creation, originally putting "all things under his feet" (Ps 8.6), granting him lordship over the whole of the Universe. But through the sin of Adam, God's purpose had failed, and now only in Christ has it been actually achieved. This idea is clearly expressed in Heb 2.9:

> For in subjecting all things to him (man), He (God) left nothing that is not subject. But in fact we do not see all things in subjection to man. In Jesus, however, we do see one who for a short while was made lower than the angels, crowned now with glory and honor because he suffered death, so that, by God's gracious will, in tasting death he should stand for us all.

The same idea appears again in Eph 1.18-23:

> I pray that your inward eyes may be illumined, so that you may know what is the hope to which he calls you, what the wealth and glory of the share he offers you among his people in their heritage, and how vast the resources of his power open to us who trust him. They are measured by his strength and the might which he exerted in Christ when he raised him from the dead, when he enthroned him at his right hand in the heavenly realms, far above all government and authority, all power and dominion, and any title of sovereignty that can be named, not only in this age but in the age to come. *He put everything in subjection beneath his feet,* and appointed him as supreme head to the church, which is his body and as such holds within it the fullness of him who himself receives the entire fullness of God.

So we see that in the event of his resurrection and exaltation, Jesus became none other than that man which God had intended Adam to be all along: "Christ as last Adam is eschatological man."[274] The glory or image of God which had been lost or defaced in Adam has been restored in the risen and glorified Christ,[275] and to become like Christ, that is, to take on his glorious image, is simply to become what God had intended humanity to be all along. In his resurrection and exaltation, the new corporate man Christ regained that ancient title of Lord which the old corporate man Adam had lost. Jesus was established as sovereign Lord of the Universe, and he received that power over all things which was intended for Adam or man in the beginning. This same power as Lord enables him even now to transform believers into his own glorious image (Phil 3.21). Salvation for Paul consists in being conformed and transformed, fashioned and shaped, into the glorious image of this risen Lord. It means being conformed to "*the pattern* which is Christ."[276] The climax of Christ's rule over all things is his own submission to God -

precisely the antithesis of what took place in the sin of Adam (1 Cor 15.24-28).

Dunn points out that during this same period there were Jews who were not afraid to worship Adam, since Adam was the image and likeness of God. For example, in the *Life of Adam and Eve* 13-14:

> When God blew into you the breath of life and your countenance and likeness were made in the image of God, Michael brought you to me and made (us) worship you in the sight of God, and the Lord God said, 'Behold Adam! I have made you in our image and likeness'. And Michael went out and called all the angels, saying, 'Worship the image of the Lord God, as the Lord has instructed'. And Michael himself worshipped first, and called me and said, 'Worship the image of God, Yahweh'.

So we find Jews at that time who felt that in worshipping the image of God, they would be expressing their obedience and submission to the one God. In the same way, the Adam christology of Paul and the other early Christians remained fundamentally Jewish in character and content, and in no way did it contradict their belief in the oneness of God as God. The really significant difference that the early Christians introduced, a difference which took them beyond what their non-Christian fellow Jews were saying, was the claim that if one really wanted to see the image or the glory of God, if one really wanted to express one's obedience and submission to God, one had to look into the Face of this risen Christ and acknowledge him as Lord. This risen Lord is the "image of God which Adam was intended to be."[277] He is the *image* of the invisible God (Col 1.15), and "in him God in all his fullness was pleased to dwell" (Col 1.18).

Paul and the early Christians were caught up in a strong current within Jewish expectation which understood that God would only reveal himself fully at the end of time. Only in the last days would all flesh come to see the glory of God. Therefore when Jesus' disciples understood that he was risen from the dead, they immediately concluded that such an event had all of the revelatory power of the long-awaited End. The thought process which led these early Christians to such a conclusion we will never understand completely, but our synthesis of modern process science opens up whole new possibilities of christological insight in this regard.

In process terms we would say that in the risen Christ we have a powerful *image* of all that man on his particular level of self-organization could possibly be. Our synthesis points to a multileveled Universe where no level is preeminent and where every level reflects and mirrors every other level. Now any image that represents the finality and fullness of any one level reflects and mirrors, in fact, the finality and fullness of the whole of the Universe. Fullness achieved on any one level mirrors the fullness of the whole of the Universe, and it is only the Universe as a whole which can reveal God as God. It is precisely this *image* of the risen Christ, as New Man, as prototype of a new humanity, as eldest brother in the eschatological family of God, which, in revealing all that man could be, points to a gloriously resurrected and life-filled Universe which in turn reveals God in all of his fullness. In other words, the Glory shining forth in the Face of the risen Lord automatically generates visions of a New Heaven and a New Earth (Rev 21.1) which in turn reveals God as God. As we look into the Face of this magnificent "Lord of glory" (James 2.1), we are beholding the glory of a Universe in becoming. There we see the wholeness of a Universe selecting and anticipating according to that which matches the brightness and beauty of his glorious image.

Christ as Wisdom

This brings us to what Dunn calls "the single most important category in the development of earliest christology - Wisdom christology."[278] The Wisdom tradition is exceedingly old, reaching back at least to the 10th Century before the common era.[279] It became quite popular after the Babylonian exile at the time when Judaism as such was in the process of emerging. Even though Wisdom literature was firmly rooted in Palestinian soil and Jewish faith, many of the images and words used to describe her were drawn from the wider religious thought and worship of the ancient Near East.[280]

We may see the influence of the Egyptian goddess, Maat - translated in a variety of ways as "truth, right, righteousness in human life, as well as right or righteousness in general and order and regularity in the cosmos."[281] We may detect the influence of the Babylonian Mesaru (righteousness) or the influence of the figure of Ishtar-Astarte, the Mesopotamian goddess of love. In the cult of Isis in Egypt, Isis proclaims herself as the divine agent who created and sustains the Universe.[282] We may detect the influence of "the myth of the Urmensch (Primordial Man) of which Ezekiel 28.1-19 preserves traces."[283] One could point perhaps to an ancient form of myth to be found in the

Ethiopian Enoch 42, "where Wisdom is said to have descended from heaven, to dwell among men. Finding no welcome, she returns to God's side."[284] Many other influences could be cited, but the main point here is that we are dealing above all else with a principle of order within the Universe. Dunn cites several passages to illustrate the function and role of Wisdom:[285]

> The Lord by wisdom founded the earth; by understanding he established the heavens.. Prov 3.19.

> She (Wisdom) is the *radiance* of eternal light, the spotless *mirror* of the working of God.. Wisd 7.26.

> For she (Wisdom) is an initiate in the knowledge of God, and *an associate in his works*. If riches are a desirable possession in life, what is richer than wisdom *who effects all things?* And if understanding is effective, who more than she is *fashioner of what exists?* Wisd 8.4-6.

> On the sixth day I commanded my wisdom to create man. 2 Enoch 30.8.

> The Lord created me (Wisdom) the beginning of his works, before all else that he made, long ago. Alone, I was fashioned in times long past, at the beginning, long before earth itself. When there was yet no ocean I was born, no springs brimming with water. Before the mountains were settled in their place, long before the hills I was born, when as yet he had made neither land nor lake nor the first clod of earth. . . Then I was at his side each day, his darling and delight, playing in his presence continually, playing on the earth, when he had finished it, while my delight was in mankind. Prov 8.22-31.

> From eternity, in the beginning, he created me, and for eternity I shall not cease to exist. Sir 24.9.

> Wisdom by whose agency the Universe was brought to completion . . . Philo. Det.54.

Not only was such Wisdom language prominent within Diaspora Judaism, as in the Hellenistic Jewish literature which emerged from Alexandria, but it was also present in the more domestic Palestinian traditions of Proverbs and ben Sira.[286] M. Gilbert points to an evolution in the concept of wisdom: from the end of the Biblical period on, there are texts which say that the Torah is authentic Wisdom, Israel's wisdom;

and later from Sir 24.23 and Bar 4.1-4, the Torah definitely appears as the "privileged expression of God's own Wisdom."[287]

This ancient tradition of Wisdom as a principle of order within the Universe served as a powerful tool for the early Christians to express the significance of Christ. We have already seen 1 Cor 8.6: the use of the prepositions "from," "through" and "to" when speaking of God and the Universe was "widespread in the ancient world and typically Stoic."[288] Here Paul describes Christ the Lord in the language of Wisdom: "his meaning then would be that the power of God in creation came so fully to expression in Christ's death and resurrection that it can be said of Christ what was said of Wisdom."[289] Another New Testament scripture showing the same influence of Wisdom is Col 1.15-20:

> He is the *image of the invisible God*, the first-born of all creation; for in him were created all things in heaven and on earth (visible and invisible, whether thrones or dominions or principalities or authorities); all things were created through him and to him. He is before all things, and in him all things hold together. And he is the head of the body (the church).
>
> He is the beginning, the firstborn from the dead, in order that in all things he might be preeminent. For in him God in all his fullness was pleased to dwell, and through him to reconcile all things to him, making peace (through the blood of his cross) through him, whether things on earth or things in heaven.

What was Paul doing in 1 Cor 8.6 and Col 1.15-20? Not only was Paul describing Jesus in the language of Wisdom, but he was actually identifying Jesus with this figure of Wisdom.[290] Just as the Jews could say that the preexistent Wisdom immanent within the Universe is most clearly expressed and embodied in the Torah, the Christians could say that this same preexistent Wisdom within the Universe is most clearly expressed and embodied in the risen and exalted Christ. We have no evidence that the use of such language with regard to Christ was seen or interpreted as a threat to the monotheism of Christian or non-Christian Jews. We may witness a lot of controversy at the time over the law, but not over christology as such, and the reason for this lack of christological controversy at this early stage most probably goes back to the fact that Wisdom, especially in the latter part of the second Temple period, was understood mainly in cosmological terms. In no way did it infringe upon or take away from the transcendent otherness of God. In his first letter to the Corinthians Paul explicitly identified the crucified Christ with this figure of Wisdom:

> For Jews demand signs and Greeks seek wisdom; but we preach Christ crucified, to Jews a stumbling-block, to Greeks folly, but to those who are called, both Jews and Greeks, he is the power of God and the wisdom of God (1 Cor 1.22-24).

A bit further within the same letter Paul said:

> He (God) has chosen things low and contemptible, mere nothings, to overthrow the existing order. And so there is no place for pride in the presence of God. You are in Christ Jesus by God's act, for God has made him our wisdom; he is our righteousness; in him we are consecrated and set free (1 Cor 1.28-31).

And again:

> And yet I do speak words of wisdom to those who are ripe for it, not a wisdom belonging to this passing age, nor to any of its governing powers, which are declining to their end; I speak God's hidden wisdom, his secret purpose framed from the beginning *to bring us to our full glory*. The *rulers of this age* have never known it; if they had, they would not have crucified *the Lord of glory* (1 Cor 2.6-9).

We cannot say with exactitude why the Corinthians were so preoccupied with wisdom, but in any case, this preoccupation went hand in hand with an elitist spirituality which Paul was attempting to combat. Wisdom for the Corinthians had cosmological ramifications: it had to do with "governing powers" and "rulers of this age," certain cosmic realities which constituted the structure of the Universe as the Corinthians understood it.[291] Perhaps they took pride in some privileged insight into these cosmological realities. Perhaps they overestimated their superior rhetorical skills, but in any case they failed to understand that the true measure of wisdom within the Universe includes that peculiar element of the foolishness and weakness of the cross of Christ. This is not a wisdom grounded in human ability, skill, power or accomplishment; not a wisdom grounded in education or training; but a wisdom grounded in that totally gratuitous yet glorious transformation of all that is weak, low, helpless, useless, redundant and despicable. Paul reminded the Corinthians that he came before them "weak, nervous and shaking with fear" (1 Cor 2.3-4) and that the word that he spoke and the gospel he proclaimed did not sway with subtle arguments. Instead "it carried conviction by spiritual power, so that your faith might be built not upon human wisdom but upon the power of God." (1 Cor 2.5). Paul spoke to the Corinthians in words found for him "not by human wisdom but by the Spirit" (1 Cor 2.13).

Another striking expression of Wisdom christology is Hebrews 1.1-4:

> In times past God spoke to the fathers through the prophets at many times and in diverse ways. But in these last days he spoke to us through a Son, whom he appointed *heir to all things, through whom also he made the universe,* who is the *radiance* of God's glory and the *stamp* of his very being, *sustaining all things by his word of power.* Having made purification for sins, he sat down at the very right hand of the majesty on high, raised as far above the angels, as the title he has inherited is superior to theirs.

This passage in Hebrews closely parallels Col 1.15-17,292 and it draws upon the Wisdom and Logos theology of Alexandrian Judaism as expressed so clearly in the Wisdom of Solomon and Philo: [293]

> Heb 1.2 - the Son whom he appointed heir to all things
> see Philo's treatise, *Who is the Heir of Divine Things.*
>
> Heb 1.2 - through whom he made the world.
> see above 1 Cor 8.6 and Col 1.15
>
> Heb 1.3 - He is the radiance of God's glory
> Wisd. Sol. 7.26 - She is the radiance of eternal light, a spotless mirror of the working of God.
>
> Heb 1.3 - and the stamp of his nature
> Philo, Plant. 18 - the stamp is the eternal Word
>
> Heb 1.3 - sustaining all things by the word of his power.
> Philo, Plant 8f. speaks of the Word as the prop which sustains the whole.

In both Hebrews and Philo we note the influence of Platonic philosophy. In Hebrews there can be no doubt that Wisdom had come to definitive and final expression in Christ. But before closing this section, we turn to the prologue of John's gospel where we find a beautiful poem considerably dependent on the Wisdom theology of second Temple

Judaism: [294]

> John 1.1 - In the beginning as the Word, and the Word was with God
> Wisd 9.9 - With you is Wisdom, who knows your works and was present when you made the world.

> John 1.4 - The life was the light of men.
> Aristobulus - All light comes from her (wisdom).

> John 1.11 - He came into his own home, and his own people received him not.
> 1 Enoch 42 - Wisdom went forth to make her dwelling place among the children of men, and found no dwelling place.

> John 1.14 - The word became flesh and dwelt (literally, pitched his tent) among us.
> Sir. 24.8 - The one who created me assigned a place for my tent. And he said, 'Make your dwelling (literally, set your tent) in Jacob.

In conclusion, we see that the first Christians addressed Jews, Stoics, Platonists and other religious seekers influenced by the syncretist speculation of the time, and they used every available means to express the significance of Christ. They saw in this crucified and risen Lord that very Wisdom by which the Universe was created and sustains itself (1 Cor 8.6, Col 1.16), so much so that this man for them could be none other than that man which preexistent Wisdom within the Universe had become.[295] We are not saying, of course, that this man Jesus who once lived in Palestine had been literally there in the beginning creating and sustaining the Universe. The Wisdom by which the Universe creates and sustains itself certainly preexisted Jesus of Nazareth, but this in no way contradicts the fundamental christological claim that, through the event of his death, resurrection and glorification, this man *became* the clearest expression and fullest embodiment of preexistent Wisdom within the Universe.

Christ as Logos

Before examining the Logos christology of John, perhaps we should go back for a moment to some of the key ideas within Stoicism and Platonism. We will examine how these two philosophies influenced one another and how they were later transformed by Philo of Alexandria.

Platonism and Stoicism

We have alluded to Plato (c. 429-347 BC) in our third chapter. For Plato, true knowledge is not obtained from the senses, but it is rooted in an independent, immaterial, eternal, transcendent world of Forms or Ideas which can be apprehended only through the intellect. These Forms are hierarchically related to one another, and above them all we find the most universal Form of all, the Form of the Good or the One. The world of sensible objects therefore represents nothing more than a shadow or copy of the real world of immaterial Forms. The former is the imperfect and evanescent world of Becoming, the latter is the perfect and unchanging world of Being.

According to Plato, the soul of an individual is immaterial and immortal: it has an existence prior to the body, and it continues to live on even after death. The soul in fact belongs to the world of Forms, and by virtue of the knowledge which it had of them in its previous other-worldly state, it can recognize them in the world of becoming through a process of recollection (αναυνησις). Plato also spoke of a World-Soul, a supreme organizing principle, animating the entire material universe. In the *Timaeus* the World-Soul is symbolized as a Demiurge or Craftsman who shapes the world out of a preexistent material according to the pattern which he observes in the world of Forms.

Stoicism, founded by Zeno of Citium (c. 300 BC), represents an altogether different theory of knowledge. The Stoics reacted vigorously against the Platonic notion of a transcendent world of Forms not perceptible through the senses, and they argued that whatever exists must be material. Within their materialistic universe they distinguished a *passive* and an *active* principle: on the one hand, a crude and unformed matter without character or quality, and on the other hand, a dynamic reason, plan, fiery vapor, breath or *logos* which forms and organizes. In the beginning passive matter emerged from this fiery vapor, and even though Logos is somewhat ethereal, it still remains quite material within classical Stoical thought. The Stoics apparently were not afraid of the strange paradox of two material bodies occupying the same space.

Immanent within the whole of the material universe, Logos was described in many ways as God, Nature, Providence or the Soul of the Universe. Since there was nothing above Logos, Stoicism in its original formulation could be characterized as a kind of pantheistic materialism. Although the Stoics distinguished nothing above Logos, they made many distinctions below Logos, all the while carefully preserving its fundamental and unbroken unity. All entities within the universe are microcosms of the whole, each containing both an active and a passive principle. The one, universal and supreme Logos stands in unbroken unity with its many *seminal logoi*. As particles of the divine Fire permeating the whole of reality, these *seminal logoi* form and organize each entity within the universe. In this view the soul of man, as an emanation of the divine Fire of Logos within the universe, is like a warm breath pervading the body. The soul survives the body after death, and it persists until the final conflagration at the end of time. In Stoical thought all came from Fire, and in the end all returns to Fire.

For several centuries before Christianity, from the time of Alexander the Great and even before, Hellenistic influence was widespread within Judaism.[296] Greek would have been widely known and used in Palestine at the beginning of the First Century, especially in the cities. We may safely say that at this time there was no such thing as a non-Hellenistic Judaism or a Judaism untouched by Hellenistic thought.[297] Platonism and Stoicism were an integral part of this larger Hellenistic influence, and these two philosophies followed the Greek language into some of the most sophisticated circles of Jewish thought. Here Platonism and Stoicism had a tendency to deviate from their original formulations. They borrowed ideas from one another to such an extent that a Platonized Stoicism or a Stoicized Platonism characterized the intellectual position of many educated Greek-speaking people of the time.[298] Within this complex philosophical and religious matrix, we situate Philo of Alexandria.

Philo of Alexandria

James Dunn argues very convincingly that if we want to get a good idea of the intellectual milieu out of which John's Logos Christology emerged, we should not look for a more specific background in some pre-Christian Gnostic myth[299] or in some "emerging mythical configuration."[300] We need turn no further than to someone like Philo (born c. 15-10 BC and died c. 45-50 AD)[301] who wrote quite extensively about fifty years before John penned his gospel. In Philo we see Judaism in intense interaction with Hellenistic philosophy, and from him we get a fairly good idea of the kind of cosmological speculation which must have been present in certain sophisticated circles of his day. Philo managed to do something quite extraordinary: he merged Platonism and Stoicism with his Jewish faith.

Philo derived from Plato the idea that the real world is the world of forms, patterns, or ideas. The contents of this world are only shadows and copies of the real world of eternal forms. Here no doubt Philo would have been greatly aided by Exodus 25.40: "See that you make them (the furniture of the tabernacle) after the *pattern* for them, which is being shown you on the mountain." From Stoicism Philo derived the idea of Logos as a principle of organization within the Universe. He identified the Logos of Stoicism with the Platonic world of forms[302] and then merged these two strands of Hellenistic thought with his Jewish faith.

In bringing these three seemingly disparate elements together, Philo, of course, had to make some fairly serious adjustments, especially with regard to Stoical thought. Stoicism as we have seen tended toward pantheism: Logos was material and was identified with God. But Philo's Platonized Logos was immaterial and quite distinct from God. It would be difficult for a monotheistic Jew to reduce God to the Universe or to Logos within the Universe. In Jewish thought nothing could encroach upon the distinctiveness or oneness of God. So beyond Logos, Philo pointed to the reality of God - a reality utterly transcendent, completely unknowable and totally incomprehensible even to the purest intellect:[303] "God is far away from all creation, and the apprehension of him is removed to a very great distance from all human power of thought."[304] Logos was as close as one could get to God: "to see the Logos or the powers is all that is attainable to man, even Abraham (Conf. 96f.: Mut. 15; Spec. Leg. I.32-50)."[305] Philo had good precedent within Jewish thought for saying that God in himself was completely unknowable, for in Exodus 33.21 the Lord told Moses: "My face you cannot see, for no mortal man may see me and live." Again in Deuteronomy 4.12: "When the Lord spoke to you from the fire you heard a voice speaking, but you saw no figure; there was only a voice."

To distinguish Logos from the one God, Philo used his favorite sun and light symbolism: the Logos is not God any more than the corona of the Sun is the Sun. Just as we cannot look directly upon the Sun, neither can we look upon God or know him directly. Philo made a distinction between the unknowable God whom he called ο θεος or *the* God - and the knowable God or Logos whom he called θεος or simply God/god.[306] Note well that this is not a distinction *within* the unknowable God. It is a distinction *between* the unknowable God and the knowable God/god, *between* the one and only God and the reality of Logos within the Universe. To make distinctions within the Unknowable is nonsensical, and moreover if Philo had distinguished Logos as a being *within God,* he would have introduced a second God within God and placed in jeopardy the central affirmation of his Jewish faith that God is one. Philo was not afraid to distinguish and identify Logos as a principle of organization *within the Universe,* and in so doing he abandoned nothing of his Jewish faith.

Many exegetes today maintain that at no point did the Old Testament writers really distinguish God's word from God himself. God's word was always the word of Yahweh, the utterance of Yahweh, nothing more and nothing less than Yahweh himself speaking.[307] God's word as well as God's wisdom and spirit always remained, in Jewish thought, well within the reality of God himself, in spite of all the awkwardness and tension involved in keeping them there.[308] Word, wisdom and spirit were nothing more than vivid personifications of certain attributes or functions of God, perhaps elaborations of a poetic imagination or good examples of a vigorous metaphorical style.[309]

No doubt the Jewish mind had locked itself into a very difficult and awkward position. The Old Testament writers were not just poets who enjoyed playing with words. Instead they were trying to come to grips with certain experiential realties which they could not deny and which at the same time they could not blend or absorb into the featureless transcendence of God. In the rich domain of experience, they could speak and make distinctions, and yet none of these distinctions corresponded in full to the unspeakable reality of God himself. The tendency within Jewish monotheism to pull so much into God in order to safeguard his preeminence and distinctiveness over and against the many gods and goddesses throughout the ancient Near East led to so much tension and contradiction that it degraded the very concept it was fighting to preserve. If they had followed this tendency to its logical conclusion, they would have pulled the entire Universe into God, only to have eliminated that all-important distinction between God and the Universe so fundamental to Jewish faith. Perhaps as no Jew in a pre-Christian setting had ever done, Philo recognized this illogical tendency within Jewish monotheism, and he was not afraid to formulate a clear and well thought out response to this most delicate and sensitive question.

In Philo we encounter the mind of a Jewish philosopher and theologian seriously engaged in dialogue with mainline Hellenistic thought. In merging Stoicism and Platonism with his Jewish faith, Philo clearly distinguished the completely unknowable and totally incomprehensible God from the knowable reality of Logos within the Universe. Philo introduced a strong cosmological perspective into the Jewish understanding of the word of God, and this we believe is the key to understanding the power and attraction of his thought. God's word according to Philo was not God. God's word was Logos - that tangible and knowable organizing power within the Universe. When Philo says that Logos is "the seal by which each thing that exists receives its shape" (Fuga 12.f) or the instrument which God employed in fashioning the Universe (Leg ALL III 95f.; Cher 127; Migr 6), should this be interpreted as nothing more than some loose formulation of a poetic imagination? If we do not understand Philo to be making a very real distinction between God and Logos, we fail to understand the unique contribution he was making relative to the wider philosophical and religious thought of his day.

On the one hand, Philo's Jewish faith dictated to him that the one God is unknowable, yet on the other hand, basic to this same faith was the conviction that God revealed his will *immediately and directly* to his people through prophetic inspiration and vision. Thus Philo hit upon a fundamental tension or contradiction right at the very heart of Jewish monotheism, and his attempt to resolve this problem was truly brilliant. Through his own experience of prophetic ecstasy[310] and through his openness to Hellenistic philosophy, Philo put forward a highly original solution to the awkward problem of having to relate to an unknowable and unreachable God. Philo said that it was Logos within the Universe that man encountered directly and immediately, not the one God as such. No doubt this was a very clear and precise distinction for a Jew to have made, and Philo's thought appears even more extraordinary when we recall that he was writing at the very moment the Christian message was breaking forth onto the world scene. Since we have no evidence that Philo was aware in any direct or explicit way of this new eschatological sect within Judaism,[311] it is hard for us to suppress the idea of several quasi-independent processes of thought all moving together to give rise to that unique cosmological understanding which later bore the name of Christian.

John

Christianity therefore did not evolve in isolation but as an integral part of a vast mental process. Hellenistic philosophy and Jewish thought had been interacting already for quite some time in a variety of pre-

Christian settings, and when John came to write his gospel, that very important distinction between God and Logos had already been made. This distinction enabled John to speak about Christ in a language which any well-educated Hellenistic Jew might readily understand. John drew upon the intense cosmological speculation of his day and found there a single word which allowed him to explain very succinctly what Jesus of Nazareth was all about: *Logos*. Let us not sever this word from its rich cosmological significance. If we do so, we run the risk of misunderstanding one of the most important aspects of John's christology.

Like Philo, John believed that God in himself was unknowable. In Jn 1.18 John explains that *"No one has ever seen God*; but God's only Son." In Jn 5.37 he explains further that "This testimony to me was given by the Father who sent me, although *you never heard his voice or saw his form*." Like Philo, John also referred to this one God as ο θεος or *"the God"* in distinction from Logos whom he called θεος or God/god. But John took things one step further than Philo by saying that Logos, who reveals himself in the Universe, in the word of prophecy and in the Torah, now also reveals himself immediately and directly as this man Jesus of Nazareth. John explained to his fellow Jews that, in seeing this man whom preexistent Logos became (Jn 1.14), one is in fact seeing God: "He who sees me sees him who sent me" (Jn 12.45).

In our reading of John we should never lose sight of the fact that John was a Jew, and even at the point of his deepest christological insight, he did not stop being a Jew. For him Logos was not some second God within God but that unique and distinct organizing principle within the Universe, who in revealing God, in no way encroaches upon the distinctiveness and oneness of God. Outside of this rich cosmological setting, the concept of Logos has a tendency to get pulled onto the same level as God with devastating consequences not only for christology but for the uniqueness and distinctiveness of the entire Christian understanding of reality. John made the absolutely startling claim that it is precisely as Logos within the Universe that this man Jesus reveals God and gives access to God. The Christian revelation in John is grounded in the belief that Logos was so fully poured forth and enfolded in the consciousness of this man Jesus of Nazareth that this man could be none other than that man in whom this preexistent organizing power with the Universe came to full expression. For the early Jewish Christians, this extraordinary man could be none other than that man whom preexistent Logos *became*. "So the Word *became* flesh; he *came to dwell* among us, and we saw his glory, such glory as befits the

Father's only Son, full of grace and truth." (Jn 1.14).

We emphasize that it was not God/θεος who became flesh, but the preexistent Word/θεος who became flesh. We underline as well the notion of his *becoming* flesh or *coming to dwell*. Even though Logos preexisted from the beginning with the Father, his becoming flesh, his coming to dwell, is linked to a specific historical figure at a particular time and place. Logos who is revealed in the Universe and through the prophetic word, and who for Philo was most clearly embodied in the Torah, now reveals himself according to John as this *man* Jesus of Nazareth.[312] Commenting on Jn 1.14 Dunn says:

> The conclusion which seems to emerge from our analysis thus far is that it is only with v. 14 that we can begin to speak of the *personal* Logos. The poem uses rather impersonal language (became flesh), but no Christian would fail to recognize a reference to Jesus Christ - the Word became not flesh in general but Jesus Christ.[313]

Following the lead of James Dunn we suggest that the revolutionary significance of this verse is that it marks the transition from an impersonal to a personal Logos. The Logos poet took the language which any thoughtful Hellenistic Jew would recognize to be the rather impersonal language of cosmology, and he did something quite remarkable: he applied it to a particular person. John affixed this expanded Logos poem to his gospel, conflating its Wisdom-Logos christology with his own dominant Son of God christology, thereby effecting a union of the two: the previously impersonal Logos within the Universe is now identified with the personal Son.[314] In juxtaposing the title of Son with the title of Logos, John assured the full personalization of the latter. The two titles belong together: the personal without the cosmological or the cosmological without the personal implies a serious distortion of John's original christological insight as well as a complete misunderstanding of the distinctive contribution he was making relative to the wider religious and philosophical thought of his day. Unfortunately in the christological reflection of the second, third and fourth centuries in the West, the two titles were separated and pulled apart. The title of Logos was displaced by the title of Son, and the emphasis swung from cosmology to soteriology.[315] *We see this loss of a cosmological perspective in christological reflection as the single greatest heresy in the history of Christian thought.*

In personalizing Logos, John left no doubt within the mind of the Hellenistic reader that this Logos/god within the Universe was quite distinct over and against the one God. It was no longer possible to absorb a particular man who had once lived in Palestine into the transcendent otherness of God. What had been implicit in Jewish thought all along, and what Philo distinguished clearly enough, became shockingly explicit in John so much so that it ran the risk of being interpreted as some second God within God. John was no longer pointing to what could be understood as some Hellenistic philosophical concept embodied within impersonal Torah. He was pointing to a living reality, to a particular person who had actually lived in Palestine and was still prophetically present among the early Christians as glorified Son, and furthermore, this living tangible Logos/Son, who himself relates so personally and intimately with the Father, who himself is the only one who can see the unseeable God, is now in the unique position to reveal God and to make Him visible.[316]

Therefore as a result of the specifically Christian re-working of Jewish monotheism, the worshipper in John does not have to deal directly with God. The inevitable tension within Jewish thought of having to relate to an unknowable and unreachable God is resolved. *Logos, no longer understood as some impersonal numinous power within the Universe, becomes deeply personalized, and precisely in the event of interacting personally and intimately with this living Logos/Son, is the unseeable and unknowable God revealed.* Not only does the Universe come alive in John, but it comes alive in a deeply personal and intimate way. The whole of John's gospel keeps on affirming and reaffirming this personal and intimate aspect.

"No one has ever seen God; but God's only Son, he who is *nearest to the Father's heart,* he has made him known." (Jn 1.18). As we interact with this living Logos/Son who is so close to the Father's heart, we come to share in the same intimate relationship which he now shares with the Father. "The man who has received my commands and obeys them - he it is who loves me; and he who loves me will be loved by my Father; and I will love him and disclose myself to him. Anyone who loves me will heed what I say; then my Father will love him, and *we will come and make our dwelling with him.*" (Jn 14.21-24). In John all is brought together in the deepest unity and love. "The *glory* which thou gavest me I have given to them, that they may be one, as we are one; I in them and thou in me, may they be *perfectly one*... Father, I desire that these men, who are thy gift to me, may be with me where I am, so that they may look upon my *glory,* which thou has given me before the world began." (Jn 17.22-25). According to John the *Universe is one in the love of God the Father.* Perhaps it all goes back to that marvelous insight in Jn 3.16: "God *loved the Universe* (κοσμον) so much that he gave his only Son, that everyone who has faith in him may not die but have eternal life."

So much religious effort in both the East and West falls far short of this personal and intimate aspect. Just as sexuality outside of a personal and intimate context easily degenerates into promiscuity and pornography, so too, religion outside of a personal and intimate context easily degenerates into magic and superstition. How easily enamored we are with rite, ritual, ceremony and sacrament. How quick we are to instruct one another on how to meditate, how to breathe, how to sit, how to stand, how to maintain inner silence and calm, how to master a variety of exercises and techniques, and yet all too often we remain fully preoccupied with ourselves. While some of us are enslaved in a stale and rigid religiosity, others float about aimlessly in a mindless enthusiasm. We may even distinguish ourselves as psychic enthusiasts, taking great pleasure in titillating displays of the paranormal and the miraculous, but in the end how easy it is for us to lose sight of worship and the fully personal and intimate address that true worship implies.

We could go on and on listing the many forms of abuse associated with the magic and superstition of the impersonal. Christianity avoided such abuse by deeply personalizing our relationship to a living Universe. Christianity distinguished itself from the many syncretist movements of the First-Century period by successfully pulling off a peculiar blend of the cosmological and the personal. When these two elements come together within religious consciousness, that is, when the Lord of the Universe is spontaneously addressed in the deepest love as "my Lord" or "our precious Lord," for example, then we know that we are walking in the presence of God himself. Only in worship do we find our deep and *intimate* place within the comprehensive subjectivity of a Universe.

In conclusion, the four christological titles which we examined - Lord, New Man, Wisdom and Logos - all have an undeniable cosmological thrust, and the last three feature this exciting notion of an image operating at the level of the whole of the Universe. Many of the nuances attached to the title Lord overlap with those of New Man (the New Adam for Paul is Lord of the Universe), and likewise some of the words used in describing the New Man overlap in part with those of Wisdom (image, glory, mirror), and Wisdom in turn overlaps in part with Logos (the Logos poet inserted the word Logos where normally Wisdom would have been featured), and finally John lets the Wisdom/Logos christology of the Logos poet conflate with his own dominant christology of the personal Son. So we end up with an array of titles, all influencing one another in very important ways, and all trying to express what the early Christians experienced in their direct and immediate, personal and intimate encounter with this risen Lord.

But strangely enough, their intimate encounter in worship with this personal Lord did not constitute the whole picture by which one obtains access to God.

> But the time approaches, indeed it is already here, when those who are real worshippers will worship the Father in spirit and truth. Such are the worshippers whom the Father wants (Jn 4.23-24).

Throughout the whole of the New Testament we never see the one God replaced by the one Lord, Wisdom, Word, Son or Christ. In John 14.16-17 we find reference to another Advocate in addition to Christ: "and I will ask the Father, and he will give you another to be your Advocate, who will be with you forever - the Spirit of Truth." Who is this other Advocate? Who is this Spirit of Truth?

Pneumatology

In the previous section we pointed out that Christianity was firmly united from the very beginning around the conviction that God had raised Jesus from the dead. But what made this event so special for the early Christians, as we have noted previously, was not simply the resurrection of a single individual. One of the characteristics of Jewish expectation at the end of time centered around the hope that the dead would rise from their tombs. Now when Jesus' disciples understood that he was raised from the dead, they could not help but conclude that the long-awaited general resurrection at the end of time was actually beginning: "Jesus was not merely alive after death; he was risen from the dead," and this meant that "the harvest of resurrected humanity was already in the process of reaping."[317]

So when the followers of Christ gathered in large numbers in Jerusalem on the occasion of the first great Jewish pilgrim festival after his death, Pentecost, awaiting with eager expectation the consummation of history already begun in the resurrection of Christ and the final dawn of the New Age, they found themselves standing precariously at the edge of time, relatively free from the confirmation of the past, radically disposed to and continually overwhelmed by that surprising element of the new and unexpected. In their eager anticipation of the consummation of the whole of universal history, they let themselves go, entering into a frenzied and drunken state of collective ecstasy. This powerful, tribal experience of Spirit on the day of Pentecost immediately gave them a whole new level of freedom with respect to the practice of their Jewish faith. In an instant they broke through centuries of stale tradition into the newness and freedom which only Spirit could bring:

> Christianity began as *a renewal movement within First-Century Judaism.* It began as an experience of liberation, as a breaking through of boundaries and recasting of traditions, as a movement of the Spirit clothing itself in *new* forms and expressing itself in *new* structures.[318]

Someone might object that our process definition of Spirit in terms of newness, unexpectedness and randomness does not quite correspond to the way the word Spirit is used within the New Testament. If we narrowed our effort to understand the reality of Spirit to nothing more than a study of words, then perhaps this would be true. But irrespective of how we understand the New Testament authors to be using or defining the word Spirit, we have only to look at what happens when Spirit is at work: we inevitably witness the emergence of "*new* forms" and "*new* structures," that "breaking through of boundaries and recasting of traditions" which Dunn so correctly associates with the movement of Spirit. It was this liberating experience of Spirit which launched Christianity as a powerful movement of renewal within First-Century Judaism:

> If any one experience can be said to have launched Christianity it is the experience of a largish group of Jesus' disciples on the day of Pentecost following Jesus' death. When gathered together in Jerusalem, presumably to await the consummation already begun in the resurrection of Jesus, they were caught up in a communal experience of ecstatic worship which manifested itself particularly in vision and glossolalia.[319]

But wait, is there not some contradiction here? In our previous section on christology we said that Christianity began with the event of the resurrection, and now Dunn also tells us that it was this experience of Spirit at Pentecost which launched Christianity. But as we examine the origin of Christianity, it soon becomes apparent that there is no contradiction here at all. Christianity defines itself only in terms of the bipolarity of Easter and Pentecost, only in terms of the bipolarity of Christ and his Spirit:

> If then we are looking for fundamental unity in the NT, in the twofold sense of elements which were a part of Christianity *from the first* and which *consistently* feature as *central* to Christianity across the range of documents which make up the NT, we must start with *Easter* and *Pentecost, Christ* and *Spirit.* Moreover, we should not ignore that it was *the manifest correlation* of these two fundamental elements which lay at the heart of Christianity's initial distinctiveness and success.[320]

Nowhere could we ever hope to find a more beautiful definition of the fundamental unity of early Christianity, and in it we cannot miss the point that the oneness of Christianity is the bipolar oneness of Christ and his Spirit.

The experience of collective ecstasy on the day of Pentecost came as the fulfillment of an ancient promise in Jewish expectation that the Spirit of God would no longer drive man from the *outside,* but rather it would be poured forth deeply *within.* "This will happen in the last days: I will pour out upon everyone a portion of my spirit; and your sons and daughters shall prophesy; your young men shall see visions, and your old men shall dream dreams. Yes, I will endue even my slaves, both men and women, with a portion of my spirit, and they shall prophesy (Acts 2.17-19)." In the last days, Spirit was not reserved for a special class of people or for those who had acquired certain knowledge or mastered certain techniques, rather according to Jewish expectation, it was to be poured forth on *all flesh* (Joel 2.28ff).

The law of God as foretold by the prophet Jeremiah would be written upon the human heart:

> The time is coming, says the Lord, when I will make a new covenant with Israel and Judah. It will not be like the covenant I made with their forefathers when I took them by the hand and led them out of Egypt. Although they broke my covenant, I was patient with them, says the Lord. But this is the covenant I will make with Israel after those days, says the Lord; *I will set my law within them and write it on their hearts*; I will become their God and they shall become my people. No longer need they teach one another to know the Lord; all of them, high and low alike, shall know me, says the Lord, for I will for-

give their wrongdoing and remember their sin no more (Jer 31.31-34).

The contrast between law written in stone and the law written on the human heart was for Paul the contrast between law and Spirit. He set the two in sharp antithesis:

> But now, having died to that which held us bound, we are discharged from the law, to serve God in a new way, the way of the spirit, in contrast to the old way, the way of a written code (Rm 7.6).

Christians are defined as those who are "discharged from the law." In 2 Cor 3.6 Paul shockingly contrasts the written law which *condemns to death* with the Spirit who gives life. In Gal 5.5 Paul says that "For to us, the hope of attaining that righteousness which we eagerly await is the work of the Spirit through faith." A bit further in Gal 5.16 he says that "if you are led by the Spirit, you are not under the law." Paul makes it clear that the answer to permissiveness and lawlessness is not law but Spirit. What a tremendous sense of freedom and renewal these early Christians experienced in the practice of their faith! Where is sin, where is guilt, where is condemnation for those who are directed by the Spirit? Paul boldly proclaims:

> The conclusion of the matter is this: *there is no condemnation* for those who are united with Christ Jesus, because in Christ Jesus the life-giving law of the Spirit has *set you free* from the law of sin and death. What the law could never do, because our lower nature robbed it of all potency, God has done: by sending his own Son in a form like that of our own sinful nature, and as a sacrifice for sin, he has passed judgement against sin within that very nature, so that the commandment of the law may find fulfillment in us, whose conduct no longer under the control of our lower nature is directed by the Spirit (Rm 8.1-4).

Just as Paul could contrast the law written on stone with the law written on the human heart, he could also contrast circumcision in the flesh with circumcision of the heart, not in an effort to abandon his Jewish faith but to define it more clearly:

> The true Jew is not he who is such in externals, neither is the true circumcision the external mark in the flesh. The true Jew is he who is such inwardly, and the true circumcision is of the heart, directed not by precepts but by the Spirit . . . Rm 2.28-29.

> Beware of those who insist on mutilation - "circumcision" I will
> not call it; we are the circumcised, we whose worship is spiritual,
> whose pride is in Christ Jesus, and who put no confidence in anything
> external (Phil 3.2-3).

Ethics for Paul, no longer a question of obedience to some written code or external mandate, consists in obedience to an inner compulsion, the law of the Spirit.[321] Paul went so far as to say that *whatever does not flow from the inner conviction of Spirit within the human heart is sin:*

> If you have a clear conviction, apply it to yourself in the sight of
> God. Happy is the man who can make his decisions with a clear con-
> science! But a man who has doubts is guilty if he eats, because his
> action does not arise from his conviction, and *anything that does not
> arise from conviction is sin* (Rm 14.22-23).

What Paul says here of Christian ethics flowing from the inner compulsion of the Spirit resembles a process view of ethical behavior. In a structured view, ethical behavior defines itself in terms of a fixed and rigid set of rules valid in an absolute sense and pre-determined from the outside in an *a priori* way. However, in a process-oriented view, concepts such as self-organization and self-determination come to the foreground. Here ethical behavior defines itself quite precisely in terms of the direct and immediate operation of Spirit within the human heart.[322] Open at all times to the newness of Spirit, it follows a development which is, in principle, wide open.[323] Ethical behavior can never be encapsulated in laws and fixed formulas, for the living law of Word never ceases to evolve and grow as it draws upon the newness and unexpectedness of Spirit.

Spirit leaves far behind all that is merely ritual and outward and brings faith and worship to a whole new level of excitement and deep inner experience. Spirit transforms a man from on the inside so that the metaphors of cleansing and purification become matters of actual experience in daily life (1 Cor 6.9-11). Spirit grounds hope within the human heart - a hope "which is no mockery, because God's love has flooded our inmost heart through the Holy Spirit he has given us." (Rm 5.5). It is no longer a question of mere words but of power and conviction which proceed from the Spirit (1 Thess 1.5): "when we brought you the Gospel, we brought it not in mere words but in the power of the Holy Spirit, and with *strong conviction,* as you know well." Spirit operates as the *source* of knowledge and life, directing our way in all things: "If the

Spirit is the *source of our life,* let the Spirit also direct our course." (Gal 5.25).[324] Spirit is that tangible and verifiable power within the human heart which cannot be concealed, that seal which marks the believer as Christ's property for all to see (2 Cor 1.22; Eph 1.13). In Gal 3.1-5 Paul reminds his readers that the reception of the Spirit was a clear and distinct experience which none of them could possibly forget:

> Answer me one question: did you receive the Spirit by keeping the law or by believing the gospel message? Can it be that you were so stupid? *You started with the spiritual; do you now look to the material* to make you perfect? Have all your great experiences been in vain - if indeed they should be? I ask then: when God gives you the Spirit and works miracles among you, why is this?

For Paul, a Christian is defined as someone who possesses the Spirit: "However, you are not in the flesh but in the Spirit, assuming that the Spirit of God does indeed *dwell* (οικει) in you - if anyone does not *have* (εχει) the Spirit of Christ, he does not belong to him." (Rm 8.9). "Certainly Paul takes it wholly for granted that possession of the Spirit is the hallmark of the Christian."[325] The idea of the Spirit *dwelling* (οικεω) denotes a *"settled relation"*[326] rather than some more passing or transitory state of possession. *Having* the Spirit (εχειν) is taken from the language of possession:

> Implicit is the understanding of the Spirit as a power which, working from within, manifests itself perceptibly (in word and deed) and determines the whole life of the one so possessed.[327]

Belonging to Christ (being a Christian) and having the Spirit cannot be understood apart from each other. Even though Paul had not been to Rome, he could assume, without the least fear of being controversial, that the members of this church knew what the experience of Spirit was all about. Paul did not hesitate to define a Christian in terms of the possession of Spirit: "You are on the spiritual level if only God's Spirit dwells in you; if a man does not possess the Spirit of Christ, *he is no Christian."* (Rm 8.9). Paul safely assumed that the members of the church at Rome had been caught up in that tangible and vivid experience of Spirit, and he stated clearly enough that only those who experienced directly and immediately the liberating power of Spirit could claim to be Christian.

But the recognition of the reality of Spirit did not originate with

Christianity. In pre-Christian times Spirit was clearly understood as the source or ground of knowledge and life. How then should one distinguish the experience of Spirit within pre-Christian Judaism from the experience of Spirit within Christianity? Judaism understood Spirit, πνευμα, as a kind of mysterious, impersonal power "whose most evident effect is in the experience and phenomenon of possession."[328] But how should one distinguish this power from other powers which possess? How to distinguish the Spirit of God from other spirits? Within Judaism it was difficult to establish any firm criteria of discernment:

> No firm criteria were ever achieved within Judaism. But the first Christians in effect resolved the issue by making Jesus himself the criterion: the Spirit for them was now to be recognized as the Spirit of Jesus, the Spirit of the Son (Acts 16.7; Gal 4.6; Phil 1.19; 1 Pet 1.11); the πνευμα θεου (v 9b) was more clearly defined as the πνευμα χριστου[329]

Within Christianity, the Spirit of God was redefined in terms of the Spirit of Christ. According to Paul, we know that we are dealing with the right Spirit when Spirit produces within us the confession that Jesus is Lord (1 Cor 12.3):

> Notice then the significance of Paul's claim: the range of possibly authentic experiences of inspiration has been narrowed to those experiences which affirm or accord with and do not deny the kerygmatic tradition about Jesus. This means that in Paul's view the Spirit has been limited or has limited himself in accord with the yardstick of Jesus. *The power of God has become determined by its relation to Jesus.*[330]

Any Spirit that does not promote and establish his Lordship is not the Spirit of a specifically Christian understanding. Furthermore we know we are dealing with the right Spirit when the Spirit within us cries out "Abba! Father!" (Rom 8.14), that is, when it establishes us as nothing less than "sons of God," thereby creating in us the same intimate relation of sonship that Jesus shared with the Father:

> In Paul's view experiences of God's Spirit can be more narrowly delimited in the light of Jesus' own experience of God and relation to God. The Spirit of God can be more precisely defined as the Spirit of Jesus' own relationship with the Father and as the Spirit which both brings about the same relationship for believers and makes it existen-

tially real. In short, we might say that *for Paul the character of the Spirit has taken its "shape" from the impress of Jesus' own relationship with God*[331]

True Spirit does not allow us to give into the magic and superstition of the impersonal. She creates and fosters the same personal and intimate relationship which Christ now shares with the Father. Finally we know that we are dealing with the right Spirit when Spirit gives rise to the reproduction of the image of Christ (2 Cor 3.18):

> Now by "image of God" Paul is clearly thinking primarily of Jesus (so explicitly in 4.4; see also Col 1.15). That is to say, the distinctive mark of the eschatological Spirit is an immediacy of relationship with God which makes the believer more like Jesus (if we may use such simple, pietistic language). Here then once again the relationship with God is seen in terms of experiencing the Spirit, but once again the experienced Spirit is seen in terms of Jesus. *Only that power which reproduces the image of Jesus Christ is to be recognized as the power of God.*[332]

Only that Spirit which sources and reproduces within us the image of Christ is the Spirit which Christianity recognizes and proclaims. Here we rejoin our basic theme of the power of an image. The image that fires the imagination of the worshipper is above all else the image of the risen Christ. He has become that "heavenly man" transformed into a "spiritual body" (1 Cor 15.49). He stands before the worshippers as the model and goal of human existence, as the concrete and vivid image of a new humanity, of all that man is called and destined to be. As the worshippers turn to him directly with "no veil over the face," they are "transfigured into his *likeness* from one degree of glory to the next" (2 Cor 3.18). As we have noted before, salvation for Paul is essentially a matter of being conformed to the pattern and image of the risen Christ. Not only do images have the power to organize, but according to Paul they also have the awesome power to save. In a sound epistemology of the sacred, the organizing and the saving power of images are inseparably connected.

Paul was not alone in redefining Spirit in terms of Christ:

> For John as for Paul the Spirit has ceased to be an impersonal divine power; the experience of new life alone does not sufficiently characterize the activity of the Spirit (3.5-8; 4.10-14; 6.63; 7.37ff.; 20.22). The Spirit has taken on a fuller or more precise character - the

character of Jesus: the personality of Jesus has become the personality of the Spirit.[333]

Thus we see that the early Christians redefined the Jewish concept of Spirit. If we situate Spirit directly within God as Judaism had done, Spirit inevitably moves from the outside of man, it lacks warmth and personal character, and it becomes difficult to discern or distinguish. Christianity involved such a fundamental reworking of Jewish monotheism that the primary reference of Spirit is no longer directly to God but to Christ. Let us not underestimate the importance of this distinction: "Crucial in understanding this whole realm of Christian spirituality is the recognition that for Paul the Spirit is the Spirit of Christ."[334] When Spirit refers directly to God, when Spirit gets pulled into the featureless transcendence of God, then it so easy to end up in a mindless mysticism or unbridled enthusiasm grounded in impersonal, empty or unknown forces. What had been within Judaism an impersonal force operating from the outside takes on within a Christian context the concrete role of sourcing and promoting the character and personality of Christ.[335] Spirit is not there to gratify the human heart in a spiritual high where all is reduced to a mindless oblivion. Spirit is not there to liberate us from the pain, struggle, tension, risk and responsibility of living in this world. On the contrary, Spirit is there to source and promote that powerful movement of Word which alone can lead and guide us in playing our true role as co-creators and partners in the evolutionary unfolding of a Universe.

Christian spirituality does not tolerate any external authority which should try to come in between the self and Spirit. Anytime we appeal to some supernatural authority transposed externally upon the natural, whether this be the absolute authority of a Pope or an Ayatollah, we have destroyed the basis of true religion. John tried to safeguard his fellow Christians from such dangers: "So much for those who would mislead you. But as for you, the anointing (that is, the Spirit) which you received from him stays with you; you need no other teacher, but learn all you need from his anointing, which is real and no illusion. As he taught you, then, dwell in him." (1 Jn 2.26-27). Dunn points out that this teaching role of Spirit is seen as a fulfillment of Jer 31.34.[336] Paul said that "A man gifted with the Spirit can judge the worth of everything, but is not himself subject to judgement by his fellow men. For (in the words of Scripture) "who knows the mind of the Lord? Who can advise him?" We, however, possess the mind of Christ" (1 Cor 2.15-16).

To operate out of the *mind of Christ* as he selects from the unfathomable richness of Spirit can only be described as a rather special psychological state. On the day of Pentecost the first Christians were involved in some rather strange and peculiar behavior, for they were accused of being drunk (Acts 2.13-17). In worship, every aspect of the self participates in this overpowering dynamic. Even the brain, divided into left and right hemispheres, reflects the bipolarity of Word and Spirit. The left hemisphere participates in the logical and organizational power of Word, while the right hemisphere participates in the newness and unexpectedness of Spirit.[337,338]

The Corporate Dimension of Worship

But true worship is not at all a private affair. Something happens in the togetherness of worship that could never happen with lone individuals. Worship begins in the togetherness of a shared experience, and in this respect we cannot help but follow Paul's strong communitarian emphasis:

> Religious experience is never reducible in Paul to an individualistic pietism - what one does with one's aloneness before God. On the contrary, the corporate dimension of religious experience is integral to Paul's whole understanding of the divine-human relationship. And when we talk about community with reference to Paul we are in fact talking about the experience of community. At the heart of the coming together of believers in the churches of the Pauline mission was the *shared experience* of God's Spirit.[339]

Spirit in Paul denotes above all else a *shared* experience:

> To some it may seem trite and obvious, but today it can hardly be stressed too much that fundamental to Christian community for Paul was the shared experience of Spirit/grace. Without this, 'fellowship' (κοινωνια) lacks all substance; it remains a jargon word or ideal and never becomes an existential reality. So too unity hinges on this common experience. There can be structural unity or formal unity; but without a common experience of grace (emphasis on both 'experience' and 'grace') unity can never be a living reality.[340]

The classical Western notion of the lone individual in worship before God is a sad caricature of Christian worship. True worship begins with the common, shared, ecstatic experience of Spirit.

The Movement of Spirit

John referred to Spirit as a "wind" which blows where it wills (Jn 3.8). "Wind" and "spirit" are translations of the same Greek word πνευμα (pneuma) which has both meanings. John also referred to Spirit as "a fountain of water bubbling up to eternal life" (John 4.14). *These wind and river metaphors are very apt in describing the fluidity and randomness of Spirit.* Luke saw Spirit as falling unexpectedly upon the believers compelling them to eye-catching action and ecstatic speech (Acts 2.4; 8.18; 10.45; 19.6), and many today incorrectly reduce the presence of Spirit to the ecstatic tongue-speaking which Luke particularly delighted in.[341] This, of course, would distort the full New Testament witness to Spirit,[342] but as a means of passing control to the right hemisphere of the brain, tongue-speaking is quite effective. However, speaking in tongues should never be separated from the context of deep communal worship, and it is best understood in its Biblical sense as languages of ecstatic praise. It is nearly impossible for someone to engage in this random flow of syllables and at the same time to remain in an ordinary state of consciousness. After a few minutes he or she is drawn to make the transition to that special state of mind where Spirit operates in full. In the freeflow of syllables comes a freeflow of Spirit, and with Spirit, a whirlwind of images infinite in number. The worshipper becomes bathed, immersed, baptized, lost or drunk in Spirit, and the resultant state of mind is far from rational.

The movement of Spirit in a worshipping community, whether in tongues or in some other freeflowing, non-associative worship mode, can always be recognized and discerned in that it comes to expression as a unified state of *collective ecstasy.*[343] Christianity was born on the feast of Pentecost in a rush and flurry of collective ecstasy, and Spirit was clearly the source of this ecstasy. Together with the apostle Paul we emphasize Spirit as a *shared experience,*[344] and the drunken ecstasy associated with Spirit does not represent a group of individuals each in their own private state of ecstasy, but a *true fellowship or communion of worshippers fused into a single ecstatic state.* They form a unified wave state, if we may be permitted to use the language of quantum physics. It is precisely this *experience of togetherness, this experience of a unified state* which we call Spirit. Getting caught up in mass ecstasy, in the frenzy and excitement of a real Pentecost, is not arbitrary or optional. Here we concretely touch that creative source out of which all knowledge and life unfolds.

We stress the tangibility of this drunken state of togetherness. If one were to walk into a room full of worshippers ecstatically fused into one another, usually one could not help but feel and touch Spirit as concretely and as tangibly as the air one breathes. During a sustained period of worship, a large number of worshippers, and this may include a significant number of newcomers, may be overpowered by Spirit to such an extent that they are literally knocked down and on the floor, rendered unconscious in the calm and blissful stupor of Spirit. Ecstatic singing-in-tongues may move spontaneously through the assembly of worshippers in a wave-like motion, rising and falling in a single mighty chorus of praise and adoration lasting sometimes for hours.[345] Ecstatic dance may erupt, slow and rhythmic among the older worshippers, wild and frenzied among the young. Through tribal song and dance, all are drawn irresistibly into the ecstatic unity and fellowship of Spirit.

Modern parallels to the collective ecstasy of the Pentecost event are certainly not widespread within the Western world, but nonetheless they can be found in increasingly growing numbers, particularly within African-American churches. Modern Pentecostalism originated among African-American Christians in Kansas and California around the turn of the century. Is it merely a coincidence that these wholly unsophisticated and uneducated people, only a few generations removed from a rich animistic setting, should have been the ones to have re-discovered in modern times some of the most essential elements of First-Century Christianity?

Christianity distinguishes itself generally from other religious or mystical traditions in that the operation of Spirit should never be experienced or understood apart from the operation of Word. Mindless mysticism or unbridled enthusiasm has no place whatsoever within Christian worship. Ecstatic collective worship is nothing at all if it does not operate at all times as the creative ground and source of Word.

The Movement of Word

In the New Age foretold by Joel, there was to be a widespread experience of prophecy, thereby fulfilling the ancient hope of Moses: "I wish that all the Lord's people were prophets and that the Lord would confer his spirit upon them all!" (Num 11.29). We would not want to limit the operation of Word to prophecy, for we see in the New Testament the role of the evangelist, the preacher, the teacher, the counselor, and so forth.

But apart from the apostles, the prophets were held in the very highest esteem within the early Christian churches (1 Cor 12.27-28).[346] Not merely speaking in the name of Word, they expressed Word in such a direct and immediate way that *they spoke the very words of living Word*.[347] Paul prized the gift of prophecy above all other gifts[348] (see 1 Cor 14.1 and 1 Thess 5.19), for unlike the purely "spirit" utterance of tongue speaking, it is a "speaking *with the mind*" (1 Cor 14.15-19).

However, we must emphasize that the operation of Word is an event proceeding from and at every moment dependent upon the random and totally unpredictable anointing and empowering of Spirit. Within Judaism a prophet was defined precisely in terms of possession of the Spirit.[349] The prophet, preacher, evangelist or even teacher[350] operates at every moment out of the mind of Logos in complete dependence upon the anointing of Spirit.[351] His authority is derived principally from the direct and unmediated charismatic authority of Spirit.

Prophecy can never be seen as a skill, aptitude or talent, but rather it is "the actual speaking forth of words given by the Spirit in a particular situation and ceases when the words cease."[352] In this way the body of worshippers is fed by every word issuing from the mouth of living Word. Only in this way is the body *built up* (οικοδομει, 1 Cor 14.4) and grows to full stature.[353] Prophecy according to Dunn is "the guarantor of spiritual health and growth. Without it, the community cannot exist as the body of Christ; it has been abandoned by God."[354] *A church defined apart from the vibrant exercise of the gift of prophecy simply cannot be called Christian.*

In so many classical Western churches the closest we come to the movement of Spirit is hymn-singing, and the closest we come to the movement of Word is some logical and rational exposition of a Biblical or moral nature, carefully prepared beforehand, generally informative perhaps, but totally lacking in power. All so narrow, so rational, so Western and so flat! Where are those prophetic images that burn deeply and intensely within the imagination of the worshippers to fulfill their every personal need so that they stand at all times transfigured and transported from one level of glory to the next? Where are the images that actually heal and make whole disturbed minds and broken bodies? Where are the images that fuse the worshippers into a single new humanity? Where are the images that give the worshippers a profound sense of unity with all of nature and establish their humble yet meaningful place at the heart of a living Universe? Without such vibrant images, Christianity displays nothing of its original First-Century power. It has nothing to do with the rather sad notion of the individual alone in silence before God. In stark contrast, it points to the primary reality of tribe or collectivity fused into single ecstatic state and organized from within by the words of living Word.

The Body of Christ

The bipolar movement of Word and Spirit serves a single purpose: to create, build up, sustain, and nourish a living Body. In 1 Cor 12.14-27 Paul understands church, εκκλεσια, as the Body of Christ: "it is clear that in this passage the dominant influence is the typical Stoic use of the metaphor of the body to describe the relationship between individual and society."[355] But Paul uses this metaphor not simply to describe a community but more specifically a *charismatic* community:

> For Paul the point is clear: as members of the body of Christ, each has a function (Rom 12.6), each has a ministry (1 Cor 12.5), each has a charism (1 Cor 12.5,7; Rom 12.4ff.). The body of Christ for Paul is essentially a 'charismatic community.'[356]

Paul does not use the metaphor of the body of Christ to describe some worldwide body of believers. Not yet a universal concept, "body" remains manifestly local and tangibly organic: it describes "Christians living or gathered in one place."[357] Since Christians did not have their own church buildings until the Third Century, the first Christian churches were all house churches. Paul saw those Christians gathered together in worship at a particular house very much as a complete Body of Christ. The accent was not at all on the place where they met, but on their coming and worshipping together. This alone made them a Body.[358]

In such a context it should not be surprising that every local worshipping body should be profoundly different, bearing witness to completely different patterns of internal self-organization, yet nonetheless they should be very much the same, insofar as they all participate in the one (meta)pattern of Word drawing upon Spirit. Dunn has written a beautiful book stressing the enormous diversity of churches within First-Century Christianity,[359] and as we stop to reflect upon this rich diversity, we are forced to rethink the traditional Catholic interpretation of the origin and development of early Christianity.

The history of Christianity has often been characterized in Catholic circles as the tale of the gradual and steady increase toward excellence and perfection. What began as a "primitive" church in the First Century gradually gave way to the more sophisticated and developed "Catholic" church of the second and third centuries. But when we examine carefully the historical record, we witness the truly explosive and highly differentiated advent of Christianity on the world scene manifesting itself not so much as a single church but as a multiplicity of churches, all fundamentally Christian, all very sophisticated and developed in their internal organization and self-understanding, yet on the whole displaying an even greater variety and diversity of form than what we see anywhere within Christianity today. As we move into the second, third and fourth centuries we witness "decimation and extinction" followed by further differentiation, but a differentiation only within a single surviving Catholic branch.

The New Testament itself bears testimony to a highly differentiated Christianity, each expression of the Christian faith quite distinct from the other, yet each fully mature and *fully Christian* in every respect. Dunn speaks generally of a Gentile Christianity, an Apocalyptic Christianity, a Jewish Christianity, and an early Catholic Christianity all within the one New Testament canon. Furthermore within each of these broad types, we witness a high degree of diversity. Far from being monochrome and homogeneous, each type contains within itself a broad spectrum of Christian churches. This richly variegated Christianity was there in its full-blown complexity right from the very beginning, and early Catholicism represents a fairly late starter within what we may call this "Christian explosion." Just as Gould argues that it is impossible for any paleontologist to go back to the Burgess seas and without the benefit of hindsight to pick out those creatures which were destined to survive and those which were destined for extinction, so too we might argue that from the viewpoint of the New Testament alone, there is nothing there to suggest that early Catholicism should or would become the normative expression of Christianity.[360]

Jewish, Hellenistic, and Apocalyptic Christianity all had tendencies which, when left unchecked, led respectively to the heresies of Ebionism, Gnosticism, and Montanism. But early Catholicism also had heretical tendencies which remained largely unchecked. By the time it reached the second and third centuries, Catholicism had lost sight of some rather important New Testament elements. Church life had become terribly overstructured. Spirit was bottled up in office, ritual, ceremony and sacrament, and prophecy was reduced to formulae and stifled within set forms.[361] If we define the fundamental unity of

Christianity in terms of Easter and Pentecost, concretely experienced within the worshipping community in terms of the direct and unmediated operation of Christ and his Spirit, in what sense was the Catholicism of the second and third centuries orthodox and Christian?

Dunn rejects John H. Newman's idea of the evolutionary development of Christian doctrine where doctrinal developments are viewed as organic growths from New Testament shoots. Newman wrote his *Essay on the Development of Christian Doctrine* in 1845, at a time when ideas on natural selection and the gradual evolutionary development of life were very much in the air. Dunn rejects this notion of the straight-line development of Christianity where each development is seen as another section in the pipeline of truth. Instead he suggests that each development within the New Testament is more like another radius of a sphere, each "formed by immediate interaction between the unifying center and the moving circumference."[362] He also offers the metaphor of a series of branches, each growing directly out of the trunk of the unifying center.[363] However, Gould's metaphor of an inverted tree might help us more in understanding the complex differentiation among surviving branches, while literally turning upside down any simplistic notion of their "primitive" origins.

When Spirit is at work, newness abounds. Unrepeatable and totally unique patterns of ecclesial self-organization emerge. *In a Pentecostal setting no two churches could ever be the same.* This never-ending thrust toward diversity, far from being an aberration, is the normal and natural outcome of the presence of Spirit within a worshipping body.

> Christianity can only exist in concrete expressions and these concrete expressions are *inescapably different* from each other. In order to be, Christianity has to be diverse.[364]

The reason why each expression of Christianity is "inescapably different" lies in the never-ending incorporation of the newness and unexpectedness of Spirit. This diversity arising from Spirit is endless, since each and every member of the Body is called to participate in Spirit:

> At no time does Paul conceive of two kinds of Christians - those who minister to others and those who are ministered to, those who manifest charismata and those who do not. To be Christian is to be charismatic; one cannot be a member of the body without sharing the charismatic Spirit.[365]

Since all members of the Body of Christ draw upon the charismatic Spirit, all are called to ministry. This leaves far behind the Jewish and later Catholic distinction between priest and people:

> Christian community is not sacerdotal in the sense that only some have particular functions, only some have ministry; charismata are many and various, and *all are charismatics, all have ministry* - for Paul the Spirit has surmounted *the old Jewish distinction* between priest and people and left it behind. Some will have more regular ministry which the community should recognize and encourage; but the idea of a mono-ministry, of all the most important gifts concentrated on one man (even an apostle) is foolish nonsense to Paul (1 Cor 12.14-27).[366]

There are no passive members, no second-class members, and no second-class functions which second-class members are called upon to exercise (see 1 Cor 12.21). All functions within the body are of *equal importance.* No function is preeminent, and therefore no function should be regarded as inferior to any other. "Every charisma, every manifestation of grace is *indispensable,* for *the Spirit's gifts are the living movements of Christ's body.*"[367] Dunn then goes on to describe the interaction of members of a worshipping body in terms which accord well with the vocabulary of the dynamics of natural systems:

> So too the interdependence of members is a dynamic process. When Paul speaks of the functioning of the members of the body he is not thinking of individuals with set functions. As each charisma is an act of grace, so the unity of Christian community cannot be a static state; rather it is *an ongoing creative event, constantly dependent on the Spirit manifesting his manifold interacting charismata.* The unity of today does not guarantee the unity of tomorrow - that depends on ever-new charismata bringing about that unity through their mutual interaction.[368]

Note well the dynamic mutual interdependence among members of the Body of Christ. Dunn then points out that the individual does not exist for himself but for the body:

> It follows . . . that *the charismatic as charismatic does not exist for himself but only for the community.* "The Corinthians are fundamentally and primarily the body of Christ and only in a secondary way individual members." If we are to appreciate Paul's emphases, the

charismata are never to be thought of as given to the individual, far less for his own personal advancement or pleasure; on the contrary, that is the very antithesis of community (14.2ff.). Rather the charismata are always to be seen as *service* (διακονια), as *gifts for the body,* given to, or better, *through* the individual "for the common good" (12.7) . . . Thus the emphasis of Rom 12.5 - "We, though many, are one body in Christ, and individually members of one another."[369]

The Body of Christ functions in every respect as a single living organism. Paul's concept of the mutual interdependence within the worshipping body reminds us of the symbiotic relationships within nature which biologists such as Margulis, Thomas, and Kirk have pointed to in recent times. The functioning of a worshipping body resembles in a profound way the functioning of any interdependent living organism within nature. The worshipping body occupies a distinct place within the multileveled structure of the Universe. The individual worshippers symbiotically take their place in a much larger autopoietic whole, a whole as natural and as organic as any other whole on any other level within a multileveled Universe. We can never relegate worship and the body engaged in worship to some supernatural realm. Called into being and sustained continually from within by the direct and immediate operation of Word and Spirit, it forms a living whole, a New Humanity as Paul would say, which represents an important step forward in the evolutionary history of mankind.

We follow Paul in emphasizing the primary reality of a Body organized from within by virtue of common Mind. Therefore we may not turn to the mind of any particular worshipper for leadership, not even to the mind of a prophet or pastor. Mind operates at all times as *collective mind,* and all members of the worshipping Body behold the same internal images as they emerge within the *collective imagination.* This corporate Mind truly leads and guides, and it alone constitutes the authority of the Body. Perhaps this is why Paul generally never made reference to any one individual or group of individuals for leadership:

> Nowhere in his letters, with the probable exception of Phil 1.1, does Paul address one single class or group of people as though they were responsible for the organization, worship or spiritual wellbeing of others.[370]

Individuals do not organize on behalf of the group, rather the body itself self-organizes by virtue of the images arising within the collective imagination: "if leadership was required, Paul assumed that the charismatic Spirit would provide it."[371] We should not understand the dynamics of a worshipping Body in terms of a control hierarchy where information flows upward and orders flow downward.[372] Leadership arises from out of the dynamics of a common Mind, and Spirit provides the source and motivation for this common Mind (Phil 2.1). To think in static terms of title and office distorts completely the Pauline understanding of leadership and authority. How we love to place emphasis on parts, to inject members of a body with power and authority, to invest them with title and office! Dunn says that offices signify "positions where certain privileges and authority are reserved for an appointed few, positions with well defined responsibilities which the 'officials' can only begin to exercise on appointment."[373] We find no support for the concept of office in writings of Paul:

> Within the Pauline churches the only ministries which *begin* to fall within this definition of "office" are apostles and teachers; but since apostles by (Paul's) definition were unrepeatable (eschatological apostles), and since teaching included charismatic teaching, the word "office" is best avoided completely in any description of the Pauline concept of ministry. As for authority and continuity, in Paul's view *that lay primarily in the Spirit* ever freshly creating a new word (prophecy) and in the gospel tradition first brought by the apostle and passed on by the teacher. In short, authority was essentially charismatic authority: *only he who ministered could have authority and that only in the actual exercise of his ministry.*[374]

We underline what Dunn says here: *Spirit ever freshly creating new Word!* The authority that comes to expression in the worshipping body is the authority of the whole:

> The community as a whole are taught by God (1 Thess 4.9), they all participate in the one Spirit (κοινωνια), they are all men of the Spirit (πνευματικοι). As such they have authority to regulate and exercise judgement concerning the charismata (1 Cor 2.15) . . . The responsibility of the church as a whole to hear, understand, test, and control is underlined.[375]

Authority expresses itself in the charismatic event of being absorbed into Word and Spirit, and it ceases the moment that the charismatic event ceases. Our churches today have become so thoroughly Westernized, with genuine prophetic and ecstatic forms of worship so little in evidence, that it is hard for us to imagine church leadership and authority evolving directly and immediately through that delicately balanced interplay between Word and Spirit.

A balance between the operation of Word and Spirit should always be maintained within the worshipping community. For Spirit without Word quickly degenerates into mindless enthusiasm, and Word without Spirit becomes dull, superficial, totally unconvincing, rigid, frozen, institutionalized and dead. In the whole of 1 Cor 14, we see Paul appealing to the church at Corinth to maintain a balance between the language of ecstasy and prophecy.[376] Once this balance has been achieved, it causes the visitor to "fall down and worship God, crying, "God is certainly among you!" (1 Cor 14.25). A binocular view into the bipolarity of Word and Spirit allows one to peer into the very heart of God himself. Any view or formulation outside of worship quickly degenerates into a dangerous distortion of what is meant by God.

In the introduction we said that through the experience of being transformed, transfigured and renewed through the fullness of a living Universe, we are given a window out onto God which no rational formulation, unitary description or mystical silence could ever provide. Can we specify a bit more precisely onto what this window opens out? At the same time we might ask how to discern the true operation of Word and Spirit, how to be sure that we have reached Word and Spirit operating at that unique and distinct level of the whole of the Universe? The only answer to these questions is love. The crucial test of charismatic phenomenon for Paul was love (see 1 Cor 13).[377] Love defines itself as that which is experienced in the balanced interaction of the selective and the random. As the driving force behind all co-evolutionary unfolding, love *builds up* the body and causes it to grow (1 Cor 8.2). Modern man may have problems with the word "God" so long associated with all of the formalism and abuse surrounding the concept of a supernatural Being, but when we return to John's insight into God, all of his doubts and fears quietly fade away: "God is love; he who dwells in love is dwelling in God, and God in him" (1 Jn 4.16).

Therefore the unknowable God is only made knowable in the deepest bipolarity of the direct and immediate, personal and intimate, ecstatic and prophetic, harmonious and balanced interaction of Word and Spirit. All of these couplets help to describe in a limited way that awesome experience of operating from on the inside of a living Universe. This book is grounded in the firm conviction that it is this bipolar experience which alone gives access to God. It might be difficult to understand what prompted Stephen J. Gould to write: "But Fortuna's gifts languish unless reinforced by her sister Diligencia under the patronage of Amor." [378] No doubt we commit a kind of literary sacrilege by borrowing this sentence and using it in an entirely different context.[379] But in any case, is Fortuna not Spirit? is Diligencia not Word? and is Amor not Love?

A Universe in Worship: Romans 8.18-39

Before bringing this last chapter to a close, we turn to that magnificent letter which Paul wrote to the church at Rome. This letter represents one of the most beautiful expressions of the early Christian faith by one of its most outstanding proponents. Romans stands as the most developed and most sophisticated exposition of Paul's thought,[380] and we turn immediately to those verses which represent the high point, the climax[381] and the center of the entire letter, Rm 8. 18-39.[382] What does Paul do at the moment of greatest insight and inspiration? We should not be surprised if he should take up the theme of a living Universe.

As an apostle to the Gentiles and perhaps the least Jewish among his fellow apostles, Paul was still very much a Jew and remained at all times a Jew.[383] Paul never used the word "conversion" to describe his encounter with the risen Christ.[384] Rather he referred to it as a calling and commission to take the gospel of God's son to the Gentiles. Paul wrote primarily as an evangelist and missionary[385] passionately absorbed, not in founding a new religion, but in preaching among the Gentiles what he saw as the final expression and full intent of his Jewish faith.[386] As a Christian Paul never stopped being a Jew.[387]

To the First-Century Jew, Israel's covenant relationship with God was fundamental, and the law was given as an expression of this covenant. Following the lead of E.P. Sanders, Dunn cautions that we should not view the function of the law within First-Century Judaism from the perspective of the problems and concerns of Martin Luther. Israel had never denied the premise of God's free and unmerited grace. The law in Israel was never meant to be a means of entering into the covenant or of gaining merit. Rather it served as means of *maintaining* the covenant, a means of *living within* the covenant.[388] Obedience to the law was Israel's response to God's free grace and not a means of meriting grace.

As a Jew, Paul did not want to abandon the mainstay of his Jewish faith - law and covenant. Rather he wanted to broaden the base by which they were supposed to function within Judaism. For Paul, the law had become much too closely identified with ethnic Israel as such. The law set the Jews apart from all other peoples, not only expressing their distinctiveness as a people but also serving as an identity marker or boundary fencing them off from everyone else. The Jews experienced a sense of privilege in being set apart by God as well as a sense of pride in the law as the mark of God's special favor. The law, in its misplaced emphasis on boundary-marking ritual, divided Jew from non-Jew. As a source of ethnic pride, it gave the Jew a distorted sense of privileged distinctiveness.

Of course, Paul did not deny law and covenant. He denied them only insofar as they were taken over and appropriated by Israel as their exclusive property. He insisted on broadening law and covenant to encompass and include much more than just ethnic Jews. Paul proclaimed to his fellow Jews that they were no longer the exclusive center of reality, and he was convinced that God's salvation in Christ completed his original purpose both in creating the Universe and in calling Israel.[389] In the verses that follow, Paul offers us a coherent and thoroughly magnificent vision where Jew and Gentile, in unity with the whole of a living Universe, await their total transformation into the fullness of God's glory made manifest in Christ.[390]

Verse 18

For I reckon that the sufferings of the present time are not to be compared with the coming glory to be revealed to us.[391]

λογιζομαι οτι, ουκ αξια τα παθηματα του νυν καιρου προς, τπν μελλουσαν δοξαν αποκαλυθηναι εις ημας,

Paul's use of the word suffering (παθημα) should be understood in its normal Pauline sense as sharing in the sufferings of Christ. The glory (δοξαν) to be revealed is clearly in the future, something waited for in hope. Paul is drawing upon a well-known Jewish suffering-vindication motif wherein the suffering of the righteous cannot be compared with their glorious vindication in the future. His language is thoroughly apocalyptic: he speaks of *revelation* (αποκαλυθηναι) and an imminent end. But still he is convinced that the work of salvation and renewal has already begun through the Abba-crying Spirit. In an earlier exposition (2 Cor 4.16-5.5), Paul expressed very much the same thought:

No wonder we do not lose heart! Though our outward humanity is in decay, yet day by day we are inwardly renewed. Our troubles are slight and short-lived; and their outcome an eternal glory which outweighs them far. Meanwhile our eyes are fixed, not on things that are seen, but on the things that are unseen: for what is seen passes away; what is unseen is eternal. For we know the earthly frame that houses us today should be demolished, we possess a building which God has provided - a house not made by human hands, eternal, and in heaven. In this present body we do indeed groan; we yearn to have our heavenly habitation put over this one - in the hope that, being this clothed, we shall not find ourselves naked. We groan indeed, we who are enclosed within this earthly frame; we are oppressed because we do not want to have the old body stripped off. Rather our desire is to have the new body put on over it, so that our mortal part may be absorbed into life immortal. God himself has shaped us for this very end; and as a pledge of it he has given us his Spirit.

Note that twice within this Corinthian passage, Paul makes reference to "groaning," a theme which will appear three times in the verses that follow. Through the overwhelming experience of Spirit, the believer operates out of an unshakable hope in the glory soon to be revealed.[392]

Verse 19

For the eager expectation of creation eagerly awaits the revelation of the sons of God.

η γαρ αποκαραδοκια τηδ κτισεως, την αποκαλυψιν των υιων του θεου απεκδεχεται,

The sense of longing is sustained. Creation eagerly and confidently awaits without any doubt or uncertainty the revelation of the sons of God at the end of time. Paul does not attempt to define what he means by *creation* (κτισεως), but he probably has non-human creation in mind. Paul speaks of this non-human creation in vivid animistic terms - a creation full of wistful and eager longing. For Paul all those who are "in Christ," all those who have been incorporated into his Body, are already "sons of God," and once these sons of God enter upon their full inheritance at the end of time and come to share in the fullness of the glory of God, then the whole of creation will be gloriously transformed, thus fulfilling God's original intention in creating the Universe. Acutely aware that its destiny is intertwined with the destiny of man, this living Universe is just bursting with eager anticipation! After all, Christ has been raised from death as the first fruits of a harvest soon to come, and his Spirit has been poured forth at Pentecost. The long-awaited End has begun, and the whole of creation excitedly awaits the final unveiling from heaven of the true status of the sons of God. Note how Paul moves far beyond any idea of a "merely personal or human redemption."[393] *Redemption for Paul is a cosmological event, encompassing the whole of the Universe.*

Verse 20

> *For creation was subjected to futility, not willingly, but on account of him who subjected it, in hope,*

τη γαρ ματαιοτητι η κτισις υπεταγη, ουχ εκουσα αλλα δια τον υποταξαντα, εφ ελπιδι,

The idea of *futility* (here as ματαιοτης) appeared earlier in Rm 1.21 (as εματαιωθησαν). As in chapter one, the primary allusion is to the narrative of Adam's creation and fall (Gen 1-3). What is this futility? Dunn explains that it is "the futility of something which does not function according to what it was designed to do (like an expensive satellite which has malfunctioned and now spins uselessly in space), or more precisely, which has been given a role for which it was not designed and which is unreal or illusory."[394] In his pride Adam broke from away from his dependency upon God (1.21), and as a consequence he was subjected to the futility of the "complete insignificance of the individual in the tides of time and the currents of human affairs."[395] But since God in subjecting all things to Adam, subjected creation to fallen Adam, creation too is faced with futility:

> As man's futility is his assumption that he is an independent creator, the failure to realize that he is but a creature, so the futility of creation is its being seen solely in relation to man (as man's to use or abuse for himself).[396]

Creation becomes futile and without meaning when seen solely in terms of its relationship to man. In describing creation's subjection as a *not willing* (ουχ εκουσα) subjection, Paul speaks from the same vivid animism which we saw in the previous verse. Note the tight interdependency between man and creation, a negative relational interlocking across levels: creation was subjected to futility because man in his ambition to be like God was subjected to futility. Creation is unwillingly subjected to futility through its relationship to man who in turn is not in proper relationship with God.

Verse 21

because creation also itself will be set free from the slavery of corruption into the liberty of the glory of the children of God.

οτι και αυτη η κτισις, ελευθερωθησεται απο της δουλειας της φθορας, εις της ελευθεριαν της δοξης των τεκνων του θεου,

To Paul's Gentile audience in Rome composed mainly of slaves and former slaves, this talk of slavery was particularly relevant. Previously in Romans Paul spoke much about liberation: liberation from sin (6.18,22) and liberation from the law (7.33; 8.2). Here he introduces the notion of liberation from *corruption* (φθορας). But it is not just believers who are to be liberated from corruption: the whole of creation awaits the same liberation and redemption. Dunn defines this slavery to corruption as "the complete inability to escape from the physical deterioration and dissolution which characterizes the created order (and on which sin has capitalized)."[397] Paul would have had little sympathy for our modern view of the Universe as aging and dying, running down inexorably to nothingness and death. For him the Universe is destined for that same fullness of life made manifest in the resurrection of Christ, destined to share in the same glory and splendor which God had in mind when he created man in the beginning. What a far cry from Gnosticism or any other kind of dualism which speaks of man's redemption or liberation from creation.

Verse 22

For we know that the whole creation groans and suffers the pains of childbirth together up till now.

οιδαμεν γαρ οτι, πασα η κτισις συστεναζει και συνωδινει αχρι του νυν,

Here Paul makes use of the powerful eschatological image of giving birth: the present labor pains give "promise of the cosmic birth of the new age."[398] The image evokes "the climactic transition from this age and created order to the new age of God's final purpose. It is an all embracing process involving the total cosmos, "the 'whole creation' joining 'together' in fractured chorus."[399] Dunn notes "how undualistic is the thought of sighing *with* rather than to escape *from* creation,"[400] but soon afterwards he talks about the "vivid personification of nature" as "typical of the more poetic strains of Jewish writing."[401] Now if we seriously want to avoid all forms of dualism, then let us take Paul's description of the Universe as a living organism at its face value. From a mechanistic standpoint Paul is just a poet, someone who is merely playing with words, for how could there ever be an intimate sighing with, a real groaning *together*? But from an organismic standpoint, Paul and his Universe truly operate from on the inside of one another. Both situate quite clearly on the same side of the Cartesian gap, and both can be legitimately analogized as two living subjects groaning and suffering together. Paul even amplifies his vision of a single living Universe with a metaphor taken from childbirth. Keep in mind that Paul was no detached 17th-Century man of the Enlightenment, and we should make no attempt to demythologize him into our modern mechanistic worldview.

Verse 23

And not only creation, but also we ourselves who have the first fruits of the Spirit, we also ourselves groan within ourselves, eagerly awaiting adoption, the redemption of our body.

ου μονον δε, αλλα και, αυτοι την απαρχην του πνευματος εχοντες, ημεις και αυτοι εν εαυτοις στεναζομεν, υιοθεσιαν απεκδεχομενοι, την απολυτρωσιν του σωματος ημῶν,

The *first fruits of the Spirit* (την απαρχην του πνευματος) is an image referring primarily to a harvest, the first fruits of the wine press or threshing floor. The Spirit in Christianity was given during the feast of Pentecost, a feast referred to in the Jewish calendar as the Feast of Weeks, the principle celebration of the first fruits of the harvest. If one gathers first fruits it means that the harvest has begun, and what one gathers as first fruits is one of a kind and continuous with the rest of the harvest soon to follow. The harvest for Paul was the final ingathering of resurrected bodies at the end of time, and he understood the gift of the Spirit to be but the beginning of this process. The believer lives in the overlap between the ages, and he groans in unity with the whole of the natural world for full liberation and redemption. Paul's second use of the word "groaning" (στεναζομεν) is deliberately intended to recall the groaning of creation in v22 (συστεναζει)[402] The believer groans in the Spirit just as the Universe groans in the Spirit. Both are groaning together for a salvation which has already begun but which at the moment is not complete. Both are groaning together for that total transformation into a "spiritual body" (1 Cor 15.44), for that total conformation to the "likeness of the heavenly man" (1 Cor 15.49).

Verses 24-25

For in terms of hope, we are saved. But hope which is seen is not hope; for who hopes for what he sees?

τη γαρ ελπδι εσωθημεν, ελπις δε βλεπομενη ουκ εστιν ελπις. ο γαρ βλεπει τις εγπιζει;

But if we hope for what we do not see, we await it eagerly with patience.

ει δε ο ου βλεπομεν ελπιζομεν, δι υπομονης απεκδεχομεθα,

The aorist tense which Paul uses in the word *we are saved* (εσωθη-μεν) is surprising and unusual. Paul is not simply saying we hope we are saved, but he expresses firm conviction and full assurance of salvation yet to come. Full salvation lies only in the future, but for those who have the Spirit and are led by the Spirit, this salvation is *certain*. There can be no doubt about salvation, since it is grounded in the powerful experience of the Spirit already given. But no matter how overwhelming this experience may be, it does not allow the believer to disengage from this world and to withdraw into some supernatural high tower. Spirit represents but a foretaste of the fullness of glory to come. Perhaps Paul feared that the Romans, like the Corinthians, might overemphasize the experience of Spirit, and this overemphasis would lead to a dualistic disregard for the believer's involvement and struggle in this world.[403]

Verse 26

In the same way also the Spirit helps us in our weakness. For we do not know what to pray for as we should, but the Spirit itself intercedes on our behalf with inarticulate groans.

ωσαυτως δε και, το πνευμα συναντιλαμβανεται τη ασθενεια ημων, το γαρ τι προσευξωμεθα καθο δει ουκ οιδαμεν, αλλα αυτο το πνευμα υπερεντυγχανει, στεναγμοις αλαλητοις.

The Spirit of God operates not out of man's strength but out of man's weakness (ασθενεια), out of man's utter dependence upon God.

> As with 8.3 the concept ασθενεια denotes the condition of man in this age, indeed in his creatureliness, as creature and not creator, with all that implies for man's need of transcendent support (see on 8.3).[404]

What is important in prayer is not the use of so many eloquent words, but the expression of one's need for and dependence upon God as expressed most appropriately through *inarticulate groans* (στεναγμοις αλαλητοις).

> Paul clearly intends with στεναγμοις to link the thought back to vv 22 and 23. αλαλητος, only here in Biblical Greek, is presumably the opposite of λαλητος (= "endowed with speech" in Job 38.14 LXX), that is, without the speech that distinguishes man from animal.[405]

In verse 22 the whole of creation groans, in verse 23 we ourselves groan, and now in verse 26 the Spirit groans. What creation was doing in verse 22 becomes clearer: it too was groaning in worship just as man and Spirit were groaning. Man's articulate speech distinguishes him from the rest of creation, but when man comes to pray through the help of the Spirit, he is not to pray out of articulate speech but through *inarticulate groans* (στεναγμοις αλαλητοις) in full solidarity with the rest of a worshipping Universe. We may view this inarticulate speech as speaking in tongues if speaking in tongues is understood, not as a "mark of spirituality" or "something to be proud of," but as "something undignifying, something beneath man's self-respect as a rational being."[406]

These "inarticulate groans" of the Spirit correspond beautifully with the free-flowing, non-rational, non-associative movement of the Spirit which we described earlier. Real prayer in the Spirit expresses our oneness and solidarity with the whole of the natural world. Not only is the whole of creation alive but it is actually *praying with man* for its full liberation into glory.

Verse 27

And he who searches the hearts knows what is the Spirit's way of thinking because he intercedes as God would have it on behalf of the saints.

ο δε εραυνων τας καρδιας, οιδεν τι το φρονημα του πνευματος, οτι κατα θεον εντυγχανει υπερ αγιων,

Paul's thought here is very Jewish. God himself, who looks beyond outward appearance and mere words, can see right into the heart of man. There he sees Spirit hidden within the weakness and inability of man. God alone knows the meaning of this inarticulate groaning of Spirit, since it expresses man's unity with all of creation as well as man's utter dependence upon Him. Note the tension within Jewish monotheism expressed in this clear distinction between God and Spirit: Spirit at the dawn of the New Age can no longer be contained within the featureless transcendence of God but is busy interceding on behalf of the saints as God would have it.[407]

Verse 28

And we know that for those who love God everything contributes toward good for those who are called according to his purpose.

οιδαμεν δε οτι τοις αγαπωσιν τον θεον, παντα συνεργει εις αγαθον, τοις κατα προθεσιν κλητοις ουσιν,

Normally in Jewish thought there would have been a link between "loving God" and "keeping his commandments" (e.g. Exod 20.6; Deut 5.10). But here Paul only talks about loving God, maintaining a strong link with his Jewish faith and yet expressing none of the Jewish preoccupation with the Law. The pious hope that everything works out for the best was common in antiquity. Even Greeks and Romans would have felt comfortable with the idea that the providence behind events, no matter how mysterious and difficult to understand, ultimately works out for the good. Paul expresses himself here in a rather vague language which could fit more than one religious system.

But he then places this familiar pious axiom in the context of "loving God," something rather strange for Greco-Roman religiosity. Moreover, since it is "loving God" unrelated to the keeping of the Law, a loving which is in no way coerced or forced, the Christian nuance of a deeply personal and intimate kind of love is implicit in this verse. God's purpose, which drives history to its intended end, works itself out in the personal response of loving God and being completely dependent upon him, and this cuts through any easy distinction between Jew and Gentile. Anyone who loves God stands in continuity with Israel and shares in its calling, and in the context of the previous verses of the one Spirit groaning within the believers and within the whole of the natural world, this calling extends outward to the whole of the Universe. If the whole of the Universe is so called, then how much more certain is the believer in his firm conviction that the purpose at work within the larger whole in no way could work against him in spite of all the suffering and frustration of the present moment.

Verses 29-30

For those he knew beforehand he also predetermined to be conformed to the image of his Son, that he should be the firstborn among many brothers.

οτι ους προεγνω, και προωρισεν, συμμορφους της εικονος του υιου αυτου, εις το ειναν αυτον πρωτοτοκον εν πολλοις αδελφοις,

And those he predetermined, he also called; and those he called, he also justified; and those he justified, he also glorified.

ους δε προωρισεν, τουτους και εκαλεσεν, και ους εκαλεσεν, τουτους και ε δικαιωσεν, ους δε εδικαιωσεν, τουτους και εδοξασεν,

God's purpose at work in bringing the whole of creation to full glory cannot be undone, since it does not work itself out accidentally or blindly. It was clearly foreseen right from the very beginning of time. "Here

Paul obviously means to embrace the whole sweep of time and history, from beginning to end."[408] Paul emphasizes the sureness of the end as set forth from the very beginning. What is this end? For Paul it meant conformation to the image of the risen and exalted Christ. In contrast to the strongly held idea in the ancient world (including Qumran) of the need for conformity to the laws of the Universe,[409] Paul speaks of conformity to the image which is Christ. The Adam motif surfaces here: "It is a transforming of believing man back into the image of God which disobedient man lost. It is the sharing of his glory with the man he had made and into which he had never fully entered (3.23)."[410] Christ is the image of the "new humanity of the last age, the firstborn (of the dead) of a new race of eschatological people in whom God's design from the beginning of creation is at last fulfilled."[411]

We see then that Paul's view of history has much in common with a process understanding of reality. History for Paul is not cyclical: it has a beginning and an end, and it unfolds within the framework of a single open-ended metapurpose stretching over an immense span of time. For Paul, history is driven not by static laws but by the image which is Christ. Nothing is predetermined in some static or fixed way except its glorious and life-filled *finale* as defined generally by the resurrection of Christ, understood as that absolute victory of life over death. Things do go wrong (Adam's sin), adjustments must be made (salvation in Christ), but the goal which God set forth from the beginning, to bring man and all of creation to full glory, will certainly be accomplished in Christ.

Verse 31

What shall we say in view of these thing? If God is for us, who is against us?[412]

τι ουν ερουμεν προς ταυτα; ει ο θεος υπερ ημων, τις καθ ημων;

Dunn underlines the Jewish character of the question: *If God is for us, who is against us?*

Its force derives from Jewish monotheism. The confidence is rooted not simply in *some* god being "for us," but the *one* God. That is why the answer to the question itself can be left open, and does not depend on the answer "No one." There may be many "against us" (cf.

vv 38-39), but in relation to the one God, they are nothing.[413]

Besides the one God, implied in Paul's question is a host of lesser gods and goddesses. Nothing could paint an animist picture more clearly. Once again we note that Paul's position is far from 17th-Century rationalism. Who are these lesser gods who could compete with God? Should we try to demythologize and explain them in more modern categories? No, let us do away with the myths and superstitions surrounding mechanistic and supernatural categories, and let us leave these gods and goddesses firmly in place as very real entities at work throughout the whole of a living Universe.

Verse 32

He who indeed did not spare his own Son but gave him up for us all, how shall he not also with him give us all things?

ος γε του ιδιου υιου ουκ εφεισατο αλλα υπερ ημων παντων παρεδωκεν αυτον, πως ουχι και συν αυτω τα παντα ημιν χαρισεται;

This talk of God not sparing even his own Son is an echo perhaps of Abraham's offering of Isaac (Gen 22.12). In Rm 3.25 and 8.3 Paul speaks of Christ's death as a sacrifice provided by God, and in 4.24 he refers to Christ's death as a handing over. But the point that Paul seems to be pushing here is "God's commitment to his own in and through Christ."[414]

Remember that through the sin of Adam man broke away from his relationship of dependence on God, and as a consequence, the Universe was transformed into a meaningless and futile reality (verse 20). It became a reality at all times under the domination of death (Rm 5.17). We might say that it no longer resembles a living and purpose-filled organism but a dead and useless machine. Modern man has modeled the Universe after a machine, declaring his independence with respect to God and establishing himself as lord over all creation. This reflects precisely that proud and independent attitude of mind which Paul described so vividly and argued against so forcefully throughout his letter to the Romans.

Here in verse 32 Paul asserts God's firm commitment to a creation marred by the sin of Adam. God gave his own Son to death on behalf of a death-filled Universe so that through his death, it might be restored to life. Paul sees Christ as God's very own commitment to the Universe. Just as we can speak of the Spirit as "the first installment and guarantee of God's redemptive purpose" on the individual level (8.23), so too we speak of Christ's death, resurrection, and exaltation as "the first installment and guarantee of the fulfillment of God's creative purpose" on the cosmic level.[415] The believer knows that through his experience of Spirit he will not be handed over to death. In the same way, the Universe knows that through its experience of what has taken place in the death and resurrection of Christ that it too will not be handed over to death but enter into the fullness of life.

The thought continues that if God has already made such a commitment and given so much, then surely he will graciously give us all things. After all it was God's original intention that man be given *all things* (τα παντα), that he be given dominion over all creation. But through the sin of Adam, man lost the rightful and proper exercise of his lordship over creation. The lordship over creation does not belong to man in this present age: it lies only in the future with the full restoration and redemption of all things in Christ. For the moment it belongs to Christ, who alone is at the right hand of God and who alone is *Lord of the Universe.*

Verses 33-34

Who will bring charges against the elect of God? It is God who justifies.

τις εγκαλεσει κατα εκλεκτων θεου; θεος ο δικαιων,

Who is there to condemn? It is Christ (Jesus) who died, rather was raised, who is also at the right hand of God, who also intercedes on our behalf.

τις ο κατακρινων; Χριστος (Ιησους) ο αποθανων, μαλλον δε εγερθεις, ος και εστιν εν δεξια του θεου, ος και εντυγχανει υπερ ημων,

Here Paul evokes a scene of the heavenly court: "Like a court officer seeking out witnesses for the prosecution, Paul challenges the whole galaxy of created beings of all ages: 'Who will bring a charge against

God's elect?'"[416] Implied in Paul's question, *Who is there to condemn?* (τις ο κατακρινων), Dunn sees "the Satan, or any other of the hostile angelic or spiritual forces who have chosen to stand out against God."[417] Among all these spiritual beings, Christ plays the unique mediatorial role as intercessor:

> The Judge's "right-hand man" is on our side, a more powerful, and more favored advocate than any who might plead against him. Here Paul takes up, unusually for him, the idea of Jesus as heavenly inter-cessor, perhaps again echoing an already familiar Christian formula. The idea was popular elsewhere in earliest Christian faith, and had obviously been adapted from the older Jewish belief in the role of archangels as heavenly intercessors. Paul's point would then be that the decisive factor for believers is Christ's exaltation to a position of special favor and authority beside God (his right hand - Ps 110.1), above that of any (other) angelic being (including the Satan). The suc-cess of his advocacy over that of any challenge is assured, since his resurrection and exaltation to God's right hand was God's own doing, the mark of God's own authorization and approval of those he repre-sents.[418]

The Universe, for Paul, is filled with whole galaxies of spiritual beings, and through his resurrection and exaltation, Christ has been raised to a position of special favor and authority beside God, far above Satan and all other angelic powers. None of these angelic beings can challenge his power and authority, for he has been established as Lord of the Universe by God himself.

Verses 35-39

> *Who will separate us from the love of Christ? Affliction, or dis-tress, or persecution, or hunger, or nakedness, or danger, or sword?*

> τις ημας χωρισει απο της αγαπης του Χριστου; θλιψις η στενοχωρια η διωγμος η λιμος η γυμνοτης η κινδυνος η μαχαιρα,

> *As it is written, For your sake we are being killed all the day; we are reckoned as sheep for the slaughter.*

> καθως γεγραπται οτι, Ενεκεν σου θανατουμεθα ολην την ημεραν, ελογισθνημεν ως προβατα σφθγης.

But in all these things we prevail completely through him who loved us.

αλλ εν τουτοις πασιν υπερνικῳμεν δια του αγαπησαντος ημας,

For I am convinced that neither death nor life, nor angels nor rulers, neither things present nor things to come, nor powers,

πεπεισμαι γαρ οτι ουτε θανατοδ ουτε ζωη, ουτε αγγελοι ουτε αρχαι, ουτε ενεστωτα ουτε μελλοντα, ουτε δυναμεις,

neither height nor depth, nor any other creature will be able to separate us from the love of God which is in Christ Jesus our Lord.

ουτε υψωμα ουτε βαθος, ουτε τις κτισις ετερα, δυνησεται ημας χωρισαι απο τνδ αγαπης του θεου τνς εν Χριστῳ Ιησου τῳ κυριω ημῳν,

Who will separate us from the love of Christ? Paul denies rhetorically the possibility of being separated from the love of Christ. It would be ridiculous even to entertain the idea that such separation is possible. Paul's free interchange of the "love of God" with the "love of Christ" is striking. That Paul could make such a statement with regard to a contemporary of his who was crucified some 25 years previous without abandoning in any way his faith in the oneness of God is truly amazing. We suggest that Paul could make such a statement because he did not confound the theological with the cosmological. A clear distinction had been made between the one and only God and the one and only Lord.

Who or what then can separate us from his love? In the midst of the incessant turmoil and pain which Paul no doubt experienced as a missionary and apostle, he could say with full assurance: "in all things we prevail completely through him *who loved us.*" His amazing strength was derived no doubt from the personal and intimate nature of his relationship with "him who loved us." Paul's use of the past tense here probably takes the reader back to the supreme love that Christ displayed on the cross. There on the cross Christ conquered the last enemy, death, in glorious resurrection, and therefore no matter what should happen, Paul's confidence could not be shaken.

Paul makes his point with the deepest personal conviction: "For I am convinced" (implying in Greek that he continues to be convinced and that his assurance on this point is unshakable) that not even the great hostile power of death, not even life itself in this age of suffering, not even angels or rulers, not even things present or things to come (a reference to time), not even powers, not even height or depth (a reference to space), nor any other creature or power within the Universe, should ever be able to separate us from the love of God which is in Christ Jesus our Lord. For Paul, the Universe is one in the love of God made manifest in Christ Jesus our Lord.

Of further interest here are Paul's *angels* (αγγελοι), rulers (αρχαι), and powers (δυναμεις). With regard to αγγελοι, Dunn says:

> Paul probably has in mind particularly the idea of angels as inhabiting the lower reaches of heaven (or lower heavens; cf. 2 Cor 12.2; Eph 6.12), and therefore as a potential barrier between God and his people on earth; but also perhaps the idea of angels as rulers of the nations (Deut 32.8; Dan 10.13; Sir 17.17; Jub 15.31-32) and therefore potential opponents to God's extending his direct rule over the Gentiles as well as the Jewish nation.[419]

With respect to αρχαι:

> Rulers is the most frequently used name for angelic and demonic powers in the different listings of the Pauline corpus.[420]

With respect to δυναμεις:

> Another title for supernatural beings, quite familiar in extraBiblical Greek as well as Judeo-Christian literature. *It was natural to conceive of heavenly beings as characterized by power.*[421]

Dunn then goes on to situate these beings in a supposedly modern context:

> What Paul actually believed about heavenly beings and their power over events and individuals on earth is never clear; the existential realities about which he was most concerned were primarily sin and death. His concern here, however, is pastoral rather than speculative.[422]

We do not believe that Paul would have introduced ideas concerning spiritual beings right at the very high point of his letter, if these spiritual beings were not very real entities in the lives of the people to whom he was writing. After all, they were "characterized by power." Some were capable of "ruling entire nations." If Lovelock, Margulis and Margalef point to autopoietic structures on a planetary level, it might not seem so strange then to speak of autopoietic structures on the level of entire nations. Not every self-organizing process submits itself to the larger whole, since as a partially autonomous subject it exercises that degree of the freedom available at its particular level of self-organization. We can easily point to runaway processes that no longer operate within the framework of the larger whole. Like cancers they have genuine power to kill and destroy. Because Paul conceived of certain spiritual entities as having very real power to separate from the love of God in Christ Jesus our Lord, he mentioned them in the very pastoral context of relativizing their awesome power (see Eph 6.10-13). If they were not perceived by Paul's readers as exercising real power, then the point which Paul was trying to get across, right at the high-point and climax of his letter, would have amounted to nothing more than a lot of pious hand-waving. What Paul seems to say quite clearly is that their power is real, but God's power as manifest in Christ Jesus is infinitely greater. The rich animistic context in which Paul's thought is grounded shines forth unequivocally. Paul was no rationalist or existentialist. His Universe was filled with whole galaxies of living voices, and Christ stood among them all as sovereign Lord.

In conclusion, we see that Paul, never departing for a moment from his Jewish faith, broadens the base of law and covenant to include not just Jews, and not just Jews and Gentiles, but the whole of a living Universe. Redemption, therefore, moves far beyond a merely personal or human affair: it is above all else a cosmological event, encompassing the whole of the Universe. Paul explicitly described this Universe as single living organism, and he even extended this picture by means of a metaphor taken from childbirth. The Universe groans in the Spirit in eager anticipation of the final glorious unveiling from heaven of the full status of the sons of God. Once these sons of God enter upon their full inheritance and come to share in the glory of God, then creation knows that it will no longer be subjected to the futility and emptiness brought into this world by the sin of Adam, that it will be set free from the slavery of corruption and sin, and that it too will be given its full share in the glory of the children of God. The Universe anxiously and painfully awaits, as a woman about to give birth, its full liberation and redemption, understood by Paul as the total conformation of all things to the glory and image made manifest in Christ.

Man also groans in the Spirit, worshipping in oneness and solidarity with the whole of a living Universe. He now operates out of the supreme confidence that nothing has the power to work against God's purpose, framed from the beginning of time, to bring this Universe into the fullness of glory. Nothing has the power to separate from the love of God made manifest in Christ Jesus the Lord, for this same Christ has been established as sovereign Lord of the Universe. That very power which organizes an entire Universe from within itself has become completely identified with the supreme love which Christ made manifest on the cross. On the cross Christ conquered the last great hostile power of death in glorious resurrection, and therefore no other angelic or demonic power could ever destroy this love or separate us from it.

Dunn argues that we should not read Paul in terms of the concerns and preoccupations of 16th-Century Martin Luther. But we suggest that an even greater hermeneutical trap awaits the exegete who reads and interprets Paul in the light of 17th-Century mechanistic and supernaturalistic categories of thought. Modern process science gives us much insight into the highly complex dynamics of natural systems, and here we acquire a whole new vocabulary with which to approach and to understand the pre-mechanistic world of Paul. We need not demythologize the angels, demons and all those other subjects or minds whom Paul described so vividly in Romans. Rather in their complex interrelatedness they constitute the very structure of a living Universe.

Like many New Testament exegetes before him, Dunn has a tendency to draw upon existentialist categories of interpretation. Existentialism arose in reaction to the crass inhumanity of a mechanistic world view, and it fights courageously to reassert the value of all that is human. But existentialism unfortunately leaves unchallenged far too many of the fundamental presuppositions underlying mechanistic thought. Existentialism represents at best a halfhearted and feeble attempt to liberate man from the mechanistic shackles of modernity. But it is not just humanity that stands in need of liberation. Every other level within our multileveled Universe also yearns to be free with all the depth of desire and eager anticipation which Paul described so beautifully in his letter to the Romans.

So as a key to unlocking the secrets of the New Testament, existentialism is extremely limited and incomplete. In our search for New Testament meaning, we gain very little insight in extracting some existential kernel or core of truth. The comprehensive categories of modern process science steer us clear of a narrow existentialism, and they establish the priority of the cosmological as a new interpretative principle within New Testament studies. We do not deny the existential but in no way does it take priority over the cosmological. Since the existential derives meaning only within the comprehensive framework of the cosmological, we arrive at the rather strange conclusion that the New Testament contains within itself its own principle of interpretation. The New Testament points to a single living reality which bridges organically both past and present. It points to the cosmological reality of Word and Spirit immediately and directly available to the exegete in the ecstatic and prophetic experience of worship. The same cosmological reality that overwhelmed Paul on the road to Damascus 2,000 years ago is available to the worshipper of today, and it is this same experiential reality which breathes meaning and life into the New Testament text.

On the one hand, the exegete knows full well that he could never go back to the past and reconstruct it objectively. An objective reconstruction and representation of a pre-given world past or present is an illusion. His reading of the New Testament could never be understood as an exercise in historical objectivity laying out the "bare facts" of what happened. He knows full well that his exegesis remains at all times highly personal and interpretative. Yet on the other hand he knows that his exegesis should not be understood as an exercise in pure subjectivity where he simply stares at himself in a mirror, naively reading back his own concerns and pre-occupations onto the First-Century text. A sound theory of knowledge does not isolate truth all in the subject or all in the object.

The exegete avoids the pitfalls of the purely objective or the purely subjective primarily in and through the act of worship. The hermeneutical bridge linking subject and object, past and present, is the Universe itself immediately and directly accessible in the ecstatic and prophetic experience of worship. Therefore worship from within the very heart of a living Universe is central to the methodology of the exegete. He may bring to bear all the resources of modern science in his critical analysis of a text, but a deep participatory experiential re-enactment within his own imagination of those vivid New Testament images that originally gave rise to a particular text constitute a vital and indispensable element in unlocking its meaning. Those powerful images arising in worship transform and restructure the entire selective apparatus by which the exegete reads and interprets a text, and every prophetic reconstruction unfolding within his imagination changes irreversibly the character of larger whole. If we really want the New Testament text to come alive, then we must operate as both exegete and prophet, as both scientist and worshipper. We are not simply dissecting words and phrases within an ancient text, but we are actually participating in the prophetic reconstruction of a Universe.

So as we return to that grand cosmological vision of Paul, not only do we uncover the principal means by which we are to read and understand the New Testament, but we also uncover the very center and core of our Christian faith. In unison with the whole of the natural world we sigh, we groan, and we cry out in the deepest adoration and praise. In so doing we find our meaningful place within this vast unfolding cosmological process.

Conclusion

Throughout this book we have set aside the explanations of the supernaturalist and the mechanist as explanations which explain everything and nothing at all. The arguments of the supernaturalist are superfluous and unnecessary, and the mechanist adopts a circular reasoning and simply postpones the demand for explanation. If the mechanist grows weary of the monotony of logical circles, he might invoke his ultimate theory of explanation: the supernatural. The supernaturalist and the mechanist derive great comfort from one another, for in the final analysis, an automaton needs an external God.[423]

An epistemology worthy of the name must arrive at a principle of explanation which really explains. In the end, it must address squarely the question of purpose. In chapter two we raised this question quite explicitly in our example of the small child. Remember he asked his parents why, and the only answer that he received was that things are so because things are so. Was the small child wrong in asking why? Was the simple thrust within him toward knowledge misguided? Instinctively we feel that the small child is not at all misguided in asking why. Although his knowledge may be partial, provisional and extremely limited, we urge him on as best we can in the hope and belief that even though he may never acquire all knowledge in his lifetime, the knowledge that he will acquire will be far better and far more meaningful than no knowledge at all.

We noted all along that the purpose of a living organism unfolds from within the dynamics of its own internal self-organization, but at the same time we emphasized that this purposeful unfolding is difficult to pin down, since it always takes place in constant interaction with that degree of the new and unexpected available to it at its particular level of self-organization. How are we to understand purpose within an organismic context when a living organism possesses a principle by which purpose continually shifts and changes? This question becomes even more complex when we go back to what we have said in our first chapter about the interrelatedness of all reality. Since nothing can be seen, understood or defined in isolation from everything else, the purpose of any one thing is inextricably tied up with the purpose of everything else. But purpose on the level of the whole becomes a very tricky concept to deal with, since we situate Spirit on the level of the whole precisely as that incredible source of newness within our Universe. We cannot deny purpose on the level of the whole, for to say there is no purpose would be equivalent to saying there is no Word and hence no self-organization on the level of the whole. But at the same time we can never pin down Word and the purpose unfolding within Word in an exact way, since Word continually evolves and grows from out of the newness and unexpectedness of Spirit. Since we cannot even appeal to the concept of God to dispel this universal fuzziness, the evolution of our Universe remains at all times an open-ended process, the only goal or purpose of which is contained fully within itself, as the ever-increasing differentiation and complexification of itself, which we understand not only as the differentiation and complexification of knowledge and life, but also as the differentiation and complexification of its own internal beauty and splendor. It knows that it is on the right track, that real progress in being made, according to that which matches the brightness and beauty of its own internally self-differentiating Glory.

In a living organism, purpose does not unfold from without but precisely from within, and when this reasoning is applied to the whole of the Universe, our search for a real explanatory principle is rooted and grounded in Spirit as the source of the inherent creativity which our Universe possesses in and of itself. When the little child asks why, or when a scientist gazes in wonder over a starry sky at night and puzzles over the origin and purpose of it all, ultimately we can go no further than to Spirit, and just as Spirit grounds the truly historical unfolding of the Universe in time, assuring that the future is not contained in a present which in turn is all preset and determined from the past, so, too, Spirit grounds our historically conditioned knowledge and guarantees that our knowledge is not simply the unfolding of some supernatural plan or eternal law which has been there all along. Time, knowledge, beauty and life, all freely unfold from that primordial source of the new-ness and unexpectedness of Spirit.

Therefore in our search for a principle of explanation that really explains, we can point no further than to the Universe itself - a Universe growing and evolving in that marvelous interaction of Word drawing all from that endlessly creative source of Spirit.

In this book we have elaborated within a modern context upon that ancient cosmological synthesis grounded in the two internal gods of Word and Spirit. We have borrowed from Stoicism the notion of an active and passive principle operating on the level of the whole of the Universe, and not unlike the Stoics, we have developed the idea that every level within our Universe is a microcosm of the whole, each reflecting and mirroring its fundamental bipolarity. At the same time we have followed Philo the Jew in dematerializing or Platonizing Logos, and we have taken great delight in the clear distinction which Philo made between the tangible reality of Logos within the Universe and the completely unknowable and unreachable God. Furthermore, we have followed the early Christians as they came to realize that the man Jesus of Nazareth, by virtue of his death, resurrection and glorification, could be none other than that man in whom this preexistent self-organizing power within the Universe came to full expression. As Jews these early followers of Christ were not afraid to take the rather impersonal lan-guage of cosmology and to apply it to a particular person. This peculiar blending of the cosmological and the personal did not infringe in any way upon the unity and distinctiveness of God, while at the same time, it gave Christianity its truly special character among the many syncretist movements of the First-Century period. It may not have been unusual for someone during this period to view the Universe as a single living organism, but it was quite unusual within the context of Greco-Roman and even Jewish spirituality to relate to the one and only Lord of this Universe in a deeply personal and intimate way.

But the experience of a personal Lord did not capture for any of the early followers of Christ the fullness of what it meant to be Christian. For over and against the person of Christ, there was always that extremely fluid and nebulous reality whom they all referred to as Spirit. The early Christians used metaphors of wind and water to describe the random and unpredictable movement of Spirit within the human heart. When the Spirit of Christ makes her presence felt, risk, excitement and newness fill the air, and in this very special state of mind, just about anything can happen. The tension between what is and what could be, between the ordinary and the extraordinary, between the commonplace and the miraculous, is stretched to the point where we inevitably witness that "breaking through of boundaries and recasting of traditions," as Dunn would say, which continually gives rise to *new* structures and *new* patterns of tribal self-organization. In this way christology remains a fully open-ended process, always operating at the apocalyptic edge, and hence always ready to move with that aspect of the new and unexpected which matches the brightness and beauty of its own internally self-differentiating Glory.

Finally, all this is set against the background of a rich pre-mechanistic animism. Together with the whole of the natural world, we groan and cry out in the deepest adoration and praise as we await in eager anticipation that final conformation of all things into the beauty of that glorious image made manifest in Christ.

So together with the Stoics, the Platonists, the Jews, Christians and animists, we proclaim with the deepest assurance, *the Universe is one.*

In our first chapter we examined the process science of Ilya Prigogine and his school of thought, and even though Prigogine has taken us far beyond the limited vocabulary of mechanistic science and right to the threshold of a self-organizing Universe, from within his science or any other science, we can never enter into this marvelous domain and experience it in a direct and immediate way. In our last chapter we examined the New Testament with the help of James D.G. Dunn, and even though Dunn focuses quite clearly on the bipolarity of Word and Spirit, he still holds at times to an existentialist interpretation which robs them of their full cosmological significance. Prigogine without Dunn and Dunn without Prigogine are both incomplete and ultimately unstable, but as soon as we bring them together, we discover the bonds of a *holy alliance.* For what meaning can we attach to the New Testament reality of Lord, Logos or Wisdom, if we continue to view it as some theological category in no way related to that awesome power capable of organizing an entire Universe from within itself? What meaning can we attach to the New Testament reality of Spirit, if we continue to view it as some theological category in no way related to the endlessly creative source of newness within our Universe? What meaning can we attach to Mind, if we do not experience it prophetically in the intimacy of true worship? What meaning can we attach to Newness, if we do not experience it ecstatically in all the fullness and excitement of a real Pentecost? In the context of a valid theory of knowledge and life, science and religion could never be happy simply living next to one another in peaceful co-existence. On the contrary, even though each operates under a completely different set of constraints, they hunger and thirst for one another, complementing and stabilizing one another so powerfully within modern consciousness, that each one of us to some extent must be both scientist and worshipper.

For in the final analysis we are living in a single Universe, and this unique *experience* carries us far beyond the language of any particular scientific discipline, far beyond the language of any particular denominational affiliation. If we really let ourselves go, we enter into a domain so vast and extensive that human consciousness is expanded and stretched as far out as the creative fullness of Spirit itself. No language but the language of ecstasy could begin to describe what takes place here. But even the most exalted ecstatic state is simply setting the stage for those precious moments when living Word selects and speaks. In the light of those leading, guiding, organizing and saving images generated through the interaction of Word and Spirit, the words of all other levels are compared, evaluated, judged and selected. Only those words of a particular level are allowed to grow which match somehow in a limited way the unspeakable beauty of the larger self-differentiating whole. This beauty leads and guides the scientist to ask the right questions and to pursue vigorously and excitedly the way of truth on whatever level it should unfold. He may stand firmly and with great proficiency within a single discipline, or he may even stand at the philosophical crossroads of several disciplines, but at every instant he humbly and freely submits all to the lordship of the larger whole. He may delve as deeply as possible into the truth of a particular level, but never for a moment does he lose sight of that larger truth in which he participates. Not only does he meet regularly with others of the same discipline to share and exchange ideas, not only does he take part in interdisciplinary research and development, but even more importantly he assembles with his fellow scientists as well as other brothers and sisters in the deepest ecstatic and prophetic praise. His worship does not represent some peculiar personal eccentricity, but rather it forms the heart and core of his method as a scientist.

Could it be then that what happens in worship is the closest we could ever come to an experience of how nature itself has been selecting, thinking, anticipating and evolving long before we humans ever came on the scene? Yes, and in tapping into the collective memory and imagination of a Universe, we actively participate in its ongoing evolution. The newness and beauty which we encounter in the act of worship have the power to transfigure and transform the entire selective apparatus by which we construct and enact the local, and every local prophetic event crystallizing within our imaginations changes irreversibly the evolution of the larger whole. Yet this dynamic involves not only the interaction of the local and the global bidirectionally impacting and illuminating one another, but it also involves the interaction of the beginning and the end, where a future is continually selected and anticipated according to that which matches the unspeakable beauty of an evolving Universe. Large, small, beginning and end, actually create and re-create one another within the comprehensive subjectivity of a Universe.

In this book we have argued for the introduction of a strong cosmological viewpoint in both science and religion, and this implies a radical and painful reformation of both science and religion as generally understood and practiced here in the West. We have called into question the science of those who hide behind the simplicity of a mechanistic universe and in no way take into account the genuine complexity of the world in which we live. These scientists fabricate far too many easy explanations which in their utter triviality, coldness and indifference, leave the majority of us entirely dissatisfied. Likewise we have called into question the supernaturalism of so many Christians, Catholic as well as Protestant, who hide behind a dying and distant God to escape the full reality of a living Universe. Sadly, most of us in the West are hidden atheists. We know nothing of the wholeness and holiness of our Universe, and consequently we know nothing of the one God revealed therein.

So the time has come to abandon the simplicity of the mechanical and the superfluity of the supernatural. As we do so, we will discover, no doubt, that our Universe not only lives, but it also contains that amazing ability to heal and renew itself. As old institutions and ideologies within the West crumble and fall, we need not be afraid. For what we are witnessing in fact is our own transformation and renewal. This then gives us every reason to turn to the future in hope. For the whole of creation always and everywhere reverberates with the power of that life-giving voice which continually cries out from the throne: "Behold! I am making all things new!" (Rev 21.5).

Appendix: Sir Isaac Newton

Modern science arose in no other place and time than Europe in the 16th and 17th centuries, and we could hardly imagine a single individual who has contributed more to the rise of modern science than Sir Isaac Newton (1642-1727). His "Mathematical Principles of Natural Science," first published in 1687, appear to most readers as the epitome of scientific rationality. Obviously we cannot doubt that Newton was a scientist in the fullest sense of the word, yet Betty J. T. Dobbs, professor of history at the University of California, makes very clear, in a very informative and thought-provoking book called *The Janus Faces of Genius,* that Newton was at the same time one of the most brilliant theologians of his day. Are we to assume that Newton's intense preoccupation with philosophical and theological questions was completely irrelevant to those great achievements of his that marked the foundation of modern science?

In the wake of the post-Reformation turmoil of early modern Europe, where much confusion surrounded the interpretation of scripture, where skepticism gnawed away at the foundations of epistemological certainty, where the twin specters of deism and atheism haunted every true effort to believe, Newton felt compelled to engage in science, not simply for the sake of science, but as one among many important ways of coming to a knowledge of God. The primary goal in all his scientific endeavors, declares Betty Dobbs, was the knowledge of God.[424] Newton stood well within the mainstream of Biblical tradition in his firm belief that "the heavens tell out the glory of God, the vault of heaven reveals his handiwork" (Psalm 19).[425] By a careful study of the "frame of nature," Newton hoped to eliminate doubt and uncertainty, and to work out those principles which might demonstrate quite clearly God's continuing activity within the world.

Many scientists today, obviously unaware of Newton's strong religious orientation, describe him very simplistically as a mechanist:

> To the ancients the world was a living organism, but to Newton and his followers it was a unified mechanism - like the interior of a giant watch. Its workings were pristine: precise, mechanical, and mathematical. Once set in motion by the Creator they continued by their own inexorable internal logic.[426]

It is true that in his early student days Newton could be described as an "eclectic corpuscularian," or a "second-generation mechanical philosopher."[427] Like other mechanical philosophers at the time, Newton, the student, unquestioningly assumed the existence of an "all-pervasive material medium which served as an agent of change in the mechanical world."[428] This material medium or ether was completely imperceptible to the senses yet capable of transmitting effects by pressure and impact. Any *apparent* attraction between material bodies could be explained by the purely mechanical encounter of material bodies with these imperceptible particles of ether. By adhering to the dynamics of "impact physics," the mechanical philosophers of Newton's day felt that they could rid natural philosophy of any "incomprehensible occult influences acting at a distance."[429]

However, due to the general passivity of matter, it did not take long for Newton to realize how difficult it would be to explain such things as the cohesion of living forms, life and even gravity in mechanistic terms. It became increasingly difficult for him to explain how the processes which produced the endless variety of living forms could "be relegated to the mechanical actions of gross corpuscles."[430] The cohesion of living forms would appear to be qualitatively different from the random collocation of bumping bits of matter, and just as the atomist philosophers of antiquity had been strongly criticized for this same reason, Newton felt compelled to question the philosophical assumptions of contemporary corpuscularianism.

The most comprehensive answer to the problem posed by atomism had been already worked out in antiquity by the Stoics, and therefore it is not surprising that Newton turned to Stoicism in his response to the problems raised by the atomists and mechanists of his day. Dobbs maintains that "virtually all of the scanty fragments of ancient Stoicism known today had been recovered by Western Europe in the Renaissance, and Newton had most of them."[431] Surely this would have enabled him to reconstruct a "reasonably sophisticated and comprehensive knowledge of Stoic thought."[432] The Stoics believed that the Universe was permeated and shaped by Logos, and not only was the entire Universe alive but it was "rational and orderly and under the benevolent, providential care of the Deity."[433] Within this context Newton could affirm: "The earth is a great animal or rather an inanimate vegetable (that) draws in ethereal breath for its daily refreshment and vital ferment and transpires again with gross exhalations."[434] Dobbs maintains that "Newton almost certainly derived that *animistic* conception of the earth from the Stoics."[435] How far we are here from Barrow's drab and inaccurate characterization of Newton's universe as "a unified mechanism - like the interior of a giant watch!"

In his fight against materialistic monism, Newton made a sharp distinction between the vegetable and the mechanical. In 1672 he spoke of a "vast and fundamental" difference between vegetable chemistry and vulgar chemistry.[436] Vulgar chemistry relates to the grosser texture of sensible matter, whereas vegetable chemistry relates to that invisible principle by which grosser substances become organized into that endless variety of living forms. The roles played by the vegetable and the mechanical are evident in Newton's understanding of putrefication: "It is putrefication that reduces matter to its ultimate state of disorganization, where the particles of matter are all alike and hence can be remodeled in any form whatsoever by the vegetable spirit."[437] For Newton putrefication was essential to all generation, for it reduced everything to a chaotic undifferentiated primordium upon which the vegetable spirit could operate in generating new life. Heavily influenced by his study of alchemy, Newton wrote that everything comes "out of black Chaos and its first matter through the separation of the elements and the illumination of matter."[438]

For Newton matter was always passive, and the activation of matter was the province of a divine, creative, illuminating principle. But how should we understand this divine principle in Newton's thought? Was the divine simply God? Although Newton was heavily influenced by Stoic thought, he nonetheless went on to modify Stoicism in important ways, especially in the firm distinction he made between God and Logos. Newton repeated over and over again in his theological writings that God was "the invisible God whom no eye hath seen nor can see,"[439] a phrase highly reminiscent of what we have seen earlier in both Philo and John. For this reason most historians agree that by early in 1673 Newton had become a convinced Arian.

As an Arian, Newton denied that the Logos was of the same substance as God, but this denial had a very positive aspect: it gave him the freedom to accord a vast cosmological significance to the Logos/Christ as the unique creator, framer and sustainer of the Universe. Even though God for Newton was wholly other and transcendent, He maintained a continued relationship with the Universe in and through Logos: "The Christ was the intermediary through whom and by whom God created the world and interacted with it."[440] Christ was the agent of the transcendent God who "formed and transformed the world of matter according to the design of God's omnipotent will."[441] Newton avoided the trap of the absentee Deity of deism by utilizing the cosmic role of Christ who, as mediator, continually puts God's will into effect.[442] Newton was a firm believer in the principle that "the supreme God doth nothing by Himself which He can do by others."[443]

The more orthodox Stoicism within antiquity had held that everything was material including Logos, but this created the problem of how to explain the total blending of corporeal logos with corporeal body. How are two corporeal bodies to occupy the same place at the same time? Philo of Alexandria solved this problem as we have seen by his Platonization of Stoicism: Logos was no longer material and corporeal but spiritual and incorporeal. We know that Philo's brilliant synthesis of Stoicism, Platonism, and Judaism had a most profound impact upon Newton, and we have very good evidence to believe that Newton read Philo directly.[444] In Philonic Stoicism Newton even found a conceptual framework that enabled him to work out an explanation for gravity. In the context of incorporeal Logos, he no longer felt obliged to hold on to any vestige of a corporeal ether.

Newton also came to deny the presence of a corporeal ether through his own careful observation and experimentation. If ether were corporeal, then one should expect to find a frictional drag as particles of matter should pass through it. Since there was no frictional drag or retardation associated with the motion of a pendulum through a vacuum, since there was no evidence for the retardation of planets and comets in their passage through the heavens, Newton rejected any notion of mechanical causation for gravity. By drawing support from ancient cosmic thought and especially from the Platonized version of ancient Stoicism he had uncovered within Philo, Newton concluded that only immaterial spirit could penetrate to the center of a body without causing retardation. For a time Newton, wavered in his Arianism and believed that God subsumed the operation of gravity directly.[445] Yet sometime between 1710 and 1720, Newton wrote a final creed in which he clearly stated that immaterial Logos was in charge of all natural active entities including the stately gravitational motions of the heavenly bodies.[446]

Yet in spite of the firm distinction Newton made between God and Logos, in spite of the fact that the invisible God could not be seen, in spite of the fact that the supreme God does nothing by himself that can be done by another, it would appear that Newton did not go far enough in his Arian christology. He continued to speak directly of such things as the omnipresence[447] and will[448] of God. This latter concept of the will of God illustrates very well the logical trap anyone inevitably falls into in an effort to speak about God in a direct and unqualified manner. A classical distinction existed within the theology of Newton's day between the *potentia dei ordinata and absoluta*. If one stressed too much the orderly aspect of God's will (ordinata), one ended up with a predetermined and necessary universe, while if one stressed too much the absolute freedom of God to do whatever he wanted (absoluta), one ended up with an arbitrary and radically contingent universe. Gassendi had criticized Descartes for not maintaining a proper balance between the *potentia ordinata* and the *potentia absoluta*. Descartes' constantly operating mechanical laws he felt placed too much emphasis on God's general providence and did not allow enough scope for God's special or extraordinary providence.

In spite of his Arian christology, Newton dove right into this most complex debate, and there he adopted what is known as a voluntarist position. He maintained that God has the *absolute* freedom to do anything that does not involve logical contradiction.[449] The Universe is as it is, therefore, not by necessity, but by the pure unlimited *free will* of God. Newton's voluntarist theology was closely linked to his empirical method in science: the *potentia absoluta* force the scientist to investigate the world in an empirical manner in accordance with its manifest uniqueness and individuality. But if Newton had been consistent in the elaboration of his Arian christology, he need not have situated the *ordinata* or the *absoluta* within God. Surely the concept of Logos should have permitted him to account for all that is ordinary and orderly within the Universe, and if Newton had developed at least a rudimentary pneumatology, the concept of Spirit would have permitted him to account for all that is extraordinary and random within the Universe. How does one combine *simultaneously* and *directly* both aspects of the selective and the random within a unitary conception of the Deity? Surely this involves a logical contradiction of the highest order.

Newton had strayed so far from the orthodox Trinitarian position of "three persons in one God" that in his final credo he did not even find it necessary to consider Spirit.[450] The vibrant New Testament experience of Spirit was certainly lacking within the budding mechanistic culture that surrounded Newton, and many proponents of the new science in the 17th Century had virtually excluded any notion of the random or extraordinary within nature. Even Newton said that "miracles are so called not because they are the works of God but because they happen seldom and for that reason create wonder."[451] His position was very much similar to that of Augustine who maintained that there was only one miracle, creation itself, and when something happens which appears miraculous, then hidden natural causes are at work.[452]

Ancient Stoicism generally had posited a materialistic monism: an active, shaping matter over and against passive, unformed matter. To overcome the problem of the blending of these two types of matter, the active matter within Stoicism was Platonized. But this created however a far more annoying problem: that unhealthy dualism between mind and matter. As much as Newton despised the mechanistic philosophy of Rene Descartes, he never arrived at an epistemological framework which allowed him to overcome the dualism which Descartes had confirmed and elaborated. Over and against the vegetable, Newton still posited the mechanical. Over and against Mind, there was still a preexisting world of passive matter. How easy it would become for the generations following Newton to focus exclusively upon the mechanical.

In conclusion, we see that Newton made a bold attempt to revive within the context of the emerging new science of his day that ancient synthesis of Stoicism, Platonism, Judaism, and Christianity. However, since the science of his day did not entertain any serious notion of the inherently unpredictable, and since the religion of his day lacked the powerful experience of Spirit, he failed to present this synthesis to his contemporaries in a convincing manner. If randomness is not an essential and irreducible feature of our Universe, then ultimately our Universe resembles the "interior of a giant watch" whose operation is perfectly reversible with respect to time. If newness does not manifest itself even within the domain of religious experience, then ultimately our Universe unfolds according to the logic of laws that never change. Only with the inclusion of a vibrant concept of Spirit does that self-organizing power with our Universe begin to evolve in a truly non-mechanistic and non-deterministic way. Only then do we have the "frame" of a Universe capable of revealing something of the glory and majesty of God.

Notes

1 Bateson (1979), p. 2.
2 Ibid., p. 18.
3 Barrow (1991), p. 135.
4 See Guitton (1991), p. 118.
5 See Capra, Steindl-Rast and Matus (1992), p. 103.
6 Jantsch (1980), p. 162.
7 Prigogine and Stengers (1984), p. 22.
8 Ibid.
9 Ibid., p. 9.
10 "Such an explanation, which shifts attention from the interpersonal field to a factitious inner tendency, principle, instinct, or whatnot, is, I suggest, very great nonsense which only hides the real questions." Bateson (1979), p. 143.
11 See Prigogine and Stengers (1984), p. 174.
12 See Barrow (1991), p. 81.
13 Ibid.
14 "Einstein, more than two hundred years after Newton, explained gravity in a surprising and wholly unexpected way. Space is not flat, he decided, but curved, and bodies moving through curved space do not travel in perfectly straight lines but, like marbles rolling across an undulating floor in an old house, are steered this way and that. The ingenious part is that the curvature of space is generated by the presence of mass, so that a heavy object causes a depression into which other objects are drawn. There is no longer a force of gravity, in the old sense. Instead, mass distorts space, and bodies traveling through curved space move

naturally along curving trajectories. If we insist that space is "flat," as in Newtonian dynamics and special relativity, we are bound to attribute the curving paths to the action of some unseen force that diverts bodies from straight lines they would otherwise follow, and this invisible force we call gravity; but if we allow space to be curved, curved trajectories become understandable without any need for a mysterious force." Lindley (1993), p. 79. See ibid, p. 137.

15 See Prigogine and Stengers (1984), p. 218.

16 Barrow (1988), p. 24.

17 Quoted from Capra (1982), p. 70.

18 See Prigogine and Stengers (1984), pp. 224-225.

19 See ibid., p. 227.

20 Davies (1987), p. 168.

21 Ibid.

22 See Prigogine and Stengers (1984), p. 228.

23 Davies (1987), pp. 175-176. Also see ibid., p. 195.

24 Bateson (1987), p. 17.

25 See Bateson (1979), p. 105.

26 See ibid., p. 116.

27 Varela, Thompson, and Rosch (1991), p. 167.

28 See Bateson (1979), p. 105.

29 Bateson (1979), p. 30.

30 See Varela, Thompson, and Rosch (1991), pp. 160-171.

31 "In primates, the participation of subensembles of neurons in color perception has been demonstrated in the thalamus (LGN), primary and extrastriate visual cortex, inferotemporal cortex, and frontal lobes. Most notable is a collection of neurons in the so-called V4 of the extrastriate cortex where even individual neuronal responses can be roughly associated with the color constancies of a visual field." Ibid., p. 161.

32 See ibid., p. 162.

33 See ibid., p. 163.

34 Varela, Thompson and Rosch give the example of an artist who due to an accident became completely color-blind: "As a result, he found foods disgusting and sexual intercourse impossible. He could no longer visually imagine colors, nor could he dream in color. His appreciation of music was also impaired, for he could no longer experience musical tones by synestheticly transforming them into plays of color." Ibid., p. 164.

35 "Our color vision is trichromatic: as we have seen, our visual sys-

tem comprises three types of photoreceptors cross-connected to three color channels. Therefore, three dimensions are needed to represent our color vision, that is, the kinds of color distinctions that we can make. Trichromacy is certainly not unique to humans; indeed, it would appear that virtually every animal class contains some species with trichromatic vision. More interesting, however, is that some animals are dichromats, others are tetrachromats, and some may even be pentachromats." Ibid., p. 182.

36 See ibid., p. 171.

37 See ibid., p. 168.

38 See Bateson (1979), p. 31.

39 "What is crucial is the presupposition that ideas (in the very wide sense of the word) have a cogency and reality. They are what we know, and we can know nothing else." Bateson (1979), p. 207. Note that in the place of "ideas" we substitute "images and pictures."

40 See Jantcsh (1980), p. 7; p. 33

41 See Monod (1972), p. 20.

42 Prigogine and Stengers (1984), p. 99.

43 See Prigogine (1996), p. 37.

44 See Prigogine and Stengers (1984)., p. 115.

45 Regarding entropy, see Prigogine and Stengers (1984), pp. 117-118.

46 Ibid., p. 111.

47 Ibid., p. 116.

48 See ibid., p. 111.

49 See Barrow (1991), p. 152.

50 Prigogine and Stengers (1984), p. 116.

51 See Lindley (1993), p. 233-235.

52 These exciting new ideas are covered in a simple way in Peat (1991): "A key theme within this book is that form and structure emerge spontaneously, for every system and every level in nature has its own authentic life . . . We will see how all systems, from atoms to galaxies, from crystals to bodies, from trees to human insights, are manifestations of spontaneous creation and coming into form." Ibid., p. 76.

53 See Prigogine and Stengers (1984), p. 127.

54 See ibid., p. 150.

55 See Prigogine and Stengers (1984), p. 178 for why it bears this name. Also see ibid., p. 206.

56 See ibid., p. 143.

57 See Prigogine and Stengers (1984), pp. 146-147.

58 See Prigogine (1996), pp. 68-69.

59 See Prigogine and Stengers (1984), p. 162.

60 See ibid, p. 178-179.

61 See Jantsch (1980), p. 46. Also see Prigogine and Stengers (1984), p. 14; p. 178.

62 See Prigogine and Stengers (1984), p. 161.

63 Ibid., p. 16. See ibid., p. 301 as well as Peat (1991), p. 133-134.

64 See Prigogine and Stengers (1984), pp. 169-170.

65 See Jantsch (1980), p. 7.

66 See ibid., pp. 8, 11, 55-56.

67 See Prigogine and Stengers (1984), p. xxiii.

68 See Jantsch (1980), p. 51-53.

69 "According to Don Juan, reality is divided into two aspects, one of which (the tonal) comprises the regularities of a world ordered by our concepts, whereas the other (the nagual) represents the unexpected." Jantsch (1980), p. 229.

70 See Jantsch (1980), p. 11 and p. 56.

71 On solipsism see Barrow (1988), p. 16.

72 See Barrow and Tipler (1986), p. 108.

73 Penrose (1989), p. 340.

74 Ibid., p. 344.

75 See Barrow and Tipler (1986), pp. 322-328 as well as Barrow (1991), p. 45.

76 Red Shift: "The reddening of light from a star that is moving away from us, due to the Doppler effect." Hawking (1988), p. 186. See also ibid., p. 38.

77 See Hawking (1988), pp. 140 and 141.

78 See Barrow abd Tipler (1986), p. 613.

79 Ibid.

80 See Barrow (1991), p. 46.

81 This is a rather inexact formulation of the weak anthropic principle. The first published discussion of the anthropic principle by Brandon Carter back in 1974 already introduced the distinction between weak and strong. See Carter (1974), p. 291. The weak version says simply that the amazing properties of our Universe are self-selected by the fact that they must be consistent with our own evolution and present existence. For a more precise definition of the weak anthropic principle, see Barrow and Tipler (1986), p. 16. The strong version says: "The Universe must have those properties which allow life to develop within it at some stage in its history." Ibid., p. 21.

82 See Hoyle (1983), p. 220; Hoyle and Wickramasinghe (1981), p. 141.

83 See Gould (1991), p. 324.

84 Ibid., p. 115.

85 Nowhere can we find better illustration of how deeply Cartesian dualism infects Western science than in Paul Davies' sausage machine (representing the laws of physics) where the input is matter and the output is mind. See Figure 13 in Davies (1992), p. 215.

86 Gould speaks often of the "bias of adaptationism." See Gould (1991), p. 60.

87 "In sum, the fit between adaptation and environment is loose. Plants and animals have dynamics, directions, limitations, and potentialities given by their entire nature formed by the accidents as well as the needs of many million years in ways much beyond our understanding and for which there can be no simple explanation." Wesson (1991), p. 105.

88 Most historians agree that Darwin was strongly influenced by the two great Scottish economists Thomas Maltus and Adam Smith: "From Malthus, Darwin received the key insight that growth in population, if unchecked, will outrun any increase in the food supply. A struggle for existence must therefore arise, leading by natural selection to survival of the fittest (to cite all three conventional Darwinian aphorisms in a single sentence). Darwin states that this insight from Malthus supplied the last piece that enabled him to complete the theory of natural selection in 1838 (though he did not publish his theory for twenty-one years). Adam Smith's influence was more indirect, but also more pervasive. We know that the Scottish economists interested Darwin greatly and that, during the crucial months of 1838, while he assembled the pieces soon to be capped by his Malthusian insight, he was studying the thought of Adam Smith. The theory of natural selection is uncannily similar to the chief doctrine of laissezfaire economics." Gould (1993), pp. 148-149.

89 Gould (1977b), p. 24.

90 Ibid.

91 Ibid.

92 See ibid., p. 33.

93 Ibid., p. 23.

94 See ibid., p. 26.

95 "It would not be an exaggeration to say that the Darwinian revolution directly triggered this influential Nineteenth-Century conceptualization of Western history as a war between two taxonomic categories

labeled science and religion." Gould (1995), p. 47.

96 Gould (1977b), p. 40.

97 See Gould (1980), p. 158.

98 Gould (1983), p. 41.

99 See ibid.

100 Gould (1977b), p. 41.

101 Ibid., p. 42.

102 Kauffman (1995), p. 202.

103 Ibid, p. 206.

104 Ibid., p. 202.

105 The Russian geneticist Nikolai Ivanovich Vavilov developed back in the 1920's his "law of homologous series in variation." Vavilov pointed to certain internal constraints of inheritance and development, a previous genetic history which channels evolution and limits the number of changes which are possible. According to Gould, Vavilov's explanation for new varities "compromises the cardinal principle of creativity for natural selection. The variations are predictable results within their genetic system. Their occurance is almost foreordained. The role of natural selection is negative. It is an executioner only." Gould (1983), p. 138. Gould defends in part the Vavilovian emphasis: "In many cases, evolutionary pathways reflect inherited patterns more than current environmental demands." Ibid., p. 156. "Each organic design is pregnant with evolutionary possibilities, but restricted in its paths of potential change." Ibid., p. 157. While we may not reduce everything to "laws of form" as we see in Vavilov, we must also take care not to reduce everything to chance alone.

106 See Levy (1992).

107 See Gould's critique of the anthropocentrism of Teilhard de Chardin in Gould (1983), pp. 246-250.

108 See Gould (1983), p. 157.

109 Gould (1987), p. 171.

110 Gould draws attention to an odd-looking parasite called a pentastome which has been remarkably stable for more than 500 million years. See Gould (1995), p. 119.

111 Quoted from Hoyle (1983), p. 38. No original source given.

112 Hoyle (1983), p. 124.

113 Gould (1989), p. 24. See also Gould (1977b), p. 271.

114 Gould (1995), p. 97.

115 Margulis and Sagan (1986), p. 113.

116 Ibid., pp.115-116.

117 Ibid., p. 118.

118 See Denton (1985), p. 44. See Gould (1980), pp. 155-156.

119 Gould (1980), pp. 155-156.

120 See Denton (1985), pp. 88-90.

121 Davies (1987), p. 16.

122 Penrose (1989), p. 306.

123 Along similar lines, Penrose says: "Moreover, the slightest 'mutation' of an algorithm (say a slight change in a Turing machine specification, or in its input tape) would tend to render it totally useless, and it is hard to see how actual improvements in algorithms could ever arise in a random way. (Even deliberate improvements are difficult without 'meanings' being available. This is particularly borne out by the not-infrequent circumstances when an inadequately documented and complicated computer program needs to be altered or corrected; and the original programmer has departed or perhaps died. Rather than try to disentangle all the various meanings and intentions that the program implicitly depended upon, it is probably easier just to scrap it and start all over again!)." Penrose (1989), p. 415.

124 On sickle-cell anemia see Salthe (1985), pp. 189-190.

125 See Denton (1985), p. 90.

126 See Gould (1980), p. 149.

127 "In short, Darwin argued that the geologic record was exceedingly imperfect - a book with few remaining pages, few lines on a page, and few words on each line." Gould (1980), p. 150.

128 Gould (1989), p. 57. See Gould (1980). pp.148-154.

129 See Gould (1989), p. 46; also pp. 263-277.

130 For a more exact chronology of the Cambrian explosion, see Gould (1995), p. 97 & 109.

131 The radically new interpretation of the Burgess Shale goes back primarily to three people: "Three people have played the focal role in these efforts: the originator of the project and the chief force throughout, Harry Whittington, professor of geology at Cambridge University (that is, in British terminology, senior figure and department head), and two men who began as graduate students under him in the early 1970s and have since built brilliant careers on their researches in the Burgess Shale - Simon Conway Morris (now also at Cambridge) and Derek Briggs (now at Bristol University). Whittington also collaborated with two junior colleagues, especially before his graduate students arrived - Chris Hughes and David Bruton." Gould (1989)., p. 83.

132 Ibid., p. 208.

133 "Prokaryotic cells have no organelles - no nucleus, no paired chromosomes, no mitochondria, no chloroplasts. The much larger eukaryotic cells of other unicellular organisms, and of all multicellular creatures, are vastly more complex and may have evolved from colonies of prokaryotes; mitochondria and chloroplasts, at least, look remarkable like entire prokaryotic organisms and retain some DNA of their own, perhaps as a vestige of this former independence. Bacteria and blue-green algae, or cyanophytes, are prokaryotes. All other common unicellular organisms - including the amoeba and paramecium of high-school biology labs - are eukaryotes." Ibid., p. 58.

134 Gould argues that since the 1950's we possess a rich record of Precambrian life. See ibid., p. 56.

135 Ibid., p. 60.

136 Ibid.

137 See ibid., pp. 48-51. Also see Gould (1991), p. 29.

138 Gould(1989), p. 236. Also see ibid., p. 188; pp. 237-239.

139 Ibid., p. 239.

140 Ibid., p. 51.

141 Ibid.

142 Ibid., p. 277.

143 Ibid., p. 278.

144 Ibid., p. 280. Also see Gould (1987), p. 176.

145 Gould (1989), p. 281.

146 Ibid., p. 288.

147 Ibid., p. 289.

148 Ibid., pp. 289-290.

149 See ibid., p. 290. See Gould (1991), p. 30.

150 Gould (1989), pp. 290-291. See also Gould (1983). p. 43.

151 Ibid., p. 44.

152 See ibid., p. 288.

153 Barrow (1991), p. 135.

154 Ibid., pp. 168-170.

155 See Prigogine and Stengers (1984), pp. 169-170.

156 See Wesson (1991), pp.45-49; Denton (1985), pp. 199-209.

157 Denton (1985), p. 209.

158 Ibid., p. 211.

159 Ibid., p. 213.

160 "In my own strongly biased opinion, the problem of reconciling evident discontinuity in macroevolution with Darwinism is largely solved by the observation that small changes early in embryology accu-

mulate through growth to yield profound differences among adults. Prolong the high prenatal rate of brain growth into early childhood and a monkey brain moves toward human size. Delay the onset of metamorphosis and the axolotl of Lake Xochimilco reproduces as a tadpole with gills and never transforms into a salamander." Gould (1980), p. 160.

161 "With preadaptation, we cut through the dilemma of function for incipient stages by accepting the standard objection and admitting that intermediate forms did not work in the same way as their perfected descendents. We avoid the excellent question, What good is five percent of an eye? By arguing that the possessor of such an incipient structure did not use it for sight." Gould (1977b), p. 107. See Gould (1980), p. 157.

162 "Those useful structures that arose for other reasons or for no conventional reason at all, and were then fortuitously available for other usages, we call exaptations." Gould (1983), p. 171.

163 Also see Gould (1977b), pp. 103-110; Gould (1983). p. 63; pp. 170-171.

164 See Gould (1993), pp. 116-117.

165 See ibid., p. 118.

166 See ibid., p. 255.

167 See ibid., p. 117.

168 See Gleick (1987), p. 94.

169 Cairns-Smith (1985), p. 39. See also Wesson (1991), p. 56.

170 Cairns-Smith (1985), p. 60.

171 Wesson (1991), p. 17.

172 Gould (1977b), p. 161. Elsewhere he says: "Correction of error cannot always arise from new discovery within an accepted conceptual system. Sometimes the theory has to crumble first, and a new framework be adopted, before the crucial facts can be seen at all." Gould (1995), p. 127.

173 See Peat (1991), pp. 148-152.

174 Abraham, McKenna, and Sheldrake (1992), p. 68.

175 Peat (1991), p. 151.

176 Abraham, McKenna, and Sheldrake (1992), p. 28.

177 See ibid., p. 68.

178 See Jantsch (1980), p. 31.

179 On communication see Prigogine and Stengers (1984), p. 148; see Peat (1991), pp. 114-117.

180 See Prigogine and Stengers (1984), p. 162.

181 On knowledge, experience and memory, see Jantsch (1980), pp. 49-50.

182 On consciousness, see Jantsch (1980), p. 40.

183 On mind, see ibid., pp. 162-163.

184 Sheldrake leaves uncontested the views of his two friends that we do not need randomness to explain the evolution of a new biological form. See Abraham, McKenna, and Sheldrake (1992), pp. 61-63.

185 Sheldrake (1990), p. 75.

186 See Abraham, McKenna, and Sheldrake (1992), pp. 9-11;14;16;18;29; 50.

187 "We can place the novelty of novelties, the novelty to the nth power of novelty, at the end of the historical process and watch it operate as an attractor without having any information concerning its particulars." Ibid., p. 13. Also see ibid., pp. 9-11; 33.

188 See Sheldrake (1995).

189 See Gould (1977b), p. 15; 44; 125; 161-162; 201. See Gould (1995), p. 94; 148.

190 "Intellectual progress is a complex network of false starts and excursions into trial and error." Gould (1993), p. 109.

191 See Lovelock (1979), p. 8.

192 Ibid., p. 9.

193 Ibid., p. 10.

194 Lovelock (1979), pp. 68-69.

195 See ibid., pp. 84-106.

196 See ibid., p. 19.

197 See Barrow and Tipler (1986), p. 567.

198 See Lovelock (1979); Lovelock (1989).

199 See Gould (1989), p. 24

200 See ibid., p. 51.

201 Gould upholds the uniqueness and individuality of planets, for he says that "planets are more like organisms than billiard balls. They are intricate and singular bodies. Their individuality matters, and size alone will not explain planetary surfaces." Gould (1991), p. 498.

202 The quantum cosmologist Jonathan Halliwell not only poses questions about the origin of the Universe, but he even gives us a possible answer! "According to the picture afforded by quantum cosmology, the universe appeared from a quantum fuzz, tunneling into existence and thereafter evolving classically." Halliwell (1991), p. 35. On tunneling see Lindley (1993), pp. 178-179.

203 See Barrow (1988), p. 2.

204 See Bohm (1980), pp. 48-49.

205 See Augros and Stanciu (1988), p. 90.

206 See ibid., p. 91.

207 "Thousands of examples are known where similar animal species coexist without competing because they eat different foods or are active at different times or otherwise occupy different niches." Ibid., p. 93.

208 "The space that defines a niche need not be large or far from others: three different species of mite occupy different areas of the honey bee's body as their niches." Ibid. p. 95.

209 "Dividing the habitat according to time is another strategy nature uses to prevent competition." Ibid.

210 "Food specialization is one of the simplest ways that animal species avoid competition." Ibid., p. 94.

211 Quoted from ibid., p. 99, originally in Colinvaux, Why Big Fierce Animals Are Rare, pp. 144, 149.

212 Quoted from ibid., p. 102, originally in Colinvaux, Why Big Fierce Animals Are Rare, p. 144.

213 Jantsch (1980), p. 66.

214 Augros and Stanciu (1988), p. 102.

215 Gould (1977b), p. 123.

216 Ibid., p. 124.

217 Ibid.

218 See Augros and Stanciu(1988), p. 103.

219 See ibid.

220 "Every living thing has a dispersal phase at some stage in its life cycle." Ibid., p. 119.

221 "The defense of territory in all species is characterized not by battles to the death, but by highly stereotyped threats, aggressive displays, and appeasement gestures that rarely result in injury." Ibid., p. 120.

222 See ibid., p. 122.

223 See ibid., p. 123.

224 See ibid.

225 See ibid., p. 125.

226 See ibid., p. 127.

227 Ibid., p. 129.

228 See ibid., p. 105; also Jantsch (1980), p. 207.

229 Jantsch (1980), p. 139.

230 Augros and Stanciu (1988), p. 105.

231 Ibid., p. 117.

232   Ibid., originally quoted from Margulis, p. 163. Also see Margulis and Sagan (1986), p. 16.

233 See Gould (1989), pp. 309-311.

234 Jantsch (1980), p. 122.

235 "The origin of multicellular organisms is still very obscure." Ibid., p. 128. Also see Gould (1989), pp. 311-314.

236 Jantsch (1980), p. 128.

237 Quoted from Augros and Stanciu (1988), p. 118, originally in Lewis Thomas, "On the Uncertainty of Science," Phi Beta Kappa, Key Reporter (1980), no. 6, p. 1.

238 Margulis and Sagan (1986), pp. 16-17.

239 Zohar (1990), p. 142.

240 Ibid.

241 Bohm (1969), p. 50.

242 Heisenberg (1974), p. 175.

243 Feynman (1965), p. 171.

244 Penrose (1989), p. 421.

245 Lovelock (1979), p. 142.

246 Gould (1995), p. 96.

247 Darwin (1872), p. 147.

248 Poincare (1958), p.8.

249 See Bateson (1979), p. 137.

250 See Zohar (1990), pp. 159-169.

251 Penrose (1989), p. 424, originally from a letter of Einstein to Hadamard.

252 Jantsch (1980), p. 179.

253 Penrose (1989, p. 427.

254 Ibid., p. 428.

255 Ibid., p. 430.

256 See ibid., p. 430.

257 See ibid., p. 411.

258 Ibid., p. 422.

259 See Briggs and Peat (1984), p. 212.

260   See Jantsch (1980), pp. 110-115; Briggs and Peat (1984), p. 209.

261 Jantsch (1980), pp. 111-112.

262 Dunn (1991), p. 183. In making this point, Dunn refers to Acts 2.24-32; 3.15, 22-26; 10.40-41; 13.30-37; 17.18; 17.31; Romans 1.3-4; 4.24-25; 10.9; 1 Cor 15.1-8.

263 Ibid., p. 184.

264 Dunn (1980), p. 254.

265 See Dunn (1977), pp. 50-54.

266 Dunn (1991), p. 188.

267 Ibid., p. 190.

268 "The point for us to note is that Paul can hail Jesus as Lord not in order to identify him with God, but rather if anything, to distinguish him from the one God (cf. particularly 1 Cor 15.24-28; see also below pp. 225f.)." Dunn (1977), p. 53. Also see Dunn (1991), pp. 190-191.

269 "For First-Century Christians generally this was the title{Lord} Jesus received on his exaltation, by virtue of his resurrection (Acts 2,36; Phil. 2.9-11; cf. Rom. 10.9f.; 1 Cor 16.22): it was the exalted Lord who had supplanted all other 'lords' and absorbed their significance and rule in regard both to the cosmos and to redemption (8.5-6)." Dunn (1980), p. 181. Also see ibid., pp. 108-113; p. 114-115; pp. 170-181.

270 See Dunn (1977), p. 14; Dunn (1991), p. 179.

271 Dunn (1980), p. 101.

272 "Thus in Gen. Rab. 12.6 and Num. Rab. 13.12 glory (or lustre) is one of the six things taken from Adam which would be restored in the world to come (see also Gen. Rab. 11.2; 21.5; Deut. Rab. 11.3). And already at Qumran the glory anticipated by the faithful covenanters is spoken of as 'all the glory of Adam/Adam' (1QS4.23; CD 3.20; IQH 7.15)." Dunn (1980), p. 106.

273 Dunn (1991), p. 191.

274 Dunn (1980), p. 126.

275 See Dunn (1991)., p. 193.

276 Dunn (1980), p. 106.

277 Dunn (1988), p. 483.

278 Dunn (1991), p. 195.

279 See Bright (1972), p. 440.

280 See Dunn (1980), pp. 169-170.

281 Ringgren (1947), p. 45.

282 See Dunn (1980), p. 169.

283 Stone (1984), p. 288

284 Ibid.

285 Dunn (1991), pp. 196-197.

286 See ibid., p. 197.

287 Stone (1984), p. 288. Also see Dunn (1980), p. 171. See Stone (1984), p. 293. "Ben Sira recognizes the Torah, now in book form (24:23), as expressing God's wisdom. As the efficacious word of God,

it governs the universe, is implanted in Jacob and radiates from the temple all over the land." Ibid., p. 295. "Now according to Ben Sira, the fullness of wisdom's activity is what one finds expressed in the Torah, and this is then the perfect expression of the order of the cosmos (chap. 24; Prov 8:22-31 laid the groundwork for this assertion)." Ibid., p. 296.

288 Dunn (1980), p. 179.

289 Ibid., p. 182.

290 See Dunn (1991), p. 197.

291 See Dunn (1980), p. 177.

292 Ibid., p. 207.

293 Dunn (1991), p. 208.

294 Ibid., pp. 226-227.

295 For Jesus as that man Wisdom became, see Dunn (1980), p. 212.

296 See Dunn (1991), p. 10.

297 Peder Borgen says that "no sharp distinction should be drawn between Hellenistic and Palestinian Judaism." Stone (1984), p. 233.

298 See Kelly (1958), p. 14.

299 "We simply have no evidence for the existence of such a pre-Christian myth (p. 99); and the developed myth as hypothesized is best explained as a syncretist attempt (which can be dated with any degree of probability no earlier than the first half of the Second Century A.D.) to incorporate Christian belief in Jesus into a wider framework of religious-philosophical world views." Dunn (1980), p. 215. Also see ibid., pp. 252-253; pp. 259-260; Dunn (1991), pp. 10-11.

300 "Thus far we have not found anything in pre-Christian sources which would warrant the description of 'an emerging mythical configuration." See Dunn (1980), p. 216.

301 See Stone (1984), p. 252.

302 See ibid., p. 265.

303 See Dunn (1980), p. 226.

304 Quoted from ibid.

305 Ibid.

306 Philo says in Som. I.227-30: "He that is truly God is one, but those that are improperly so called are more than one. Accordingly the holy word in the present instance has indicated him who is truly God by means of the articles saying 'I am the God', while it omits the article when mentioning him who is improperly so called, saying 'Who appeared to thee in the place' not 'of the God', but simply 'of God' (Gen. 31.13). Here it gives the title of 'God' to his chief Word..."

Quoted from Dunn (1980), p. 241.

307 See ibid., p. 218.

308 "But basically all three phrases (Spirit, Wisdom, Word) are simply variant ways of speaking of the creative, revelatory or redemptive act of God." Ibid., p. 219.

309 See ibid., pp. 219-220.

310 Ibid., p. 228.

311 See ibid., p. 216.

312 See Dunn (1980), p. 242.

313 Ibid., p. 243.

314 See ibid., pp. 244-245.

315 See ibid., p. 214.

316 See ibid., p. 250.

317 Dunn (1975), p. 111.

318 Dunn (1991), p. 279.

319 Dunn (1975), p. 155. For a fuller treatment see ibid., pp. 141-155. Also see Ibid., p. 193.

320 Dunn (1991), p. 266.

321 See Dunn (1975), p. 223.

322 See Jantsch (1980), p. 263.

323 See ibid.

324 See Dunn (1975), p. 202.

325 Ibid., p. 142.

326 Dunn (1988), p. 429.

327 Ibid.

328 Ibid.

329 Ibid.

330 Dunn (1975), p. 319.

331 Ibid., p. 320.

332 Ibid.

333 Ibid., p. 351.

334 Dunn (1988), p. 429. Also, note in Acts 16:7 the term 'Spirit of Jesus': see Dunn (1975), p. 195.

335 See ibid., p. 325.

336 See Dunn (1975), p. 352.

337 We find considerable evidence that, in split-brain experiments as conducted by Donald Wilson, the two hemispheres of the split-brain can be treated as two distinct centers of consciousness. See Penrose (1989), pp. 385-386.

338 "Results of a group of researchers at the University of British

Columbia in Canada seem to indicate that the left half of the brain serves primarily the recognition of relations and the association of former experience, whereas the right half of the brain acts in a non-referential and integrative way (Brain/Mind Bulletin, 1977c). In other words, the right half of the brain furthers novelty, and the left half confirmation." Jantsch (1980), p. 180.

339 Dunn (1975), p. 260.

340 Ibid.

341 See Dunn's relativization of tongue-speaking, in Dunn (1975), pp. 191-192, especially on page 192 where he says: "Certainly anyone who is familiar with the history of enthusiastic Christianity would recognize the danger of placing too much significance on any particular type of experience or physical manifestation."

342 Shortly we will examine the non-rational 'inarticulate groans' of Romans 8:26 - which should be understood in a broader sense than tongue-speaking. It does not exclude tongue-speaking but should not be confined to it. See Dunn (1975), p. 243. Dunn points to other examples of the non-rational movement of the Spirit: see Dunn (1975), pp. 239-240; pp. 245-246.

343 Collective ecstasy is, perhaps, the best historical interpretation of the Pentecost event. For a simple and thorough analysis, see Dunn (1975), pp. 146-152.

344 See Dunn (1991), p. 278.

345 In 1 Cor 14:15, Paul even speaks of a singing in tongues. Dunn emphasizes the non-rational (tongue-speaking) character of the 'spiritual songs' of Eph 5:19 and Col 3:16 by pointing to Eph 5:18 where Paul exhorts that one should not get drunk with wine but should instead be filled with the Spirit. See Dunn (1975), p. 236.

346 See ibid., p. 227.

347 See ibid., p. 173.

348 See ibid., p. 227.

349 See ibid., p. 82.

350 See ibid., p. 186, on charismatic teaching.

351 "The authority of leadership, of evangelism, of counselling, or teaching, was the charismatic authority of the Spirit." Ibid., p. 176.

352 Ibid., p. 229.

353 For further on the Pauline concept of 'building up', see ibid., pp. 295-296.

354 Ibid., p. 233.

355 Ibid., p. 262. Also see Dunn (1991), p. 76.

356 Ibid., p. 77.

357 Dunn (1975), p. 263.

358 See Dunn (1991), pp. 76-77.

359 See Dunn (1977).

360 See ibid., p. 381.

361 See ibid., p. 365.

362 Ibid., p. 381.

363 See ibid.

364 Dunn (1991), p. 274.

365 Dunn (1975), p. 264.

366 Ibid., p. 298. Also see Dunn (1991), p. 77.

367 Dunn (1975), p. 264.

368 Ibid.

369 Ibid., pp. 264-265.

370 Ibid., p. 285.

371 Ibid.

372 See again Jantsch (1980), p. 248.

373 Dunn (1975), p. 290.

374 Ibid., p. 291.

375 Ibid., p. 292.

376 Dunn points to Jude 19f. as another appeal for charismatic balance: "His aim seems to be to achieve the same sort of charismatic balance that Paul strives for in 1 Cor 14." Dunn (1975), p. 246.

377 See Dunn (1975), p. 294.

378 Gould (1995), p.xii.

379 Gould also admits to doing the same. See ibid., pp. 131-132.

380 "And of all Paul's letters the one to Rome is the fullest and most carefully constructed statement of the Christian gospel and of the faith it called for during the foundation period of Christianity. To grapple with Romans is to engage in dialogue with one of the most creative theological minds of all time from the most creative period of Christian thought." Dunn (1988), p. xii.

381 See ibid., p. 467.

382 Dunn, referring to verses 31-39, quotes Schmidt: "In this victory song of salvation assurance the whole letter has its center." Ibid., p. 497, original source not given.

383 "Paul was a Jew. He was born and brought up a Jew. He never ceased to be a Jew." Dunn (1988), p. xxxix. Also see Dunn (1977), p. 239.

384 See Dunn (1988), p. xli; Dunn (1975), p. 110; Dunn (1991), p.

122.

385 See Dunn (1988), p. xli.

386 See ibid.

387 All the early Christians considered themselves to be loyal Jews. See Dunn (1991), p. 117.

388 See Dunn (1983); Dunn (1988), pp. lxiii-lxxii.

389 "This conviction that God's salvation completes both his purpose in creation and his purpose in calling Israel is part of the genius and one of the too little appreciated strengths of Paul's theology." Dunn (1988), p. 467.

390 We consider the following verses so central to a proper understanding of Paul's thought, and we consider Paul's thought here so central to the thrust of this book, that we depart from our fairly general analysis of the New Testament and of Paul, and we undertake to examine these verses in Romans on a verse by verse basis.

391 The translations of verses 18-30 are taken from ibid., pp. 465-466.

392 See ibid., p. 444.

393 Ibid., p. 487

394 Ibid. p. 470.

395 Ibid., p. 488.

396 Ibid., p. 470.

397 Ibid., p. 488.

398 Ibid., p. 473.

399 Ibid., p. 489.

400 Ibid., p. 472.

401 Ibid.

402 See ibid., p. 474.

403 See ibid., p. 491.

404 Ibid., p. 477.

405 Ibid., p. 478.

406 Ibid., p. 493.

407 See ibid., p. 480.

408 Ibid., p. 482.

409 See ibid., p. 483.

410 Ibid., p. 495.

411 Ibid., p. 484.

412 The translation of verses 31-39 are taken from ibid., pp. 496-497.

413 Ibid., p. 500.

414 Ibid., p. 509.
415 Ibid., p. 510.
416 Ibid.
417 Ibid.
418 Ibid., p. 511.
419 Ibid., p. 507.
420 Ibid.
421 Ibid.
422 Ibid., p. 513.
423 See Prigogine and Stengers (1984), p. 7.
424 See Dobbs (1991), p. 7.
425 See ibid., pp. 6-7 and p. 255.
426 Barrow (1988), p. 69.
427 See Dobbs (1991), 19.
428 Ibid., p. 20.
429 Ibid.,
430 Ibid., pp. 26-27.
431 Ibid., p. 28.
432 Ibid., p. 29.
433 Ibid., p. 27
434 Ibid., p. 29
435 Ibid., p. 100.
436 Ibid., p. 30.
437 Ibid., p. 32.
438 Ibid., p. 80.
439 Ibid., p. 82.
440 Ibid., pp. 108-109.
441 Ibid., p. 150.
442 See ibid., p. 246.
443 Ibid., p. 109.
444 Ibid., p. 204.
445 See ibid., p. 211 and p. 233.
446 See ibid. p. 248.
447 See ibid., p. 93 and "There can be no doubt that Newton thought God to be literally omnipresent." ibid., p. 191. See also ibid., p. 229.
448 See ibid., p. 112.
449 See ibid., pp. 113-114.
450 See ibid., p. 245.
451 Ibid., pp. 230-231.
452 See ibid., p. 231.

Bibliography

Asimov, I. 1987. *Asimov's New Guide to Science.* London: Penguin Books.

Attenborough, D. 1979. *Life on Earth: A Natural History.* London: William Collins Sons.

Attenborough, D. 1984. *The Living Planet: A Portrait of the Earth.* London: William Collins Sons.

Augros, R., and G. Stanciu. 1984. *The New Story of Science.* New York: Bantam Books.

Augros, R. and G. Stanciu. 1988. *The New Biology.* Boston: Shambhala Publications.

Bacon, F. 1627. *New Atlantis.* London: Rawley.

Barrow, J.D. 1988. *The World within the World.* Oxford: Oxford University Press.

Barrow, J.D. 1991. Theories of Everything: The Quest for Ultimate Explanation. Oxford: Clarendon Press.

Barrow, J.D. 1995. *The Artful Universe: The Cosmic Source of Human Creativity.* Boston: Little, Brown and Company.

Barrow, J.D., and F.J. Tipler. 1986. *The Anthropic Cosmological Principle.* Oxford: Clarendon Press.

Bateson, G. 1973. *Steps to an Ecology of Mind.* London: Paladin.

Bateson, G. 1979. *Mind and Nature.* London: Wildwood House.

Bateson, G., and M. C. Bateson. 1987. *Angels Fear.* New York: Macmillan.

Becker, R.O. and G. Selden. 1985. *The Body Electric.* New York: William Morrow.

Bergson, H. 1911. *Creative Evolution.* Lanham: The University Press of America.

Berry, T. 1988. *The Dream of the Earth.* San Francisco: Sierra Club Books.

Birch, C. and J.B. Cobb, Jr. 1981. *The Liberation of Life.* Cambridge: Cambridge University Press.

Bohm, D. 1969. in Towards a Theoretical Biology. ed. by C.H. Waddington. Chicago: Aldine.

Bohm, D. 1980. *Wholeness and the Implicate Order.* London: Routledge and Kegan Paul.

Bohm, D. 1985. *Unfolding Meaning.* London: Routledge and Kegan Paul.

Bohm, D. and B. Hiley. 1975. *On the Intuitive Understanding of Non-Locality as Implied by Quantum Theory. Foundations of Physics, vol. 5.*

Bohm, D. and F.D. Peat. 1987. *Science, Order, and Creativity.* New York: Bantam Books.

Bohr, N. 1934. *Atomic Physics and the Description of Nature.* Cambridge: Cambridge University Press.

Briggs, J.P. and F.D. Peat. 1984. *Looking Glass Universe.* New York: Simon and Schuster.

Butler, S. 1878. *Life and Habit.* London: Cape.

Butler, S. 1880. *Unconscious Memory.* London: Cape.

Cairns-Smith, A.G. 1985. *Seven Clues to the Origin of Life.* Cambridge: Cambridge University Press.

Capra, F. 1974. *The Tao of Physics.* London: Wildwood House.

Capra, F. 1982. *The Turning Point.* London: Wildwood House.

Capra, F. 1988. *Uncommon Wisdom.* London: Century Hutchinson.

Carter, B. 1974. *In Confrontation of Cosmological Theories with Observation,* ed. M.S. Longair. Dordrecht: Reidel.

Clements, R.E. 1992. *Wisdom in Theology.* Carlisle: The Paternoster Press.

Coveney, P. and R. Highfield. 1991. *The Arrow of Time.* London: Flamingo.

Crawford, M. and D. Marsh. 1989. *The Driving Force.* London: Heinemann.

Darwin, C. 1859. *The Origin of Species,* 1st ed. London: Murray.

Darwin, C. 1872. *The Origin of Species,* 6th ed. London: Murray.

Davies, P. 1979. *The Forces of Nature.* Cambridge: Cambridge University Press.

Davies, P. 1983. *God and the New Physics.* London: Penguin Books.

Davies, P. 1984. *Superforce.* London: Heinemann.

Davies, P. 1987. *The Cosmic Blueprint.* London: Heinemann.

Davies, P. and J.R. Brown. 1986. *The Ghost in the Atom.* Cambridge: Cambridge University Press.

Dawkins, R. 1976. *The Selfish Gene.* Oxford: Oxford University Press.

Dawkins, R. 1986. *The Blind Watchmaker.* London: Longmans.

Denton, M. 1985. *Evolution: A Theory in Crisis.* London: Hutchinson.

Dunn, J.D.G. 1970. *Baptism in the Holy Spirit.* London: SCM Press.

Dunn, J.D.G. 1975. *Jesus and the Spirit.* London: SCM Press.

Dunn, J.D.G. 1977. *Unity and Diversity in the New Testament: An Inquiry into the Character of the Earliest Christianity.* London: SCM Press.

Dunn, J.D.G. 1980. *Christology in the Making: An Inquiry into the Origins of the Doctrine of the Incarnation.* London: SCM Press.

Dunn, J.D.G. 1983. *The New Perspective on Paul.* Manchester: The John Rylands University Library of Manchester.

Dunn, J.D.G. 1985. *The Evidence for Jesus: The Impact of Scholarship on our Understanding of How Christianity Began.* London: SCM Press.

Dunn, J.D.G. 1986. *The Kingdom of God and North-East England.* London SCM Press.

Dunn, J.D.G. 1987. *The Living Word.* London: SCM Press.

Dunn, J.D.G. 1988. *Romans*: vols 1 & 2. Word Biblical Commentary - 38a & 38b. Dallas: Word Books.

Dunn, J.D.G. 1990. *Jesus, Paul and the Law.* London: SPCK.

Dyson, F. 1988. *Infinite in All Directions.* London: Penguin Books.

Eccles, J.C. 1989. *Evolution of the Brain: Creation of the Self.* London & New York: Routledge.

Eldredge, N. 1987. *The Natural History Reader in Evolution.* New York: Columbia University Press.

Eldredge, N. 1987. *Life Pulse: Episodes From the Story of the Fossil Record.* New York: Facts on File Publications.

Einstein, A. 1952. *Relativity: The Special and the General Theory.* 15th ed. New York: Crown Publishers.

Epstein, L.C. 1981. *Relativity Visualized.* San Francisco: Insight Press.

Feyerabend, P. 1987. *Farewell to Reason.* New York: Verso.

Feynman, R. 1965. *The Character of Physical Law.* Cambridge: MIT Press.

Feynman, R. 1985. *QED: The Strange Theory of Light and Matter.* London: Penguin Books.

Fox, M. 1988. *The Coming of the Cosmic Christ. San Francisco*: Harper and Row.

Fox, R.F. 1988. *Energy and the Evolution of Life.* New York: W.H. Freeman.

Gleick, J. 1987. *Chaos: Making a New Science.* New York: Penguin.

Gould, S.J. 1977. *Ontogeny and Phylogeny.* Cambridge, Mass.: Harvard University Press.

Gould, S.J. 1977. *Ever Since Darwin: Reflections in Natural History.* London: Penguin Books.

Gould, S.J. 1980. *The Panda's Thumb: More Reflections in Natural History.* London: Penguin Books.

Gould, S.J. 1981. *The Mismeasure of Man.* London: Penguin Books.

Gould, S.J. 1983. *Hen's Teeth and Horse's Toes.* New York: Norton.

Gould, S.J. 1987. *Time's Arrow, Time's Cycle: Myth and Metaphor in the Discovery of Geological Time.* London: Penguin Books.

Gould, S.J. 1989. *Wonderful Life: The Burgess Shale and the Nature of History.* New York: Norton.

Gould, S.J. 1991. *Bully for Brontosaurus.* London: Penguin Books.

Gould, S.J. 1993. *Eight Little Piggies.* New York: W.W. Norton & Company.

Gould, S.J. 1996. *Full House: The Spread of Excellence from Plato to Darwin.* New York: Harmony Books.

Gould, S.J. 1997. *Questioning the Millennium: A Rationalist's Guide to a Precisely Arbitrary Countdown.* New York: Harmony Books.

Gould, S.J. and N. Eldredge. 1977. Punctuated equilibria: the tempo and mode of evolution reconsidered. *Paleobiology* 3:115-151.

Gregory, R.L. 1986. *Odd Perceptions.* London: Routledge.

Gribbin, J. 1984. *In Search of Schrodinger's Cat: Quantum Physics and Reality.* New York: Bantam Books.

Gribbin, J. 1986. *In Search of the Big Bang: Quantum Physics and Cosmology.* New York: Bantam Books.

Gribbin, J. and M. Rees. 1989. *Cosmic Coincidences: Dark Matter, Mankind, and Anthropic Cosmology.* New York: Bantam Books.

Guiton, J. 1991. *Dieu et la Science.* Paris: Bernard Grasset.

Halliwell, J. 1991. Quantum Cosmology and the Creation of the Universe in *Scientific American,* Dec., Vol 265, Num 6:28-35.

Hawking, S. 1980. *Is the End in Sight for Theoretical Physics?* Cambridge: Cambridge University Press.

Hawking, S. 1988. *A Brief History of Time.* New York: Bantam Books.

Heisenberg, W. 1963. *Physics and Philosophy.* London: Allen and Unwin.

Heisenberg, W. 1974. *Across the Frontier.* New York: Harper and Row.

Hofstader, D. 1979. *Godel, Escher, Bach.* Brighton: Harvester Press.

Horgan, J. 1996. *The End of Science: Facing the Limits of Knowledge in the Twilight of the Scientific Age.* New York: Helix Books.

Hoyle, F. 1960. *The Black Cloud.* London: Penguin Books.

Hoyle, F. 1982. *Ice - A Chilling Scientific Forecast of a New Age.* Sevenoaks: New English Library.

Hoyle, F. 1983. *The Intelligent Universe.* London: Michael Joseph.

Hoyle, F. 1989. *The Small World of Fred Hoyle.* London: Michael Joseph.

Hoyle, F. and Chandra Wickramasinghe. 1981. *Evolution From Space.* New York: Simon and Schuster.

Jaki, S.L. 1989. *God and the Cosmologists.* Washington, D.C.: Regnery Gateway.

Jantsch, E. 1980. *The Self-Organizing Universe: Scientific and Human Implications of the Emerging Paradigm of Evolution.* Oxford: Pergamon.

Jeans, J. H. 1981. *Physics and Philosophy.* New York: Dover Publications.

Kelly, J.N.D. 1958. *Early Christian Doctrines.* London: Adam & Charles Black.

Koestler, A. 1967. *The Ghost in the Machine.* London: Hutchinson.

Koestler, A. 1970. *The Act of Creation.* London: Pan Books.

Koestler, A. 1971. *The Case of the Midwife Toad.* London: Hutchinson.

Koestler, A. 1978. *Janus: A Summing Up.* London: Hutchinson.

Krishnamurti, J. 1972. *You Are the World.* New York: Harper and Row.

Kuhlewind, G. 1985. *Becoming Aware of the Logos: The Way of St. John the Evangelist.* West Stockbridge, Ma.: Lindisfarne Press.

Kuhn, T.S. 1970. *The Structure of Scientific Revolutions,* 2d ed. Chicago: University of Chicago Press.

Kuschel, K-J. 1992. *Born Before All Time?* London: SCM Press Ltd.

Layzer, D. 1990. *Cosmogenesis: The Growth of Order in the Universe.* Oxford: Oxford University Press.

Leakey, R.E. 1981. *The Making of Mankind.* London: Michael Joseph.

Leshan, L. and H. Margenau. 1982. *Einstein's Space & Van Gogh's Sky.* New York: Macmillan.

Levy, S. 1992. *Artificial Life: The Quest for a New Creation.* London: Penguin Books.

Lindley, D. 1993. *The End of Physics.* New York: BasicBooks.

Lovelock, J. 1979. *Gaia: A New Look at Life on Earth.* Oxford: Oxford University Press.

Lovelock, J. 1989. *The Ages of Gaia: A Biography of our Living Earth.* Oxford: Oxford University Press.

Luckiesh, M. 1922. *Visual Illusions: Their Causes, Characteristics & Applications.* New York: Dover Publications.

Maltz, M. 1960. *Psycho-Cybernetics.* Englewood Cliffs: Prentice-Hall.

Maltz, M. 1964. *The Magic Power of Self Image Psychology.* Englewood Cliffs: Prentice-Hall.

Mandelbrot, B. 1977. *The Fractal Geometry of Nature.* New York: Freeman.

Margenau, H. 1984. *The Miracle of Existence.* Woodbridge: Ox Bow Press.

Margulis, Lynn and C. Sagan. 1986. *Microcosmos.* New York. Summit Books.

Margulis, Lynn and D. Sagan. 1986. *Origins of Sex: Three Billion Years of Genetic Recombination.* New Haven: Yale University Press.

Maturana, H.R. and F.J. Varela. 1988. *The Tree of Knowledge.* Boston: Shambhala.

Mayr, E. 1982. *The Growth of Biological Thought.* Cambridge, Mass.: Harvard University Press.

Medewar, P. 1986. *The Limits of Science.* Oxford: Oxford University Press.

Monod, J. 1972. *Chance and Necessity.* London: Collins.

Morgan, E. 1982. *The Aquatic Ape: A Theory of Human Evolution.* London: Souvenir Press.

Pagels, H.R. 1983. *The Cosmic Code.* London: Joeseph.

Pagels, H.R. 1985. *Perfect Symmetry.* London: Joseph.

Peacocke, A. 1986. *God and the New Biology.* London: J.M. Dent & Sons.

Peat, F.D. 1988. *Superstrings and the Search for The Theory of Everything.* Chicago: Contemporary Books.

Peat, F.D. 1991. *The Philosopher's Stone: Chaos, Synchronicity, and the Hidden Order of the World.* New York: Bantam Books.

Penfield, W. 1975. *The Mystery of the Mind.* Princeton: Princeton University Press.

Penrose, R. 1989. *The Emperor's New Mind: Concerning Computers, Minds, and the Laws of Physics.* Oxford: Oxford University Press.

Penrose, R. 1994. *Shadows of the Mind: The Search for the Missing Science of Consciousness.* Oxford: Oxford University Press.

Perry, N. 1983. *Symbiosis: Nature in Partnership.* London: Blandford.

Pirie, N.W. 1937. *The Meaninglessness of the Terms Life and Living, in Perspectives in Biochemistry,* ed. by J. Needham and D. Green. Cambridge:

University of Cambridge Press.

Poincaré, H. 1958. *The Value of Science*. New York: Dover.

Polanyi, M. 1958. *Personal Knowledge: Towards a Post-Critical Philosophy*. London: Routledge & Kegan Paul.

Polkinghorne, J. 1989. *Science and Creation: The Search for Understanding*. Boston: New Science Library Shambhala.

Popper, K.R. 1982. *Quantum Theory and the Schism in Physics*. London: Hutchinson.

Popper, K.R. 1983. *Realism and the Aim of Science*. London: Hutchinson.

Popper, K.R. and J.C. Eccles. 1977. *The Self and Its Brain*. Berlin: Springer International.

Powers, J. 1982. *Philosophy and the New Physics*. London: Methuen.

Pribram, K.H. 1971. *Languages of the Brain*. Engelwood Cliffs: Prentice Hall.

Prigogine, I. 1980. *From Being to Becoming*. San Francisco: Freeman.

Prigogine, I. 1996. *The End of Certainty: Time, Chaos, and the New Laws of Nature*. New York: The Free Press.

Prigogine, I. and Isabelle Stengers. 1984. *Order Out of Chaos*. London: Heinemann.

Rahner, K. and K. Rawer. 1981. *Weltall-Erde-Mensch, in Christlicher Glaube* in Moderner Gesellschaft, 3. Freiburg, Basel, Wien.

Raup, D. 1991. Extinction: *Bad Genes or Bad Luck?* Oxford: Oxford University Press

Rowan, J. 1990. *Subpersonalities: The People Inside Us*. London: Routledge.

Rucker, R. 1982. *Infinity and the Mind: The Science and Philosophy of the Infinite*. New York: Bantam Books.

Rucker, R. 1986. *The Fourth Dimension*. New York: Penguin Books.

Rucker, R. 1988. *Mind Tools.* New York: Penguin Books.

Russell, B. 1975. *Why I am Not a Christian.* New York: Simon & Schuster.

Salthe, S. 1985. *Evolving Hierarchical Systems.* New York: Columbia University Press.

Sciama, D.S. 1980. *The Origin of the Universe, in The State of the Universe,* ed; Geoffrey Bath. Oxford: Clarendon Press.

Scott, A. 1986. *The Creation of Life: From Chemical to Animal.* Oxford: Basil Blackwell.

Sheldrake, A.R. 1981. *A New Science of Life: The Hypothesis of Formative Causation.* London: Blond and Briggs.

Sheldrake, A.R. 1985. *A New Science of Life: The Hypothesis of Formative Causation,* new ed. London: Blond.

Sheldrake, A.R. 1988. *The Presence of the Past.* New York: Times Books.

Sheldrake, A.R. 1990. *The Rebirth of Nature.* London: Century .

Sheldrake, A.R. 1994. *Seven Experiments That Could Change the World.* London: Fourth Estate.

Sheldrake, A.R. and D. Bohm. 1982. *Morphogenetic Fields and the Implicate Order.* Revision 5:41-48.

Sheldrake, A.R., Abraham, R. and McKenna, T. 1992. *Trialogues at the Edge of the West.* Santa Fe: Bear & Company.

Sherburne, D.W. 1966. *A Key to Whitehead's Process and Reality.* Bloomington: Indiana University Press.

Stapp, H.P. 1971. *S-Matrix Interpretation of Quantum Theory.* Physical Review, vol. D3.

Stewart, I. 1990. *Does God Play Dice?* London: Penguin Books.

Stone, M. 1980. *Scriptures, Sects and Visions.* Oxford: Basil Blackwell.

Suzuki, D.T. 1957. *Mysticism Christian and Buddhist.* London: Unwin Paperbacks.

Talbot, M. 1988. *Beyond the Quantum*. New York; Bantam Books.

Teilhard de Chardin, P.T. 1959. *The Phenomenon of Man*. London: Collins.

Theissen, G. 1978. *Sociology of Early Palestinian Christianity*. Philadelphia: Fortress Press.

Thomas, L. 1974. *The Lives of a Cell*. New York: Bantam Books.

Thomas, L. 1974. *The Medusa and the Snail*. New York: Bantam Books.

Thompson, W.I. 1987. *Gaia: A Way of Knowing*. Great Barrington, Ma.: Lindisfarne Press.

Van der Veken, J. 1984. *Faith and Science: Possibility for a New Dialogue*, in Tripod - 22: Christianity and Contemporary China.

Varela, F.J. 1979. *Principles of Biological Autonomy*. New York: North Holland.

Varela, F.J., Thompson, E., and Rosch, E. 1991. *The Embodied Mind: Cognitive Science and Human Experience*. Cambridge: The MIT Press.

von Bertalanffy, L. 1971. *General Systems Theory*. London: Allen Lane.

Watson, L. 1973. *Supernature: A Natural History of the Supernatural*. Sevenoaks: Hodder and Stoughton.

Watson, L. 1974. *The Romeo Error*. Sevenoaks: Hodder and Stoughton.

Watson, L. 1984. *Heaven's Breath*. New York: William Morrow.

Watson, L. 1986. *Supernature II: A New Natural History of the Supernatural*. Sevenoaks: Hodder and Stoughton.

Watson, L. 1986. *Dreams of Dragons: Ideas on the Edge of Natural History*. Sevenoaks: Hodder and Stoughton.

Watson, L. 1988. *Omnivore: The Role of Food in Human Evolution*. Sevenoaks: Hodder and Stoughton.

Watson, L. 1989. Neophilia: *The Tradition of the New*. Sevenoaks: Hodder and Stoughton.

Watson, L. 1990. *The Nature of Things: The Secret Life of Inanimate*

Objects. London: Hodder & Stoughton.

Weeks, S. 1994. *Early Israelite Wisdom.* Oxford: Clarendon Press.

Weinberg, S. 1977. *The First Three Minutes.* London: Deutsch.

Wheeler, J.A. 1994. *At Home in the Universe.* Woodbury: AIP Press.

Whitehead, A.N. 1925. *Science and the Modern World.* New York: Macmillan.

Whitehead, A.N. 1929. *Process and Reality: An Essay in Cosmology.* New York: Free Press.

Wilber, K., ed. 1982. *The Holographic Paradigm and Other Paradoxes.* Boulder: Shambala.

Wilber, K. ed. 1984. *Quantum Questions.* Boulder: Shambala.

Wildiers, M. 1982. *The Theologian and his Universe. Theology and Cosmology from the Middle Ages to the Present.* New York: The Seabury Press.

Wilson, E.O. 1971. *The Social Insects.* Cambridge, Mass.: Harvard University Press.

Wilson, E.O. 1980. *Sociology* (abridged edition). Cambridge, Mass.: Harvard University Press.

Wolf, F.A. 1989. *Taking the Quantum Leap: The New Physics for Nonscientists.* New York: Harper & Row.

Zdenek, Marilee. 1983. *The Right-Brain Experience: An Intimate Programme to Free the Powers of Your Imagination.* London: Transworld Publishers.

Zohar, Danah. 1990. *The Quantum Self.* London: Bloomsbury.

Index